MOSES AND THE EXODUS

MOSES AND THE EXODUS

The Story as Found in Ancient Sources

Including the Holy Bible and *Antiquities of the Jews,*
by Flavius Josephus

MASTERWORKS CLASSICS

Cover design: Nathaniel J. Parry

ISBN 978-1-62730-111-4

Published by Masterworks Classics, an imprint of Stonewell Press
Salt Lake City, UT
Stonewellpress.com

CONTENTS

PREFACE

Moses is one of the towering figures of history, a man whose feats truly were of epic proportions. What other mortal has conversed with God face to face, turned rivers of water to blood, and divided a sea so his people could walk through on dry ground? Who else almost single-handedly freed hundreds of thousands of slaves and then led them to freedom in a new land? Who else has presided over a monumental, decades-long exodus where the travelers were led by a heavenly pillar of fire?

Those who doubt the reality of miracles consider Moses to be simply a grand mythological figure. But hundreds of millions of people in three major religions regard him as a true prophet of God, a man who communed with God himself and was granted access to God's power. Both groups likely agree that the image of Moses is one of a hero for the ages.

Whether one regards the story as a true account or an embellishment of a similar event in history, Moses' experience makes for fascinating reading or viewing. That story has been told and retold for millennia. In recent generations, theologians, scholars, novelists, dramatists, poets, and film makers have all contributed to our appreciation and understanding of this remarkable account.

Popular film has been particularly influential in shaping our thinking about Moses, his miracles, and Israel's forty-year exodus across the barren desert between Egypt and Palestine. Cecil B. DeMille set an imposing standard in *The Ten Commandments* (which he filmed twice, first as a silent film in 1923 and then as a ground-breaking blockbuster in 1956). The 1956 version is still regarded as one of the best movies ever made. In 1998 DreamWorks gave us an animated version, *The Prince of Egypt*. And in 2014 another blockbuster movie was released: Ridley Scott's *Exodus: Gods and Kings,* starring Christian Bale.

Each retelling of the story had its own focus—and sometimes its own agenda. But where does the Moses story come from? Where among documents of the ancient world can we find this incredible story of slavery, deliverance by divine power—and then the generation-long wandering in the wilderness?

The primary source, of course, is the account recorded in the Holy Bible, found particularly in the books of Exodus, Numbers, and Deuteronomy. Moses himself is traditionally regarded as the author of those books, though many scholars argue that these books are all of a later date. This present collection includes selections from those books, as well as a few chapters from the book of Joshua, which brings the story to completion.

Another excellent source is *Antiquities of the Jews,* a very early Jewish history written by Flavius Josephus, a Jewish scholar of the first century C.E. *Antiquities* tells the story of Adam, Noah, Moses, Esther, and others. This volume reproduces the part of Josephus's work that focuses on Moses and the Exodus.

Finally, a helpful synthesis of material is found in the *Jewish Encyclopedia;* the encyclopedia's lengthy entry on Moses is included as an appendix to this work.

Taken together, these resources will give the reader new appreciation and enhanced respect for Moses of Egypt—leader of the Israelites and lawgiver to countless generations of those who worship the God of the Bible—and for the phenomenal exodus he led across the barren, trackless deserts of Sinai.

Part I

SELECTIONS FROM THE OLD TESTAMENT

(FROM THE AMERICAN STANDARD VERSION)

Chapter 1

Exodus, the Second Book of Moses

EXODUS 1

¹Now these are the names of the sons of Israel, who came into Egypt (every man and his household came with Jacob): ²Reuben, Simeon, Levi, and Judah, ³Issachar, Zebulun, and Benjamin, ⁴Dan and Naphtali, Gad and Asher. ⁵And all the souls that came out of the loins of Jacob were seventy souls: and Joseph was in Egypt already. ⁶And Joseph died, and all his brethren, and all that generation. ⁷And the children of Israel were fruitful, and increased abundantly, and multiplied, and waxed exceeding mighty; and the land was filled with them.

⁸Now there arose a new king over Egypt, who knew not Joseph. ⁹And he said unto his people, Behold, the people of the children of Israel are more and mightier than we: ¹⁰come, let us deal wisely with them, lest they multiply, and it come to pass, that, when there falleth out any war, they also join themselves unto our enemies, and fight against us, and get them up out of the land.

¹¹Therefore they did set over them taskmasters to afflict them with their burdens. And they built for Pharaoh store-cities, Pithom and Raamses. ¹²But the more they afflicted them, the more they multiplied and the more they spread abroad. And they were grieved because of the children of Israel. ¹³And the Egyptians made the children of Israel to serve with rigor: ¹⁴and they made their lives bitter with hard service, in mortar and in brick, and in all manner of service in the field, all their service, wherein they made them serve with rigor.

¹⁵And the king of Egypt spake to the Hebrew midwives, of whom the name of the one was Shiphrah, and the name of the other Puah: ¹⁶and he said, When ye do the office of a midwife to the Hebrew women, and see them upon the birth-stool; if it be a son, then ye shall kill him; but if it be

a daughter, then she shall live. [17]But the midwives feared God, and did not as the king of Egypt commanded them, but saved the men-children alive.

[18]And the king of Egypt called for the midwives, and said unto them, Why have ye done this thing, and have saved the men-children alive? [19]And the midwives said unto Pharaoh, Because the Hebrew women are not as the Egyptian women; for they are lively, and are delivered ere the midwife come unto them. [20]And God dealt well with the midwives: and the people multiplied, and waxed very mighty. [21]And it came to pass, because the midwives feared God, that he made them households. [22]And Pharaoh charged all his people, saying, Every son that is born ye shall cast into the river, and every daughter ye shall save alive.

EXODUS 2

[1]And there went a man of the house of Levi, and took to wife a daughter of Levi. [2]And the woman conceived, and bare a son: and when she saw him that he was a goodly child, she hid him three months. [3]And when she could not longer hide him, she took for him an ark of bulrushes, and daubed it with slime and with pitch; and she put the child therein, and laid it in the flags by the river's brink. [4]And his sister stood afar off, to know what would be done to him.

[5]And the daughter of Pharaoh came down to bathe at the river; and her maidens walked along by the river-side; and she saw the ark among the flags, and sent her handmaid to fetch it. [6]And she opened it, and saw the child: and, behold, the babe wept. And she had compassion on him, and said, This is one of the Hebrews' children.

[7]Then said his sister to Pharaoh's daughter, Shall I go and call thee a nurse of the Hebrew women, that she may nurse the child for thee? [8]And Pharaoh's daughter said to her, Go. And the maiden went and called the child's mother. [9]And Pharaoh's daughter said unto her, Take this child away, and nurse it for me, and I will give thee thy wages. And the woman took the child, and nursed it.

[10]And the child grew, and she brought him unto Pharaoh's daughter, and he became her son. And she called his name Moses, and said, Because I drew him out of the water.

[11]And it came to pass in those days, when Moses was grown up, that he went out unto his brethren, and looked on their burdens: and he saw an Egyptian smiting a Hebrew, one of his brethren. [12]And he looked this way and that way, and when he saw that there was no man, he smote the Egyptian, and hid him in the sand. [13]And he went out the second day, and, behold, two men of the Hebrews were striving together: and he said

to him that did the wrong, Wherefore smitest thou thy fellow? [14]And he said, Who made thee a prince and a judge over us? Thinkest thou to kill me, as thou killedst the Egyptian? And Moses feared, and said, Surely the thing is known. [15]Now when Pharaoh heard this thing, he sought to slay Moses. But Moses fled from the face of Pharaoh, and dwelt in the land of Midian: and he sat down by a well.

[16]Now the priest of Midian had seven daughters: and they came and drew water, and filled the troughs to water their father's flock. [17]And the shepherds came and drove them away; but Moses stood up and helped them, and watered their flock. [18]And when they came to Reuel their father, he said, How is it that ye are come so soon today? [19]And they said, An Egyptian delivered us out of the hand of the shepherds, and moreover he drew water for us, and watered the flock. [20]And he said unto his daughters, And where is he? Why is it that ye have left the man? Call him, that he may eat bread.

[21]And Moses was content to dwell with the man: and he gave Moses Zipporah his daughter. [22]And she bare a son, and he called his name Gershom; for he said, I have been a sojourner in a foreign land.

[23]And it came to pass in the course of those many days, that the king of Egypt died: and the children of Israel sighed by reason of the bondage, and they cried, and their cry came up unto God by reason of the bondage. [24]And God heard their groaning, and God remembered his covenant with Abraham, with Isaac, and with Jacob. [25]And God saw the children of Israel, and God took knowledge of them.

EXODUS 3

[1]Now Moses was keeping the flock of Jethro his father-in-law, the priest of Midian: and he led the flock to the back of the wilderness, and came to the mountain of God, unto Horeb. [2]And the angel of Jehovah appeared unto him in a flame of fire out of the midst of a bush: and he looked, and, behold, the bush burned with fire, and the bush was not consumed. [3]And Moses said, I will turn aside now, and see this great sight, why the bush is not burnt. [4]And when Jehovah saw that he turned aside to see, God called unto him out of the midst of the bush, and said, Moses, Moses. And he said, Here am I. [5]And he said, Draw not nigh hither: put off thy shoes from off thy feet, for the place whereon thou standest is holy ground. [6]Moreover he said, I am the God of thy father, the God of Abraham, the God of Isaac, and the God of Jacob. And Moses hid his face; for he was afraid to look upon God.

[7]And Jehovah said, I have surely seen the affliction of my people that are in Egypt, and have heard their cry by reason of their taskmasters; for I know their sorrows; [8]and I am come down to deliver them out of the hand of the Egyptians, and to bring them up out of that land unto a good land and a large, unto a land flowing with milk and honey; unto the place of the Canaanite, and the Hittite, and the Amorite, and the Perizzite, and the Hivite, and the Jebusite. [9]And now, behold, the cry of the children of Israel is come unto me: moreover I have seen the oppression wherewith the Egyptians oppress them. [10]Come now therefore, and I will send thee unto Pharaoh, that thou mayest bring forth my people the children of Israel out of Egypt.

[11]And Moses said unto God, Who am I, that I should go unto Pharaoh, and that I should bring forth the children of Israel out of Egypt? [12]And he said, Certainly I will be with thee; and this shall be the token unto thee, that I have sent thee: when thou hast brought forth the people out of Egypt, ye shall serve God upon this mountain.

[13]And Moses said unto God, Behold, when I come unto the children of Israel, and shall say unto them, The God of your fathers hath sent me unto you; and they shall say to me, What is his name? What shall I say unto them? [14]And God said unto Moses, I AM THAT I AM: and he said, Thus shalt thou say unto the children of Israel, I AM hath sent me unto you. [15]And God said moreover unto Moses, Thus shalt thou say unto the children of Israel, Jehovah, the God of your fathers, the God of Abraham, the God of Isaac, and the God of Jacob, hath sent me unto you: this is my name forever, and this is my memorial unto all generations.

[16]Go, and gather the elders of Israel together, and say unto them, Jehovah, the God of your fathers, the God of Abraham, of Isaac, and of Jacob, hath appeared unto me, saying, I have surely visited you, and seen that which is done to you in Egypt: [17]and I have said, I will bring you up out of the affliction of Egypt unto the land of the Canaanite, and the Hittite, and the Amorite, and the Perizzite, and the Hivite, and the Jebusite, unto a land flowing with milk and honey. [18]And they shall hearken to thy voice: and thou shalt come, thou and the elders of Israel, unto the king of Egypt, and ye shall say unto him, Jehovah, the God of the Hebrews, hath met with us: and now let us go, we pray thee, three days' journey into the wilderness, that we may sacrifice to Jehovah our God. [19]And I know that the king of Egypt will not give you leave to go, no, not by a mighty hand. [20]And I will put forth my hand, and smite Egypt with all my wonders which I will do in the midst thereof: and after that he will let you go. [21]And I will give this people favor in the sight of the Egyptians: and it shall come to pass, that, when ye go, ye shall not go empty. [22]But every woman shall ask of

her neighbor, and of her that sojourneth in her house, jewels of silver, and jewels of gold, and raiment: and ye shall put them upon your sons, and upon your daughters; and ye shall despoil the Egyptians.

EXODUS 4

[1]And Moses answered and said, But, behold, they will not believe me, nor hearken unto my voice; for they will say, Jehovah hath not appeared unto thee. [2]And Jehovah said unto him, What is that in thy hand? And he said, A rod. [3]And he said, Cast in on the ground. And he cast it on the ground, and it became a serpent; and Moses fled from before it. [4]And Jehovah said unto Moses, Put forth thy hand, and take it by the tail: (and he put forth his hand, and laid hold of it, and it became a rod in his hand:) [5]That they may believe that Jehovah, the God of their fathers, the God of Abraham, the God of Isaac, and the God of Jacob, hath appeared unto thee.

[6]And Jehovah said furthermore unto him, Put now thy hand into thy bosom. And he put his hand into his bosom: and when he took it out, behold, his hand was leprous, as white as snow. [7]And he said, Put thy hand into thy bosom again. (And he put his hand into his bosom again; and when he took it out of his bosom, behold, it was turned again as his other flesh.) [8]And it shall come to pass, if they will not believe thee, neither hearken to the voice of the first sign, that they will believe the voice of the latter sign.

[9]And it shall come to pass, if they will not believe even these two signs, neither hearken unto thy voice, that thou shalt take of the water of the river, and pour it upon the dry land: and the water which thou takest out of the river shall become blood upon the dry land.

[10]And Moses said unto Jehovah, Oh, Lord, I am not eloquent, neither heretofore, nor since thou hast spoken unto thy servant; for I am slow of speech, and of a slow tongue. [11]And Jehovah said unto him, Who hath made man's mouth? Or who maketh a man dumb, or deaf, or seeing, or blind? Is it not I, Jehovah? [12]Now therefore go, and I will be with thy mouth, and teach thee what thou shalt speak.

[13]And he said, Oh, Lord, send, I pray thee, by the hand of him whom thou wilt send. [14]And the anger of Jehovah was kindled against Moses, and he said, Is there not Aaron thy brother the Levite? I know that he can speak well. And also, behold, he cometh forth to meet thee: and when he seeth thee, he will be glad in his heart. [15]And thou shalt speak unto him, and put the words in his mouth: and I will be with thy mouth, and with his mouth, and will teach you what ye shall do. [16]And he shall be thy

spokesman unto the people; and it shall come to pass, that he shall be to thee a mouth, and thou shalt be to him as God. [17]And thou shalt take in thy hand this rod, wherewith thou shalt do the signs.

[18]And Moses went and returned to Jethro his father-in-law, and said unto him, Let me go, I pray thee, and return unto my brethren that are in Egypt, and see whether they be yet alive. And Jethro said to Moses, Go in peace. [19]And Jehovah said unto Moses in Midian, Go, return into Egypt; for all the men are dead that sought thy life.

[20]And Moses took his wife and his sons, and set them upon an ass, and he returned to the land of Egypt: and Moses took the rod of God in his hand. [21]And Jehovah said unto Moses, When thou goest back into Egypt, see that thou do before Pharaoh all the wonders which I have put in thy hand: but I will harden his heart and he will not let the people go. [22]And thou shalt say unto Pharaoh, Thus saith Jehovah, Israel is my son, my first-born: [23]and I have said unto thee, Let my son go, that he may serve me; and thou hast refused to let him go: behold, I will slay thy son, thy first-born.

[24]And it came to pass on the way at the lodging-place, that Jehovah met him, and sought to kill him. [25]Then Zipporah took a flint, and cut off the foreskin of her son, and cast it at his feet; and she said, Surely a bridegroom of blood art thou to me. [26]So he let him alone. Then she said, A bridegroom of blood art thou, because of the circumcision.

[27]And Jehovah said to Aaron, Go into the wilderness to meet Moses. And he went, and met him in the mountain of God, and kissed him. [28]And Moses told Aaron all the words of Jehovah wherewith he had sent him, and all the signs wherewith he had charged him. [29]And Moses and Aaron went and gathered together all the elders of the children of Israel: [30]and Aaron spake all the words which Jehovah had spoken unto Moses, and did the signs in the sight of the people. [31]And the people believed: and when they heard that Jehovah had visited the children of Israel, and that he had seen their affliction, then they bowed their heads and worshipped.

EXODUS 5

[1]And afterward Moses and Aaron came, and said unto Pharaoh, Thus saith Jehovah, the God of Israel, Let my people go, that they may hold a feast unto me in the wilderness. [2]And Pharaoh said, Who is Jehovah, that I should hearken unto his voice to let Israel go? I know not Jehovah, and moreover I will not let Israel go. [3]And they said, The God of the Hebrews hath met with us: let us go, we pray thee, three days' journey into the wilderness, and sacrifice unto Jehovah our God, lest he fall upon us with

pestilence, or with the sword. [4]And the king of Egypt said unto them, Wherefore do ye, Moses and Aaron, loose the people from their works? get you unto your burdens. [5]And Pharaoh said, Behold, the people of the land are now many, and ye make them rest from their burdens.

[6]And the same day Pharaoh commanded the taskmasters of the people, and their officers, saying, [7]Ye shall no more give the people straw to make brick, as heretofore: let them go and gather straw for themselves. [8]And the number of the bricks, which they did make heretofore, ye shall lay upon them; ye shall not diminish aught thereof: for they are idle; therefore they cry, saying, Let us go and sacrifice to our God. [9]Let heavier work be laid upon the men, that they may labor therein; and let them not regard lying words.

[10]And the taskmasters of the people went out, and their officers, and they spake to the people, saying, Thus saith Pharaoh, I will not give you straw. [11]Go yourselves, get you straw where ye can find it: for nought of your work shall be diminished. [12]So the people were scattered abroad throughout all the land of Egypt to gather stubble for straw. [13]And the taskmasters were urgent saying, Fulfil your works, your daily tasks, as when there was straw. [14]And the officers of the children of Israel, whom Pharaoh's taskmasters had set over them, were beaten, and demanded, Wherefore have ye not fulfilled your task both yesterday and today, in making brick as heretofore?

[15]Then the officers of the children of Israel came and cried unto Pharaoh, saying, Wherefore dealest thou thus with thy servants? [16]There is no straw given unto thy servants, and they say to us, Make brick: and, behold, thy servants are beaten; but the fault it in thine own people. [17]But he said, Ye are idle, ye are idle: therefore ye say, Let us go and sacrifice to Jehovah. [18]Go therefore now, and work; for there shall no straw be given you, yet shall ye deliver the number of bricks. [19]And the officers of the children of Israel did see that they were in evil case, when it was said, Ye shall not diminish aught from your bricks, your daily tasks.

[20]And they met Moses and Aaron, who stood in the way, as they came forth from Pharaoh: [21]and they said unto them, Jehovah look upon you, and judge: because ye have made our savor to be abhorred in the eyes of Pharaoh, and in the eyes of his servants, to put a sword in their hand to slay us.

[22]And Moses returned unto Jehovah, and said, Lord, wherefore hast thou dealt ill with this people? why is it that thou hast sent me? [23]For since I came to Pharaoh to speak in thy name, he hath dealt ill with this people; neither hast thou delivered thy people at all.

EXODUS 6

[1]And Jehovah said unto Moses, Now shalt thou see what I will do to Pharaoh: for by a strong hand shall he let them go, and by a strong hand shall he drive them out of his land.

[2]And God spake unto Moses, and said unto him, I am Jehovah: [3]and I appeared unto Abraham, unto Isaac, and unto Jacob, as God Almighty; but by my name Jehovah I was not known to them. [4]And I have also established my covenant with them, to give them the land of Canaan, the land of their sojournings, wherein they sojourned. [5]And moreover I have heard the groaning of the children of Israel, whom the Egyptians keep in bondage; and I have remembered my covenant. [6]Wherefore say unto the children of Israel, I am Jehovah, and I will bring you out from under the burdens of the Egyptians, and I will rid you out of their bondage, and I will redeem you with an outstretched arm, and with great judgments: [7]and I will take you to me for a people, and I will be to you a God; and ye shall know that I am Jehovah your God, who bringeth you out from under the burdens of the Egyptians. [8]And I will bring you in unto the land which I sware to give to Abraham, to Isaac, and to Jacob; and I will give it you for a heritage: I am Jehovah. [9]And Moses spake so unto the children of Israel: but they hearkened not unto Moses for anguish of spirit, and for cruel bondage.

[10]And Jehovah spake unto Moses, saying, [11]Go in, speak unto Pharaoh king of Egypt, that he let the children of Israel go out of his land. [12]And Moses spake before Jehovah, saying, Behold, the children of Israel have not hearkened unto me; how then shall Pharaoh hear me, who am of uncircumcised lips? [13]And Jehovah spake unto Moses and unto Aaron, and gave them a charge unto the children of Israel, and unto Pharaoh king of Egypt, to bring the children of Israel out of the land of Egypt. . . .

[28]And it came to pass on the day when Jehovah spake unto Moses in the land of Egypt, [29]that Jehovah spake unto Moses, saying, I am Jehovah: speak thou unto Pharaoh king of Egypt all that I speak unto thee. [30]And Moses said before Jehovah, Behold, I am of uncircumcised lips, and how shall Pharaoh hearken unto me?

EXODUS 7

[1]And Jehovah said unto Moses, See, I have made thee as God to Pharaoh; and Aaron thy brother shall be thy prophet. [2]Thou shalt speak all that I command thee; and Aaron thy brother shall speak unto Pharaoh, that he let the children of Israel go out of his land. [3]And I will harden Pharaoh's heart,

and multiply my signs and my wonders in the land of Egypt. ⁴But Pharaoh will not hearken unto you, and I will lay my hand upon Egypt, and bring forth my hosts, my people the children of Israel, out of the land of Egypt by great judgments. ⁵And the Egyptians shall know that I am Jehovah, when I stretch forth my hand upon Egypt, and bring out the children of Israel from among them. ⁶And Moses and Aaron did so; as Jehovah commanded them, so did they. ⁷And Moses was fourscore years old, and Aaron fourscore and three years old, when they spake unto Pharaoh.

⁸And Jehovah spake unto Moses and unto Aaron, saying, ⁹When Pharaoh shall speak unto you, saying, Show a wonder for you; then thou shalt say unto Aaron, Take thy rod, and cast it down before Pharaoh, that it become a serpent. ¹⁰And Moses and Aaron went in unto Pharaoh, and they did so, as Jehovah had commanded: and Aaron cast down his rod before Pharaoh and before his servants, and it became a serpent. ¹¹Then Pharaoh also called for the wise men and the sorcerers: and they also, the magicians of Egypt, did in like manner with their enchantments. ¹²For they cast down every man his rod, and they became serpents: but Aaron's rod swallowed up their rods. ¹³And Pharaoh's heart was hardened, and he hearkened not unto them; as Jehovah had spoken.

¹⁴And Jehovah said unto Moses, Pharaoh's heart is stubborn, he refuseth to let the people go. ¹⁵Get thee unto Pharaoh in the morning; lo, he goeth out unto the water; and thou shalt stand by the river's brink to meet him; and the rod which was turned to a serpent shalt thou take in thy hand. ¹⁶And thou shalt say unto him, Jehovah, the God of the Hebrews, hath sent me unto thee, saying, Let my people go, that they may serve me in the wilderness: and, behold, hitherto thou hast not hearkened. ¹⁷Thus saith Jehovah, In this thou shalt know that I am Jehovah: behold, I will smite with the rod that is in my hand upon the waters which are in the river, and they shall be turned to blood. ¹⁸And the fish that are in the river shall die, and the river shall become foul; and the Egyptians shall loathe to drink water from the river. ¹⁹And Jehovah said unto Moses, Say unto Aaron, Take thy rod, and stretch out thy hand over the waters of Egypt, over their rivers, over their streams, and over their pools, and over all their ponds of water, that they may become blood; and there shall be blood throughout all the land of Egypt, both in vessels of wood and in vessels of stone.

²⁰And Moses and Aaron did so, as Jehovah commanded; and he lifted up the rod, and smote the waters that were in the river, in the sight of Pharaoh, and in the sight of his servants; and all the waters that were in the river were turned to blood. ²¹And the fish that were in the river died; and the river became foul, and the Egyptians could not drink water from the river; and the blood was throughout all the land of Egypt. ²²And the magicians of

Egypt did in like manner with their enchantments: and Pharaoh's heart was hardened, and he hearkened not unto them; as Jehovah had spoken. [23]And Pharaoh turned and went into his house, neither did he lay even this to heart. [24]And all the Egyptians digged round about the river for water to drink; for they could not drink of the water of the river. [25]And seven days were fulfilled, after that Jehovah had smitten the river.

EXODUS 8

[1]And Jehovah spake unto Moses, Go in unto Pharaoh, and say unto him, Thus saith Jehovah, Let my people go, that they may serve me. [2]And if thou refuse to let them go, behold, I will smite all thy borders with frogs: [3]and the river shall swarm with frogs, which shall go up and come into thy house, and into thy bedchamber, and upon thy bed, and into the house of thy servants, and upon thy people, and into thine ovens, and into thy kneading-troughs: [4]and the frogs shall come up both upon thee, and upon thy people, and upon all thy servants. [5]And Jehovah said unto Moses, Say unto Aaron, Stretch forth thy hand with thy rod over the rivers, over the streams, and over the pools, and cause frogs to come up upon the land of Egypt. [6]And Aaron stretched out his hand over the waters of Egypt; and the frogs came up, and covered the land of Egypt. [7]And the magicians did in like manner with their enchantments, and brought up frogs upon the land of Egypt.

[8]Then Pharaoh called for Moses and Aaron, and said, Entreat Jehovah, that he take away the frogs from me, and from my people; and I will let the people go, that they may sacrifice unto Jehovah. [9]And Moses said unto Pharaoh, Have thou this glory over me: against what time shall I entreat for thee, and for thy servants, and for thy people, that the frogs be destroyed from thee and thy houses, and remain in the river only? [10]And he said, Against tomorrow. And he said, Be it according to thy word; that thou mayest know that there is none like unto Jehovah our God. [11]And the frogs shall depart from thee, and from thy houses, and from thy servants, and from thy people; they shall remain in the river only. [12]And Moses and Aaron went out from Pharaoh: and Moses cried unto Jehovah concerning the frogs which he had brought upon Pharaoh. [13]And Jehovah did according to the word of Moses; and the frogs died out of the houses, out of the courts, and out of the fields. [14]And they gathered them together in heaps; and the land stank. [15]But when Pharaoh saw that there was respite, he hardened his heart, and hearkened not unto them, as Jehovah had spoken.

[16]And Jehovah said unto Moses, Say unto Aaron, Stretch out thy rod, and smite the dust of the earth, that is may become lice throughout all

the land of Egypt. [17]And they did so; and Aaron stretched out his hand with his rod, and smote the dust of the earth, and there were lice upon man, and upon beast; all the dust of the earth became lice throughout all the land of Egypt. [18]And the magicians did so with their enchantments to bring forth lice, but they could not: and there were lice upon man, and upon beast. [19]Then the magicians said unto Pharaoh, This is the finger of God: and Pharaoh's heart was hardened, and he hearkened not unto them; as Jehovah had spoken.

[20]And Jehovah said unto Moses, Rise up early in the morning, and stand before Pharaoh; lo, he cometh forth to the water; and say unto him, Thus saith Jehovah, Let my people go, that they may serve me. [21]Else, if thou wilt not let my people go, behold, I will send swarms of flies upon thee, and upon they servants, and upon thy people, and into thy houses: and the houses of the Egyptians shall be full of swarms of flies, and also the ground whereon they are. [22]And I will set apart in that day the land of Goshen, in which my people dwell, that no swarms of flies shall be there; to the end thou mayest know that I am Jehovah in the midst of the earth. [23]And I will put a division between my people and thy people: by tomorrow shall this sign be. [24]And Jehovah did so; and there came grievous swarms of flies into the house of Pharaoh, and into his servants' houses: and in all the land of Egypt the land was corrupted by reason of the swarms of flies.

[25]And Pharaoh called for Moses and for Aaron, and said, Go ye, sacrifice to your God in the land. [26]And Moses said, It is not meet so to do; for we shall sacrifice the abomination of the Egyptians to Jehovah our God: lo, shall we sacrifice the abomination of the Egyptians before their eyes, and will they not stone us? [27]We will go three days' journey into the wilderness, and sacrifice to Jehovah our God, as he shall command us. [28]And Pharaoh said, I will let you go, that ye may sacrifice to Jehovah your God in the wilderness; only ye shall not go very far away: entreat for me. [29]And Moses said, Behold, I go out from thee, and I will entreat Jehovah that the swarms of flies may depart from Pharaoh, from his servants, and from his people, tomorrow: only let not Pharaoh deal deceitfully any more in not letting the people go to sacrifice to Jehovah. [30]And Moses went out from Pharaoh, and entreated Jehovah. [31]And Jehovah did according to the word of Moses; and he removed the swarms of flies from Pharaoh, from his servants, and from his people; there remained not one. [32]And Pharaoh hardened his heart this time also, and he did not let the people go.

EXODUS 9

[1]Then Jehovah said unto Moses, Go in unto Pharaoh, and tell him, Thus saith Jehovah, the God of the Hebrews, Let my people go, that they

may serve me. [2]For if thou refuse to let them go, and wilt hold them still, [3]behold, the hand of Jehovah is upon thy cattle which are in the field, upon the horses, upon the asses, upon the camels, upon the herds, and upon the flocks: there shall be a very grievous murrain. [4]And Jehovah shall make a distinction between the cattle of Israel and the cattle of Egypt; and there shall nothing die of all that belongeth to the children of Israel. [5]And Jehovah appointed a set time, saying, Tomorrow Jehovah shall do this thing in the land. [6]And Jehovah did that thing on the morrow; and all the cattle of Egypt died; but of the cattle of the children of Israel died not one. [7]And Pharaoh sent, and, behold, there was not so much as one of the cattle of the Israelites dead. But the heart of Pharaoh was stubborn, and he did not let the people go.

[8]And Jehovah said unto Moses and unto Aaron, Take to you handfuls of ashes of the furnace, and let Moses sprinkle it toward heaven in the sight of Pharaoh. [9]And it shall become small dust over all the land of Egypt, and shall be a boil breaking forth with blains upon man and upon beast, throughout all the land of Egypt. [10]And they took ashes of the furnace, and stood before Pharaoh; and Moses sprinkled it up toward heaven; and it became a boil breaking forth with blains upon man and upon beast. [11]And the magicians could not stand before Moses because of the boils; for the boils were upon the magicians, and upon all the Egyptians. [12]And Jehovah hardened the heart of Pharaoh, and he hearkened not unto them, as Jehovah had spoken unto Moses.

[13]And Jehovah said unto Moses, Rise up early in the morning, and stand before Pharaoh, and say unto him, Thus saith Jehovah, the God of the Hebrews, Let my people go, that they may serve me. [14]For I will this time send all my plagues upon thy heart, and upon thy servants, and upon thy people; that thou mayest know that there is none like me in all the earth. [15]For now I had put forth my hand, and smitten thee and thy people with pestilence, and thou hadst been cut off from the earth: [16]but in very deed for this cause have I made thee to stand, to show thee my power, and that my name may be declared throughout all the earth. [17]As yet exaltest thou thyself against my people, that thou wilt not let them go? [18]Behold, tomorrow about this time I will cause it to rain a very grievous hail, such as hath not been in Egypt since the day it was founded even until now. [19]Now therefore send, hasten in thy cattle and all that thou hast in the field; for every man and beast that shall be found in the field, and shall not be brought home, the hail shall come down upon them, and they shall die.

[20]He that feared the word of Jehovah among the servants of Pharaoh made his servants and his cattle flee into the houses. [21]And he that regarded not the word of Jehovah left his servants and his cattle in the field.

²²And Jehovah said unto Moses, Stretch forth thy hand toward heaven, that there may be hail in all the land of Egypt, upon man, and upon beast, and upon every herb of the field, throughout the land of Egypt. ²³And Moses stretched forth his rod toward heaven: and Jehovah sent thunder and hail, and fire ran down unto the earth; and Jehovah rained hail upon the land of Egypt. ²⁴So there was hail, and fire mingled with the hail, very grievous, such as had not been in all the land of Egypt since it became a nation. ²⁵And the hail smote throughout all the land of Egypt all that was in the field, both man and beast; and the hail smote every herb of the field, and brake every tree of the field. ²⁶Only in the land of Goshen, where the children of Israel were, was there no hail.

²⁷And Pharaoh sent, and called for Moses and Aaron, and said unto them, I have sinned this time: Jehovah is righteous, and I and my people are wicked. ²⁸Entreat Jehovah; for there hath been enough of these mighty thunderings and hail; and I will let you go, and ye shall stay no longer. ²⁹And Moses said unto him, As soon as I am gone out of the city, I will spread abroad my hands unto Jehovah; the thunders shall cease, neither shall there be any more hail; that thou mayest know that the earth is Jehovah's. ³⁰But as for thee and thy servants, I know that ye will not yet fear Jehovah God. ³¹And the flax and the barley were smitten: for the barley was in the ear, and the flax was in bloom. ³²But the wheat and the spelt were not smitten: for they were not grown up.

³³And Moses went out of the city from Pharaoh, and spread abroad his hands unto Jehovah: and the thunders and hail ceased, and the rain was not poured upon the earth. ³⁴And when Pharaoh saw that the rain and the hail and the thunders were ceased, he sinned yet more, and hardened his heart, he and his servants. ³⁵And the heart of Pharaoh was hardened, and he did not let the children of Israel go, as Jehovah had spoken by Moses.

EXODUS 10

¹And Jehovah said unto Moses, Go in unto Pharaoh: for I have hardened his heart, and the heart of his servants, that I may show these my signs in the midst of them, ²and that thou mayest tell in the ears of thy son, and of thy son's son, what things I have wrought upon Egypt, and my signs which I have done among them; that ye may know that I am Jehovah. ³And Moses and Aaron went in unto Pharaoh, and said unto him, Thus saith Jehovah, the God of the Hebrews, How long wilt thou refuse to humble thyself before me? let my people go, that they may serve me. ⁴Else, if thou refuse to let my people go, behold, tomorrow will I bring locusts into thy border: ⁵and they shall cover the face of the earth, so that one shall not be

able to see the earth: and they shall eat the residue of that which is escaped, which remaineth unto you from the hail, and shall eat every tree which groweth for you out of the field: 6and thy houses shall be filled, and the houses of all thy servants, and the houses of all the Egyptians; as neither thy fathers nor thy fathers' fathers have seen, since the day that they were upon the earth unto this day. And he turned, and went out from Pharaoh.

7And Pharaoh's servants said unto him, How long shall this man be a snare unto us? let the men go, that they may serve Jehovah their God: knowest thou not yet that Egypt is destroyed? 8And Moses and Aaron were brought again unto Pharaoh: and he said unto them, Go, serve Jehovah your God; but who are they that shall go? 9And Moses said, We will go with our young and with our old; with our sons and with our daughters, with our flocks and with our herds will we go; for we must hold a feast unto Jehovah. 10And he said unto them, So be Jehovah with you, as I will let you go, and your little ones: look to it; for evil is before you. 11Not so: go now ye that are men, and serve Jehovah; for that is what ye desire. And they were driven out from Pharaoh's presence.

12And Jehovah said unto Moses, Stretch out thy hand over the land of Egypt for the locusts, that they may come up upon the land of Egypt, and eat every herb of the land, even all that the hail hath left. 13And Moses stretched forth his rod over the land of Egypt, and Jehovah brought an east wind upon the land all that day, and all the night; and when it was morning, the east wind brought the locusts. 14And the locusts went up over all the land of Egypt, and rested in all the borders of Egypt; very grievous were they; before them there were no such locusts as they, neither after them shall be such. 15For they covered the face of the whole earth, so that the land was darkened; and they did eat every herb of the land, and all the fruit of the trees which the hail had left: and there remained not any green thing, either tree or herb of the field, through all the land of Egypt.

16Then Pharaoh called for Moses and Aaron in haste; and he said, I have sinned against Jehovah your God, and against you. 17Now therefore forgive, I pray thee, my sin only this once, and entreat Jehovah your God, that he may take away from me this death only. 18And he went out from Pharaoh, and entreated Jehovah. 19And Jehovah turned an exceeding strong west wind, which took up the locusts, and drove them into the Red Sea; there remained not one locust in all the border of Egypt. 20But Jehovah hardened Pharaoh's heart, and he did not let the children of Israel go.

21And Jehovah said unto Moses, Stretch out thy hand toward heaven, that there may be darkness over the land of Egypt, even darkness which may be felt. 22And Moses stretched forth his hand toward heaven; and there was a thick darkness in all the land of Egypt three days; ²³they saw not one another, neither rose any one from his place for three days: but all the children of Israel had light in their dwellings.

²⁴And Pharaoh called unto Moses, and said, Go ye, serve Jehovah; only let your flocks and your herds be stayed: let your little ones also go with you. ²⁵And Moses said, Thou must also give into our hand sacrifices and burnt-offerings, that we may sacrifice unto Jehovah our God. ²⁶Our cattle also shall go with us; there shall not a hoof be left behind: for thereof must we take to serve Jehovah our God; and we know not with what we must serve Jehovah, until we come thither. ²⁷But Jehovah hardened Pharaoh's heart, and he would not let them go. ²⁸And Pharaoh said unto him, Get thee from me, take heed to thyself, see my face no more; for in the day thou seest my face thou shalt die. ²⁹And Moses said, Thou hast spoken well. I will see thy face again no more.

EXODUS 11

¹And Jehovah said unto Moses, Yet one plague more will I bring upon Pharaoh, and upon Egypt; afterwards he will let you go hence: when he shall let you go, he shall surely thrust you out hence altogether. ²Speak now in the ears of the people, and let them ask every man of his neighbor, and every woman of her neighbor, jewels of silver, and jewels of gold. ³And Jehovah gave the people favor in the sight of the Egyptians. Moreover the man Moses was very great in the land of Egypt, in the sight of Pharaoh's servants, and in the sight of the people.

⁴And Moses said, Thus saith Jehovah, About midnight will I go out into the midst of Egypt: ⁵and all the first-born in the land of Egypt shall die, from the first-born of Pharaoh that sitteth upon his throne, even unto the first-born of the maid-servant that is behind the mill; and all the first-born of cattle. ⁶And there shall be a great cry throughout all the land of Egypt, such as there hath not been, nor shall be any more. ⁷But against any of the children of Israel shall not a dog move his tongue, against man or beast: that ye may know how that Jehovah doth make a distinction between the Egyptians and Israel. ⁸And all these thy servants shall come down unto me, and bow down themselves unto me, saying, Get thee out, and all the people that follow thee: and after that I will go out. And he went out from Pharaoh in hot anger.

⁹And Jehovah said unto Moses, Pharaoh will not hearken unto you; that my wonders may be multiplied in the land of Egypt. ¹⁰And Moses and Aaron did all these wonders before Pharaoh: and Jehovah hardened Pharaoh's heart, and he did not let the children of Israel go out of his land.

EXODUS 12

¹And Jehovah spake unto Moses and Aaron in the land of Egypt, saying, ²This month shall be unto you the beginning of months: it shall be the first month of the year to you. ³Speak ye unto all the congregation of Israel, saying, In the tenth day of this month they shall take to them every man a lamb, according to their fathers' houses, a lamb for a household: ⁴and if the household be too little for a lamb, then shall he and his neighbor next unto his house take one according to the number of the souls; according to every man's eating ye shall make your count for the lamb. ⁵Your lamb shall be without blemish, a male a year old: ye shall take it from the sheep, or from the goats: ⁶and ye shall keep it until the fourteenth day of the same month; and the whole assembly of the congregation of Israel shall kill it at even. ⁷And they shall take of the blood, and put it on the two side-posts and on the lintel, upon the houses wherein they shall eat it. ⁸And they shall eat the flesh in that night, roast with fire, and unleavened bread; with bitter herbs they shall eat it. ⁹Eat not of it raw, nor boiled at all with water, but roast with fire; its head with its legs and with the inwards thereof. ¹⁰And ye shall let nothing of it remain until the morning; but that which remaineth of it until the morning ye shall burn with fire. ¹¹And thus shall ye eat it: with your loins girded, your shoes on your feet, and your staff in your hand; and ye shall eat it in haste: it is Jehovah's passover. ¹²For I will go through the land of Egypt in that night, and will smite all the first-born in the land of Egypt, both man and beast; and against all the gods of Egypt I will execute judgments: I am Jehovah. ¹³And the blood shall be to you for a token upon the houses where ye are: and when I see the blood, I will pass over you, and there shall no plague be upon you to destroy you, when I smite the land of Egypt. ¹⁴And this day shall be unto you for a memorial, and ye shall keep it a feast to Jehovah: throughout your generations ye shall keep it a feast by an ordinance for ever.

¹⁵Seven days shall ye eat unleavened bread; even the first day ye shall put away leaven out of your houses: for whosoever eateth leavened bread from the first day until the seventh day, that soul shall be cut off from Israel. ¹⁶And in the first day there shall be to you a holy convocation, and in the seventh day a holy convocation; no manner of work shall be done in them, save that which every man must eat, that only may be done by you. ¹⁷And ye shall observe the feast of unleavened bread; for in this selfsame day have I brought your hosts out of the land of Egypt: therefore shall ye observe this day throughout your generations by an ordinance for ever. ¹⁸In the first month, on the fourteenth day of the month at even, ye shall eat unleavened bread, until the one and twentieth day of the month

at even. ¹⁹Seven days shall there be no leaven found in your houses: for whosoever eateth that which is leavened, that soul shall be cut off from the congregation of Israel, whether he be a sojourner, or one that is born in the land. ²⁰Ye shall eat nothing leavened; in all your habitations shall ye eat unleavened bread.

²¹Then Moses called for all the elders of Israel, and said unto them, Draw out, and take you lambs according to your families, and kill the passover. ²²And ye shall take a bunch of hyssop, and dip it in the blood that is in the basin, and strike the lintel and the two side-posts with the blood that is in the basin; and none of you shall go out of the door of his house until the morning. ²³For Jehovah will pass through to smite the Egyptians; and when he seeth the blood upon the lintel, and on the two side-posts, Jehovah will pass over the door, and will not suffer the destroyer to come in unto your houses to smite you.

²⁴And ye shall observe this thing for an ordinance to thee and to thy sons for ever. ²⁵And it shall come to pass, when ye are come to the land which Jehovah will give you, according as he hath promised, that ye shall keep this service. ²⁶And it shall come to pass, when your children shall say unto you, What mean ye by this service? ²⁷that ye shall say, It is the sacrifice of Jehovah's passover, who passed over the houses of the children of Israel in Egypt, when he smote the Egyptians, and delivered our houses. And the people bowed the head and worshipped. ²⁸And the children of Israel went and did so; as Jehovah had commanded Moses and Aaron, so did they.

²⁹And it came to pass at midnight, that Jehovah smote all the first-born in the land of Egypt, from the first-born of Pharaoh that sat on his throne unto the first-born of the captive that was in the dungeon; and all the first-born of cattle. ³⁰And Pharaoh rose up in the night, he, and all his servants, and all the Egyptians; and there was a great cry in Egypt, for there was not a house where there was not one dead. ³¹And he called for Moses and Aaron by night, and said, Rise up, get you forth from among my people, both ye and the children of Israel; and go, serve Jehovah, as ye have said. ³²Take both your flocks and your herds, as ye have said, and be gone; and bless me also. ³³And the Egyptians were urgent upon the people, to send them out of the land in haste; for they said, We are all dead men. ³⁴And the people took their dough before it was leavened, their kneading-troughs being bound up in their clothes upon their shoulders. ³⁵And the children of Israel did according to the word of Moses; and they asked of the Egyptians jewels of silver, and jewels of gold, and raiment. ³⁶And Jehovah gave the people favor in the sight of the Egyptians, so that they let them have what they asked. And they despoiled the Egyptians.

[37] And the children of Israel journeyed from Rameses to Succoth, about six hundred thousand on foot that were men, besides children. [38] And a mixed multitude went up also with them; and flocks, and herds, even very much cattle. [39] And they baked unleavened cakes of the dough which they brought forth out of Egypt; for it was not leavened, because they were thrust out of Egypt, and could not tarry, neither had they prepared for themselves any victuals. [40] Now the time that the children of Israel dwelt in Egypt was four hundred and thirty years. [41] And it came to pass at the end of four hundred and thirty years, even the selfsame day it came to pass, that all the hosts of Jehovah went out from the land of Egypt. [42] It is a night to be much observed unto Jehovah for bringing them out from the land of Egypt: this is that night of Jehovah, to be much observed of all the children of Israel throughout their generations.

[43] And Jehovah said unto Moses and Aaron, This is the ordinance of the passover: there shall no foreigner eat thereof; [44] but every man's servant that is bought for money, when thou hast circumcised him, then shall he eat thereof. [45] A sojourner and a hired servant shall not eat thereof. [46] In one house shall it be eaten; thou shalt not carry forth aught of the flesh abroad out of the house; neither shall ye break a bone thereof. [47] All the congregation of Israel shall keep it. [48] And when a stranger shall sojourn with thee, and will keep the passover to Jehovah, let all his males be circumcised, and then let him come near and keep it; and he shall be as one that is born in the land: but no uncircumcised person shall eat thereof. [49] One law shall be to him that is home-born, and unto the stranger that sojourneth among you.

[50] Thus did all the children of Israel; as Jehovah commanded Moses and Aaron, so did they. [51] And it came to pass the selfsame day, that Jehovah did bring the children of Israel out of the land of Egypt by their hosts.

EXODUS 13

[1] And Jehovah spake unto Moses, saying, [2] Sanctify unto me all the first-born, whatsoever openeth the womb among the children of Israel, both of man and of beast: it is mine.

[3] And Moses said unto the people, Remember this day, in which ye came out from Egypt, out of the house of bondage; for by strength of hand Jehovah brought you out from this place: there shall no leavened bread be eaten. [4] This day ye go forth in the month Abib. [5] And it shall be, when Jehovah shall bring thee into the land of the Canaanite, and the Hittite, and the Amorite, and the Hivite, and the Jebusite, which he sware unto thy fathers to give thee, a land flowing with milk and honey,

that thou shalt keep this service in this month. ⁶Seven days thou shalt eat unleavened bread, and in the seventh day shall be a feast to Jehovah. ⁷Unleavened bread shall be eaten throughout the seven days; and there shall no leavened bread be seen with thee, neither shall there be leaven seen with thee, in all thy borders. ⁸And thou shalt tell thy son in that day, saying, It is because of that which Jehovah did for me when I came forth out of Egypt. ⁹And it shall be for a sign unto thee upon thy hand, and for a memorial between thine eyes, that the law of Jehovah may be in thy mouth: for with a strong hand hath Jehovah brought thee out of Egypt. ¹⁰Thou shalt therefore keep this ordinance in its season from year to year.

¹¹And it shall be, when Jehovah shall bring thee into the land of the Canaanite, as he sware unto thee and to thy fathers, and shall give it thee, ¹²that thou shalt set apart unto Jehovah all that openeth the womb, and every firstling which thou hast that cometh of a beast; the males shall be Jehovah's. ¹³And every firstling of an ass thou shalt redeem with a lamb; and if thou wilt not redeem it, then thou shalt break its neck: and all the first-born of man among thy sons shalt thou redeem. ¹⁴And it shall be, when thy son asketh thee in time to come, saying, What is this? that thou shalt say unto him, By strength of hand Jehovah brought us out from Egypt, from the house of bondage: ¹⁵and it came to pass, when Pharaoh would hardly let us go, that Jehovah slew all the first-born in the land of Egypt, both the first-born of man, and the first-born of beast: therefore I sacrifice to Jehovah all that openeth the womb, being males; but all the first-born of my sons I redeem. ¹⁶And it shall be for a sign upon thy hand, and for frontlets between thine eyes: for by strength of hand Jehovah brought us forth out of Egypt.

¹⁷And it came to pass, when Pharaoh had let the people go, that God led them not by the way of the land of the Philistines, although that was near; for God said, Lest peradventure the people repent when they see war, and they return to Egypt: ¹⁸but God led the people about, by the way of the wilderness by the Red Sea: and the children of Israel went up armed out of the land of Egypt. ¹⁹And Moses took the bones of Joseph with him: for he had straitly sworn the children of Israel, saying, God will surely visit you; and ye shall carry up my bones away hence with you. ²⁰And they took their journey from Succoth, and encamped in Etham, in the edge of the wilderness. ²¹And Jehovah went before them by day in a pillar of cloud, to lead them the way, and by night in a pillar of fire, to give them light, that they might go by day and by night: ²²the pillar of cloud by day, and the pillar of fire by night, departed not from before the people.

EXODUS 14

[1]And Jehovah spake unto Moses, saying, [2]Speak unto the children of Israel, that they turn back and encamp before Pihahiroth, between Migdol and the sea, before Baal-zephon: over against it shall ye encamp by the sea. [3]And Pharaoh will say of the children of Israel, They are entangled in the land, the wilderness hath shut them in. [4]And I will harden Pharaoh's heart, and he shall follow after them; and I will get me honor upon Pharaoh, and upon all his host: and the Egyptians shall know that I am Jehovah. And they did so.

[5]And it was told the king of Egypt that the people were fled: and the heart of Pharaoh and of his servants was changed towards the people, and they said, What is this we have done, that we have let Israel go from serving us? [6]And he made ready his chariot, and took his people with him: [7]and he took six hundred chosen chariots, and all the chariots of Egypt, and captains over all of them. [8]And Jehovah hardened the heart of Pharaoh king of Egypt, and he pursued after the children of Israel: for the children of Israel went out with a high hand. [9]And the Egyptians pursued after them, all the horses and chariots of Pharaoh, and his horsemen, and his army, and overtook them encamping by the sea, beside Pihahiroth, before Baal-zephon.

[10]And when Pharaoh drew nigh, the children of Israel lifted up their eyes, and, behold, the Egyptians were marching after them; and they were sore afraid: and the children of Israel cried out unto Jehovah. [11]And they said unto Moses, Because there were no graves in Egypt, hast thou taken us away to die in the wilderness? wherefore hast thou dealt thus with us, to bring us forth out of Egypt? [12]Is not this the word that we spake unto thee in Egypt, saying, Let us alone, that we may serve the Egyptians? For it were better for us to serve the Egyptians, than that we should die in the wilderness. [13]And Moses said unto the people, Fear ye not, stand still, and see the salvation of Jehovah, which he will work for you today: for the Egyptians whom ye have seen today, ye shall see them again no more for ever. [14]Jehovah will fight for you, and ye shall hold your peace.

[15]And Jehovah said unto Moses, Wherefore criest thou unto me? speak unto the children of Israel, that they go forward. [16]And lift thou up thy rod, and stretch out thy hand over the sea, and divide it: and the children of Israel shall go into the midst of the sea on dry ground. [17]And I, behold, I will harden the hearts of the Egyptians, and they shall go in after them: and I will get me honor upon Pharaoh, and upon all his host, upon his chariots, and upon his horsemen. [18]And the Egyptians shall know that I am Jehovah, when I have gotten me honor upon Pharaoh, upon his chariots, and upon his horsemen.

¹⁹And the angel of God, who went before the camp of Israel, removed and went behind them; and the pillar of cloud removed from before them, and stood behind them: ²⁰and it came between the camp of Egypt and the camp of Israel; and there was the cloud and the darkness, yet gave it light by night: and the one came not near the other all the night.

²¹And Moses stretched out his hand over the sea; and Jehovah caused the sea to go back by a strong east wind all the night, and made the sea dry land, and the waters were divided. ²²And the children of Israel went into the midst of the sea upon the dry ground: and the waters were a wall unto them on their right hand, and on their left. ²³And the Egyptians pursued, and went in after them into the midst of the sea, all Pharaoh's horses, his chariots, and his horsemen. ²⁴And it came to pass in the morning watch, that Jehovah looked forth upon the host of the Egyptians through the pillar of fire and of cloud, and discomfited the host of the Egyptians. ²⁵And he took off their chariot wheels, and they drove them heavily; so that the Egyptians said, Let us flee from the face of Israel; for Jehovah fighteth for them against the Egyptians.

²⁶And Jehovah said unto Moses, Stretch out thy hand over the sea, that the waters may come again upon the Egyptians, upon their chariots, and upon their horsemen. ²⁷And Moses stretched forth his hand over the sea, and the sea returned to its strength when the morning appeared; and the Egyptians fled against it; and Jehovah overthrew the Egyptians in the midst of the sea. ²⁸And the waters returned, and covered the chariots, and the horsemen, even all the host of Pharaoh that went in after them into the sea; there remained not so much as one of them. ²⁹But the children of Israel walked upon dry land in the midst of the sea; and the waters were a wall unto them on their right hand, and on their left.

³⁰Thus Jehovah saved Israel that day out of the hand of the Egyptians; and Israel saw the Egyptians dead upon the sea-shore. ³¹And Israel saw the great work which Jehovah did upon the Egyptians, and the people feared Jehovah: and they believed in Jehovah, and in his servant Moses.

EXODUS 15

¹*Then sang Moses and the children of Israel this song unto*
Jehovah, and spake, saying,
I will sing unto Jehovah, for he hath triumphed gloriously:
The horse and his rider hath he thrown into the sea.
²*Jehovah is my strength and song,*
And he is become my salvation:
This is my God, and I will praise him;

My father's God, and I will exalt him.
³Jehovah is a man of war:
Jehovah is his name.
⁴Pharaoh's chariots and his host hath he cast into the sea;
And his chosen captains are sunk in the Red Sea.
⁵The deeps cover them:
They went down into the depths like a stone.
⁶Thy right hand, O Jehovah, is glorious in power,
Thy right hand, O Jehovah, dasheth in pieces the enemy.
⁷And in the greatness of thine excellency thou overthrowest
*   them that rise up against thee:*
Thou sendest forth thy wrath,
it consumeth them as stubble.
⁸And with the blast of thy nostrils the waters were
*   piled up,*
The floods stood upright as a heap;
The deeps were congealed in the heart of the sea.
⁹The enemy said, I will pursue, I will overtake,
I will divide the spoil;
My desire shall be satisfied upon them;
I will draw my sword, my hand shall destroy them.
¹⁰Thou didst blow with thy wind, the sea covered them:
They sank as lead in the mighty waters.
¹¹Who is like unto thee, O Jehovah, among the gods?
Who is like thee, glorious in holiness,
Fearful in praises, doing wonders?
¹²Thou stretchedst out thy right hand,
The earth swallowed them.
¹³Thou in thy lovingkindness hast led the people that thou
*   hast redeemed:*
Thou hast guided them in thy strength to thy holy
*   habitation.*
¹⁴The peoples have heard, they tremble:
Pangs have taken hold on the inhabitants of Philistia.
¹⁵Then were the chiefs of Edom dismayed;
The mighty men of Moab, trembling taketh hold
*   upon them:*
All the inhabitants of Canaan are melted away.
¹⁶Terror and dread falleth upon them;
By the greatness of thine arm they are as still as a stone;
Till thy people pass over, O Jehovah,

Till the people pass over that thou hast purchased.
[17]Thou wilt bring them in, and plant them in the
mountain of thine inheritance,
The place, O Jehovah, which thou hast made for thee to
dwell in,
The sanctuary, O Lord, which thy hands have established.
[18]Jehovah shall reign for ever and ever.
[19]For the horses of Pharaoh went in with his chariots and
with his horsemen into the sea,
and Jehovah brought back the waters of the sea
upon them;
but the children of Israel walked on dry land in the midst
of the sea.

[20]And Miriam the prophetess, the sister of Aaron, took a timbrel in her hand; and all the women went out after her with timbrels and with dances. [21]And Miriam answered them,

Sing ye to Jehovah, for he hath triumphed gloriously;
The horse and his rider hath he thrown into the sea.

[22]And Moses led Israel onward from the Red Sea, and they went out into the wilderness of Shur; and they went three days in the wilderness, and found no water. [23]And when they came to Marah, they could not drink of the waters of Marah, for they were bitter: therefore the name of it was called Marah. [24]And the people murmured against Moses, saying, What shall we drink? [25]And he cried unto Jehovah; And Jehovah showed him a tree, and he cast it into the waters, and the waters were made sweet. There he made for them a statute and an ordinance, and there he proved them; [26]and he said, If thou wilt diligently hearken to the voice of Jehovah thy God, and wilt do that which is right in his eyes, and wilt give ear to his commandments, and keep all his statutes, I will put none of the diseases upon thee, which I have put upon the Egyptians: for I am Jehovah that healeth thee. [27]And they came to Elim, where were twelve springs of water, and threescore and ten palm-trees: and they encamped there by the waters.

EXODUS 16

[1]And they took their journey from Elim, and all the congregation of the children of Israel came unto the wilderness of Sin, which is between Elim and Sinai, on the fifteenth day of the second month after their departing

out of the land of Egypt. ²And the whole congregation of the children of Israel murmured against Moses and against Aaron in the wilderness: ³and the children of Israel said unto them, Would that we had died by the hand of Jehovah in the land of Egypt, when we sat by the flesh-pots, when we did eat bread to the full; for ye have brought us forth into this wilderness, to kill this whole assembly with hunger.

⁴Then said Jehovah unto Moses, Behold, I will rain bread from heaven for you; and the people shall go out and gather a day's portion every day, that I may prove them, whether they will walk in my law, or not. ⁵And it shall come to pass on the sixth day, that they shall prepare that which they bring in, and it shall be twice as much as they gather daily. ⁶And Moses and Aaron said unto all the children of Israel, At even, then ye shall know that Jehovah hath brought you out from the land of Egypt; ⁷and in the morning, then ye shall see the glory of Jehovah; for that he heareth your murmurings against Jehovah: and what are we, that ye murmur against us? ⁸And Moses said, This shall be, when Jehovah shall give you in the evening flesh to eat, and in the morning bread to the full; for that Jehovah heareth your murmurings which ye murmur against him: and what are we? your murmurings are not against us, but against Jehovah. ⁹And Moses said unto Aaron, Say unto all the congregation of the children of Israel, Come near before Jehovah; for he hath heard your murmurings. ¹⁰And it came to pass, as Aaron spake unto the whole congregation of the children of Israel, that they looked toward the wilderness, and, behold, the glory of Jehovah appeared in the cloud. ¹¹And Jehovah spake unto Moses, saying, ¹²I have heard the murmurings of the children of Israel: speak unto them, saying, At even ye shall eat flesh, and in the morning ye shall be filled with bread: and ye shall know that I am Jehovah your God.

¹³And it came to pass at even, that the quails came up, and covered the camp: and in the morning the dew lay round about the camp. ¹⁴And when the dew that lay was gone up, behold, upon the face of the wilderness a small round thing, small as the hoar-frost on the ground. ¹⁵And when the children of Israel saw it, they said one to another, What is it? For they knew not what it was. And Moses said unto them, It is the bread which Jehovah hath given you to eat. ¹⁶This is the thing which Jehovah hath commanded, Gather ye of it every man according to his eating; an omer a head, according to the number of your persons, shall ye take it, every man for them that are in his tent. ¹⁷And the children of Israel did so, and gathered some more, some less. ¹⁸And when they measured it with an omer, he that gathered much had nothing over, and he that gathered little had no lack; they gathered every man according to his eating. ¹⁹And Moses said unto them, Let no man leave of it till the morning. ²⁰Notwithstanding

they hearkened not unto Moses; but some of them left of it until the morning, and it bred worms, and became foul: and Moses was wroth with them. [21]And they gathered it morning by morning, every man according to his eating: and when the sun waxed hot, it melted. [22]And it came to pass, that on the sixth day they gathered twice as much bread, two omers for each one: and all the rulers of the congregation came and told Moses.

[23]And he said unto them, This is that which Jehovah hath spoken, Tomorrow is a solemn rest, a holy sabbath unto Jehovah: bake that which ye will bake, and boil that which ye will boil; and all that remaineth over lay up for you to be kept until the morning. [24]And they laid it up till the morning, as Moses bade: and it did not become foul, neither was there any worm therein. [25]And Moses said, Eat that today; for today is a sabbath unto Jehovah: today ye shall not find it in the field. [26]Six days ye shall gather it; but on the seventh day is the sabbath, in it there shall be none. [27]And it came to pass on the seventh day, that there went out some of the people to gather, and they found none. [28]And Jehovah said unto Moses, How long refuse ye to keep my commandments and my laws? [29]See, for that Jehovah hath given you the sabbath, therefore he giveth you on the sixth day the bread of two days; abide ye every man in his place, let no man go out of his place on the seventh day. [30]So the people rested on the seventh day.

[31]And the house of Israel called the name thereof Manna: and it was like coriander seed, white; and the taste of it was like wafers made with honey. [32]And Moses said, This is the thing which Jehovah hath commanded, Let an omerful of it be kept throughout your generations, that they may see the bread wherewith I fed you in the wilderness, when I brought you forth from the land of Egypt. [33]And Moses said unto Aaron, Take a pot, and put an omerful of manna therein, and lay it up before Jehovah, to be kept throughout your generations. [34]As Jehovah commanded Moses, so Aaron laid it up before the Testimony, to be kept. [35]And the children of Israel did eat the manna forty years, until they came to a land inhabited; they did eat the manna, until they came unto the borders of the land of Canaan. [36]Now an omer is the tenth part of an ephah.

EXODUS 17

[1]And all the congregation of the children of Israel journeyed from the wilderness of Sin, by their journeys, according to the commandment of Jehovah, and encamped in Rephidim: and there was no water for the people to drink. [2]Wherefore the people stove with Moses, and said, Give us water that we may drink. And Moses said unto them, Why strive ye with me? Wherefore do ye tempt Jehovah? [3]And the people thirsted there

for water; and the people murmured against Moses, and said, Wherefore hast thou brought us up out of Egypt, to kill us and our children and our cattle with thirst?

[4]And Moses cried unto Jehovah, saying, What shall I do unto this people? They are almost ready to stone me. [5]And Jehovah said unto Moses, Pass on before the people, and take with thee of the elders of Israel; and they rod, wherewith thou smotest the river, take in thy hand, and go. [6]Behold, I will stand before thee there upon the rock in Horeb; and thou shalt smite the rock, and there shall come water out of it, that the people may drink. And Moses did so in the sight of the elders of Israel. [7]And he called the name of the place Massah, and Meribah, because of the striving of the children of Israel, and because they tempted Jehovah, saying, Is Jehovah among us, or not?

[8]Then came Amalek, and fought with Israel in Rephidim. [9]And Moses said unto Joshua, Choose us out men, and go out, fight with Amalek: tomorrow I will stand on the top of the hill with the rod of God in my hand. [10]So Joshua did as Moses had said to him, and fought with Amalek: and Moses, Aaron, and Hur went up to the top of the hill. [11]And it came to pass, when Moses held up his hand, that Israel prevailed; and when he let down his hand, Amalek prevailed. [12]But Moses' hands were heavy; and they took a stone, and put it under him, and he sat thereon; and Aaron and Hur stayed up his hands, the one on the one side, and the other on the other side; And his hands were steady until the going down of the sun. [13]And Joshua discomfited Amalek and his people with the edge of the sword.

[14]And Jehovah said unto Moses, Write this for a memorial in a book, and rehearse it in the ears of Joshua: that I will utterly blot out the remembrance of Amalek from under heaven. [15]And Moses built an altar, and called the name of it Jehovah-nissi; [16]And he said, Jehovah hath sworn: Jehovah will have war with Amalek from generation to generation.

EXODUS 18

[1]Now Jethro, the priest of Midian, Moses' father-in-law, heard of all that God had done for Moses, and for Israel his people, how that Jehovah had brought Israel out of Egypt. [2]And Jethro, Moses' father-in-law, took Zipporah, Moses' wife, after he had sent her away, [3]and her two sons; of whom the name of the one was Gershom; for he said, I have been a sojourner in a foreign land: [4]and the name of the other was Eliezer; for he said, The God of my father was my help, and delivered me from the sword of Pharaoh. [5]And Jethro, Moses' father-in-law, came with his sons and his wife unto Moses into the wilderness where he was encamped, at the

mount of God: [6]and he said unto Moses, I, thy father-in-law Jethro, am come unto thee, and thy wife, and her two sons with her.

[7]And Moses went out to meet his father-in-law, and did obeisance, and kissed him: and they asked each other of their welfare; and they came into the tent. [8]And Moses told his father-in-law all that Jehovah had done unto Pharaoh and to the Egyptians for Israel's sake, all the travail that had come upon them by the way, and how Jehovah delivered them. [9]And Jethro rejoiced for all the goodness which Jehovah had done to Israel, in that he had delivered them out of the hand of the Egyptians. [10]And Jethro said, Blessed be Jehovah, who hath delivered you out of the hand of the Egyptians, and out of the hand of Pharaoh; who hath delivered the people from under the hand of the Egyptians. [11]Now I know that Jehovah is greater than all gods; yea, in the thing wherein they dealt proudly against them. [12]And Jethro, Moses' father-in-law, took a burnt-offering and sacrifices for God: and Aaron came, and all the elders of Israel, to eat bread with Moses' father-in-law before God.

[13]And it came to pass on the morrow, that Moses sat to judge the people: and the people stood about Moses from the morning unto the evening. [14]And when Moses' father-in-law saw all that he did to the people, he said, What is this thing that thou doest to the people? why sittest thou thyself alone, and all the people stand about thee from morning unto even? [15]And Moses said unto his father-in-law, Because the people come unto me to inquire of God: [16]when they have a matter, they come unto me; and I judge between a man and his neighbor, and I make them know the statutes of God, and his laws.

[17]And Moses' father-in-law said unto him, The thing that thou doest is not good. [18]Thou wilt surely wear away, both thou, and this people that is with thee: for the thing is too heavy for thee; thou art not able to perform it thyself alone. [19]Hearken now unto my voice, I will give thee counsel, and God be with thee: be thou for the people to God-ward, and bring thou the causes unto God: [20]and thou shalt teach them the statutes and the laws, and shalt show them the way wherein they must walk, and the work that they must do. [21]Moreover thou shalt provide out of all the people able men, such as fear God, men of truth, hating unjust gain; and place such over them, to be rulers of thousands, rulers of hundreds, rulers of fifties, and rulers of tens: [22]and let them judge the people at all seasons: and it shall be, that every great matter they shall bring unto thee, but every small matter they shall judge themselves: so shall it be easier for thyself, and they shall bear the burden with thee. [23]If thou shalt do this thing, and God command thee so, then thou shalt be able to endure, and all this people also shall go to their place in peace.

²⁴So Moses hearkened to the voice of his father-in-law, and did all that he had said. ²⁵And Moses chose able men out of all Israel, and made them heads over the people, rulers of thousands, rulers of hundreds, rulers of fifties, and rulers of tens. ²⁶And they judged the people at all seasons: the hard causes they brought unto Moses, but every small matter they judged themselves. ²⁷And Moses let his father-in-law depart; and he went his way into his own land.

EXODUS 19

¹In the third month after the children of Israel were gone forth out of the land of Egypt, the same day came they into the wilderness of Sinai. ²And when they were departed from Rephidim, and were come to the wilderness of Sinai, they encamped in the wilderness; and there Israel encamped before the mount. ³And Moses went up unto God, and Jehovah called unto him out of the mountain, saying, Thus shalt thou say to the house of Jacob, and tell the children of Israel: ⁴Ye have seen what I did unto the Egyptians, and how I bare you on eagles' wings, and brought you unto myself. ⁵Now therefore, if ye will obey my voice indeed, and keep my covenant, then ye shall be mine own possession from among all peoples: for all the earth is mine: ⁶and ye shall be unto me a kingdom of priests, and a holy nation. These are the words which thou shalt speak unto the children of Israel.

⁷And Moses came and called for the elders of the people, and set before them all these words which Jehovah commanded him. ⁸And all the people answered together, and said, All that Jehovah hath spoken we will do. And Moses reported the words of the people unto Jehovah. ⁹And Jehovah said unto Moses, Lo, I come unto thee in a thick cloud, that the people may hear when I speak with thee, and may also believe thee for ever. And Moses told the words of the people unto Jehovah. ¹⁰And Jehovah said unto Moses, Go unto the people, and sanctify them today and tomorrow, and let them wash their garments, ¹¹and be ready against the third day; for the third day Jehovah will come down in the sight of all the people upon mount Sinai. ¹²And thou shalt set bounds unto the people round about, saying, Take heed to yourselves, that ye go not up into the mount, or touch the border of it: whosoever toucheth the mount shall be surely put to death: ¹³no hand shall touch him, but he shall surely be stoned, or shot through; whether it be beast or man, he shall not live: when the trumpet soundeth long, they shall come up to the mount.

¹⁴And Moses went down from the mount unto the people, and sanctified the people; and they washed their garments. ¹⁵And he said unto the people, Be ready against the third day: come not near a woman.

[16]And it came to pass on the third day, when it was morning, that there were thunders and lightnings, and a thick cloud upon the mount, and the voice of a trumpet exceeding loud; and all the people that were in the camp trembled. [17]And Moses brought forth the people out of the camp to meet God; and they stood at the nether part of the mount. [18]And mount Sinai, the whole of it, smoked, because Jehovah descended upon it in fire; and the smoke thereof ascended as the smoke of a furnace, and the whole mount quaked greatly. [19]And when the voice of the trumpet waxed louder and louder, Moses spake, and God answered him by a voice. [20]And Jehovah came down upon mount Sinai, to the top of the mount: and Jehovah called Moses to the top of the mount; and Moses went up.

[21]And Jehovah said unto Moses, Go down, charge the people, lest they break through unto Jehovah to gaze, and many of them perish. [22]And let the priests also, that come near to Jehovah, sanctify themselves, lest Jehovah break forth upon them. [23]And Moses said unto Jehovah, The people cannot come up to mount Sinai: for thou didst charge us, saying, Set bounds about the mount, and sanctify it. [24]And Jehovah said unto him, Go, get thee down; and thou shalt come up, thou, and Aaron with thee: but let not the priests and the people break through to come up unto Jehovah, lest he break forth upon them. [25]So Moses went down unto the people, and told them.

EXODUS 20

[1]And God spake all these words, saying, [2]I am Jehovah thy God, who brought thee out of the land of Egypt, out of the house of bondage. [3]Thou shalt have no other gods before me.

[4]Thou shalt not make unto thee a graven image, nor any likeness of any thing that is in heaven above, or that is in the earth beneath, or that is in the water under the earth. [5]Thou shalt not bow down thyself unto them, nor serve them, for I Jehovah thy God am a jealous God, visiting the iniquity of the fathers upon the children, upon the third and upon the fourth generation of them that hate me, [6]and showing lovingkindness unto thousands of them that love me and keep my commandments.

[7]Thou shalt not take the name of Jehovah thy God in vain; for Jehovah will not hold him guiltless that taketh his name in vain.

[8]Remember the sabbath day, to keep it holy. [9]Six days shalt thou labor, and do all thy work; [10]but the seventh day is a sabbath unto Jehovah thy God: in it thou shalt not do any work, thou, nor thy son, nor thy daughter, thy man-servant, nor thy maid-servant, nor thy cattle, nor thy stranger that is within thy gates: [11]for in six days Jehovah made heaven and earth,

the sea, and all that in them is, and rested the seventh day: wherefore Jehovah blessed the sabbath day, and hallowed it.

¹²Honor thy father and thy mother, that thy days may be long in the land which Jehovah thy God giveth thee.

¹³Thou shalt not kill.

¹⁴Thou shalt not commit adultery.

¹⁵Thou shalt not steal.

¹⁶Thou shalt not bear false witness against thy neighbor.

¹⁷Thou shalt not covet thy neighbor's house, thou shalt not covet thy neighbor's wife, nor his man-servant, nor his maid-servant, nor his ox, nor his ass, nor anything that is thy neighbor's.

¹⁸And all the people perceived the thunderings, and the lightnings, and the voice of the trumpet, and the mountain smoking: and when the people saw it, they trembled, and stood afar off. ¹⁹And they said unto Moses, Speak thou with us, and we will hear; but let not God speak with us, lest we die. ²⁰And Moses said unto the people, Fear not: for God is come to prove you, and that his fear may be before you, that ye sin not. ²¹And the people stood afar off, and Moses drew near unto the thick darkness where God was.

²²And Jehovah said unto Moses, Thus thou shalt say unto the children of Israel, Ye yourselves have seen that I have talked with you from heaven. ²³Ye shall not make other gods with me; gods of silver, or gods of gold, ye shall not make unto you. ²⁴An altar of earth thou shalt make unto me, and shalt sacrifice thereon thy burnt-offerings, and thy peace-offerings, thy sheep, and thine oxen: in every place where I record my name I will come unto thee and I will bless thee. ²⁵And if thou make me an altar of stone, thou shalt not build it of hewn stones; for if thou lift up thy tool upon it, thou hast polluted it. ²⁶Neither shalt thou go up by steps unto mine altar, that thy nakedness be not uncovered thereon. . . .

[Additional laws are covered in chapters 21-22.]

EXODUS 23

¹Thou shalt not take up a false report: put not thy hand with the wicked to be an unrighteous witness. ²Thou shalt not follow a multitude to do evil; neither shalt thou speak in a cause to turn aside after a multitude to wrest justice: ³neither shalt thou favor a poor man in his cause.

⁴If thou meet thine enemy's ox or his ass going astray, thou shalt surely bring it back to him again. ⁵If thou see the ass of him that hateth thee lying under his burden, thou shalt forbear to leave him, thou shalt surely release it with him.

[6]Thou shalt not wrest the justice due to thy poor in his cause. [7]Keep thee far from a false matter; and the innocent and righteous slay thou not: for I will not justify the wicked. [8]And thou shalt take no bribe: for a bribe blindeth them that have sight, and perverteth the words of the righteous. [9]And a sojourner shalt thou not oppress: for ye know the heart of a sojourner, seeing ye were sojourners in the land of Egypt.

[10]And six years thou shalt sow thy land, and shalt gather in the increase thereof: [11]but the seventh year thou shalt let it rest and lie fallow; that the poor of thy people may eat: and what they leave the beast of the field shall eat. In like manner thou shalt deal with thy vineyard, and with thy oliveyard. [12]Six days thou shalt do thy work, and on the seventh day thou shalt rest; that thine ox and thine ass may have rest, and the son of thy handmaid, and the sojourner, may be refreshed. [13]And in all things that I have said unto you take ye heed: and make no mention of the name of other gods, neither let it be heard out of thy mouth.

[14]Three times thou shalt keep a feast unto me in the year. [15]The feast of unleavened bread shalt thou keep: seven days thou shalt eat unleavened bread, as I commanded thee, at the time appointed in the month Abib (for in it thou camest out from Egypt); and none shall appear before me empty: [16]and the feast of harvest, the first-fruits of thy labors, which thou sowest in the field: and the feast of ingathering, at the end of the year, when thou gatherest in thy labors out of the field. [17]Three times in the year all thy males shall appear before the Lord Jehovah.

[18]Thou shalt not offer the blood of my sacrifice with leavened bread; neither shall the fat of my feast remain all night until the morning. [19]The first of the first-fruits of thy ground thou shalt bring into the house of Jehovah thy God. Thou shalt not boil a kid in it mother's milk.

[20]Behold, I send an angel before thee, to keep thee by the way, and to bring thee into the place which I have prepared. [21]Take ye heed before him, and hearken unto his voice; provoke him not; for he will not pardon your transgression: for my name is in him. [22]But if thou shalt indeed hearken unto his voice, and do all that I speak; then I will be an enemy unto thine enemies, and an adversary unto thine adversaries. [23]For mine angel shall go before thee, and bring thee in unto the Amorite, and the Hittite, and the Perizzite, and the Canaanite, the Hivite, and the Jebusite: and I will cut them off. [24]Thou shalt not bow down to their gods, nor serve them, nor do after their works; but thou shalt utterly overthrow them, and break in pieces their pillars.

[25]And ye shall serve Jehovah your God, and he will bless thy bread, and thy water; and I will take sickness away from the midst of thee. [26]There shall none cast her young, nor be barren, in thy land: the number of thy

days I will fulfil. [27]I will send my terror before thee, and will discomfit all the people to whom thou shalt come, and I will make all thine enemies turn their backs unto thee. [28]And I will send the hornet before thee, which shall drive out the Hivite, the Canaanite, and the Hittite, from before thee. [29]I will not drive them out from before thee in one year, lest the land become desolate, and the beasts of the field multiply against thee. [30]By little and little I will drive them out from before thee, until thou be increased, and inherit the land. [31]And I will set thy border from the Red Sea even unto the sea of the Philistines, and from the wilderness unto the River: for I will deliver the inhabitants of the land into your hand: and thou shalt drive them out before thee. [32]Thou shalt make no covenant with them, nor with their gods. [33]They shall not dwell in thy land, lest they make thee sin against me; for if thou serve their gods, it will surely be a snare unto thee.

EXODUS 24

[1]And he said unto Moses, Come up unto Jehovah, thou, and Aaron, Nadab, and Abihu, and seventy of the elders of Israel; and worship ye afar off: [2]and Moses alone shall come near unto Jehovah; but they shall not come near; neither shall the people go up with him. [3]And Moses came and told the people all the words of Jehovah, and all the ordinances: and all the people answered with one voice, and said, All the words which Jehovah hath spoken will we do.

[4]And Moses wrote all the words of Jehovah, and rose up early in the morning, and builded an altar under the mount, and twelve pillars, according to the twelve tribes of Israel. [5]And he sent young men of the children of Israel, who offered burnt-offerings, and sacrificed peace-offerings of oxen unto Jehovah. [6]And Moses took half of the blood, and put it in basins; and half of the blood he sprinkled on the altar. [7]And he took the book of the covenant, and read in the audience of the people: and they said, All that Jehovah hath spoken will we do, and be obedient. [8]And Moses took the blood, and sprinkled it on the people, and said, Behold the blood of the covenant, which Jehovah hath made with you concerning all these words.

[9]Then went up Moses, and Aaron, Nadab, and Abihu, and seventy of the elders of Israel. [10]And they saw the God of Israel; and there was under his feet as it were a paved work of sapphire stone, and as it were the very heaven for clearness. [11]And upon the nobles of the children of Israel he laid not his hand: and they beheld God, and did eat and drink.

[12]And Jehovah said unto Moses, Come up to me into the mount, and be there: and I will give thee the tables of stone, and the law and the commandment, which I have written, that thou mayest teach them. [13]And

Moses rose up, and Joshua his minister: and Moses went up into the mount of God. [14]And he said unto the elders, Tarry ye here for us, until we come again unto you: and, behold, Aaron and Hur are with you: whosoever hath a cause, let him come near unto them. [15]And Moses went up into the mount, and the cloud covered the mount. [16]And the glory of Jehovah abode upon mount Sinai, and the cloud covered it six days: and the seventh day he called unto Moses out of the midst of the cloud. [17]And the appearance of the glory of Jehovah was like devouring fire on the top of the mount in the eyes of the children of Israel. [18]And Moses entered into the midst of the cloud, and went up into the mount: and Moses was in the mount forty days and forty nights. . . .

[Chapters 25-30 include instructions on the tabernacle.]

EXODUS 31

[1]And Jehovah spake unto Moses, saying, [2]See, I have called by name Bezalel the son of Uri, the son of Hur, of the tribe of Judah: [3]and I have filled him with the Spirit of God, in wisdom, and in understanding, and in knowledge, and in all manner of workmanship, [4]to devise skilful works, to work in gold, and in silver, and in brass, [5]and in cutting of stones for setting, and in carving of wood, to work in all manner of workmanship. [6]And I, behold, I have appointed with him Oholiab, the son of Ahisamach, of the tribe of Dan; and in the heart of all that are wise-hearted I have put wisdom, that they may make all that I have commanded thee: [7]the tent of meeting, and the ark of the testimony, and the mercy-seat that is thereupon, and all the furniture of the Tent, [8]and the table and its vessels, and the pure candlestick with all its vessels, and the altar of incense, [9]and the altar of burnt-offering with all its vessels, and the laver and its base, [10]and the finely wrought garments, and the holy garments for Aaron the priest, and the garments of his sons, to minister in the priest's office, [11]and the anointing oil, and the incense of sweet spices for the holy place: according to all that I have commanded thee shall they do.

[12]And Jehovah spake unto Moses, saying, [13]Speak thou also unto the children of Israel, saying, Verily ye shall keep my sabbaths: for it is a sign between me and you throughout your generations; that ye may know that I am Jehovah who sanctifieth you. [14]Ye shall keep the sabbath therefore; for it is holy unto you: every one that profaneth it shall surely be put to death; for whosoever doeth any work therein, that soul shall be cut off from among his people. [15]Six days shall work be done, but on the seventh day is a sabbath of solemn rest, holy to Jehovah: whosoever doeth any work on the sabbath day, he shall surely be put to death. [16]Wherefore the

children of Israel shall keep the sabbath, to observe the sabbath throughout their generations, for a perpetual covenant. [17]It is a sign between me and the children of Israel for ever: for in six days Jehovah made heaven and earth, and on the seventh day he rested, and was refreshed.

[18]And he gave unto Moses, when he had made an end of communing with him upon mount Sinai, the two tables of the testimony, tables of stone, written with the finger of God.

EXODUS 32

[1]And when the people saw that Moses delayed to come down from the mount, the people gathered themselves together unto Aaron, and said unto him, Up, make us gods, which shall go before us; for as for this Moses, the man that brought us up out of the land of Egypt, we know not what is become of him. [2]And Aaron said unto them, Break off the golden rings, which are in the ears of your wives, of your sons, and of your daughters, and bring them unto me. [3]And all the people brake off the golden rings which were in their ears, and brought them unto Aaron. [4]And he received it at their hand, and fashioned it with a graving tool, and made it a molten calf: and they said, These are thy gods, O Israel, which brought thee up out of the land of Egypt.

[5]And when Aaron saw this, he built an altar before it; and Aaron made proclamation, and said, Tomorrow shall be a feast to Jehovah. [6]And they rose up early on the morrow, and offered burnt-offerings, and brought peace-offerings; and the people sat down to eat and to drink, and rose up to play.

[7]And Jehovah spake unto Moses, Go, get thee down; for thy people, that thou broughtest up out of the land of Egypt, have corrupted them-selves: [8]they have turned aside quickly out of the way which I commanded them: they have made them a molten calf, and have worshipped it, and have sacrificed unto it, and said, These are thy gods, O Israel, which brought thee up out of the land of Egypt. [9]And Jehovah said unto Moses, I have seen this people, and, behold, it is a stiffnecked people: [10]now therefore let me alone, that my wrath may wax hot against them, and that I may consume them: and I will make of thee a great nation.

[11]And Moses besought Jehovah his God, and said, Jehovah, why doth thy wrath wax hot against thy people, that thou hast brought forth out of the land of Egypt with great power and with a mighty hand? [12]Wherefore should the Egyptians speak, saying, For evil did he bring them forth, to slay them in the mountains, and to consume them from the face of the earth? Turn from thy fierce wrath, and repent of this evil against thy

people. [13]Remember Abraham, Isaac, and Israel, thy servants, to whom thou swarest by thine own self, and saidst unto them, I will multiply your seed as the stars of heaven, and all this land that I have spoken of will I give unto your seed, and they shall inherit it for ever. [14]And Jehovah repented of the evil which he said he would do unto his people.

[15]And Moses turned, and went down from the mount, with the two tables of the testimony in his hand; tables that were written on both their sides; on the one side and on the other were they written. [16]And the tables were the work of God, and the writing was the writing of God, graven upon the tables. [17]And when Joshua heard the noise of the people as they shouted, he said unto Moses, There is a noise of war in the camp. [18]And he said, It is not the voice of them that shout for mastery, neither is it the voice of them that cry for being overcome; but the noise of them that sing do I hear. [19]And it came to pass, as soon as he came nigh unto the camp, that he saw the calf and the dancing: and Moses' anger waxed hot, and he cast the tables out of his hands, and brake them beneath the mount. [20]And he took the calf which they had made, and burnt it with fire, and ground it to powder, and strewed it upon the water, and made the children of Israel drink of it.

[21]And Moses said unto Aaron, What did this people unto thee, that thou hast brought a great sin upon them? [22]And Aaron said, Let not the anger of my lord wax hot: thou knowest the people, that they are set on evil. [23]For they said unto me, Make us gods, which shall go before us; for as for this Moses, the man that brought us up out of the land of Egypt, we know not what is become of him. [24]And I said unto them, Whosoever hath any gold, let them break it off: so they gave it me; and I cast it into the fire, and there came out this calf.

[25]And when Moses saw that the people were broken loose, (for Aaron had let them loose for a derision among their enemies,) [26]then Moses stood in the gate of the camp, and said, Whoso is on Jehovah's side, let him come unto me. And all the sons of Levi gathered themselves together unto him. [27]And he said unto them, Thus saith Jehovah, the God of Israel, Put ye every man his sword upon his thigh, and go to and fro from gate to gate throughout the camp, and slay every man his brother, and every man his companion, and every man his neighbor. [28]And the sons of Levi did according to the word of Moses: and there fell of the people that day about three thousand men. [29]And Moses said, Consecrate yourselves today to Jehovah, yea, every man against his son, and against his brother; that he may bestow upon you a blessing this day.

[30]And it came to pass on the morrow, that Moses said unto the people, Ye have sinned a great sin: and now I will go up unto Jehovah; peradventure

I shall make atonement for your sin. [31]And Moses returned unto Jehovah, and said, Oh, this people have sinned a great sin, and have made them gods of gold. [32]Yet now, if thou wilt forgive their sin—; and if not, blot me, I pray thee, out of thy book which thou hast written. [33]And Jehovah said unto Moses, Whosoever hath sinned against me, him will I blot out of my book. [34]And now go, lead the people unto the place of which I have spoken unto thee: behold, mine angel shall go before thee; nevertheless in the day when I visit, I will visit their sin upon them. [35]And Jehovah smote the people, because they made the calf, which Aaron made.

EXODUS 33

[1]And Jehovah spake unto Moses, Depart, go up hence, thou and the people that thou hast brought up out of the land of Egypt, unto the land of which I sware unto Abraham, to Isaac, and to Jacob, saying, Unto thy seed will I give it: [2]and I will send an angel before thee; and I will drive out the Canaanite, the Amorite, and the Hittite, and the Perizzite, the Hivite, and the Jebusite: [3]unto a land flowing with milk and honey: for I will not go up in the midst of thee, for thou art a stiffnecked people, lest I consume thee in the way.

[4]And when the people heard these evil tidings, they mourned: and no man did put on him his ornaments. [5]And Jehovah said unto Moses, Say unto the children of Israel, Ye are a stiffnecked people; if I go up into the midst of thee for one moment, I shall consume thee: therefore now put off thy ornaments from thee, that I may know what to do unto thee. [6]And the children of Israel stripped themselves of their ornaments from mount Horeb onward.

[7]Now Moses used to take the tent and to pitch it without the camp, afar off from the camp; and he called it, The tent of meeting. And it came to pass, that every one that sought Jehovah went out unto the tent of meeting, which was without the camp. [8]And it came to pass, when Moses went out unto the Tent, that all the people rose up, and stood, every man at his tent door, and looked after Moses, until he was gone into the Tent. [9]And it came to pass, when Moses entered into the Tent, the pillar of cloud descended, and stood at the door of the Tent: and Jehovah spake with Moses. [10]And all the people saw the pillar of cloud stand at the door of the Tent: and all the people rose up and worshipped, every man at his tent door. [11]And Jehovah spake unto Moses face to face, as a man speaketh unto his friend. And he turned again into the camp: but his minister Joshua, the son of Nun, a young man, departed not out of the Tent.

¹²And Moses said unto Jehovah, See, thou sayest unto me, Bring up this people: and thou hast not let me know whom thou wilt send with me. Yet thou hast said, I know thee by name, and thou hast also found favor in my sight. ¹³Now therefore, I pray thee, if I have found favor in thy sight, show me now thy ways, that I may know thee, to the end that I may find favor in thy sight: and consider that this nation is thy people. ¹⁴And he said, My presence shall go with thee, and I will give thee rest. ¹⁵And he said unto him, If thy presence go not with me, carry us not up hence. ¹⁶For wherein now shall it be known that I have found favor in thy sight, I and thy people? is it not in that thou goest with us, so that we are separated, I and thy people, from all the people that are upon the face of the earth?

¹⁷And Jehovah said unto Moses, I will do this thing also that thou hast spoken; for thou hast found favor in my sight, and I know thee by name. ¹⁸And he said, Show me, I pray thee, thy glory. ¹⁹And he said, I will make all my goodness pass before thee, and will proclaim the name of Jehovah before thee; and I will be gracious to whom I will be gracious, and will show mercy on whom I will show mercy. ²⁰And he said, Thou canst not see my face; for man shall not see me and live. ²¹and Jehovah said, Behold, there is a place by me, and thou shalt stand upon the rock: ²²and it shall come to pass, while my glory passeth by, that I will put thee in a cleft of the rock, and will cover thee with my hand until I have passed by: ²³and I will take away my hand, and thou shalt see my back; but my face shall not be seen.

EXODUS 34

¹And Jehovah said unto Moses, Hew thee two tables of stone like unto the first: and I will write upon the tables the words that were on the first tables, which thou brakest. ²And be ready by the morning, and come up in the morning unto mount Sinai, and present thyself there to me on the top of the mount. ³And no man shall come up with thee; neither let any man be seen throughout all the mount; neither let the flocks nor herds feed before that mount. ⁴And he hewed two tables of stone like unto the first; and Moses rose up early in the morning, and went up unto mount Sinai, as Jehovah had commanded him, and took in his hand two tables of stone.

⁵And Jehovah descended in the cloud, and stood with him there, and proclaimed the name of Jehovah. ⁶And Jehovah passed by before him, and proclaimed, Jehovah, Jehovah, a God merciful and gracious, slow to anger, and abundant in lovingkindness and truth, ⁷keeping lovingkindness for thousands, forgiving iniquity and transgression and sin; and that will by no means clear the guilty, visiting the iniquity of the fathers upon the

children, and upon the children's children, upon the third and upon the fourth generation. [8]And Moses made haste, and bowed his head toward the earth, and worshipped. [9]And he said, If now I have found favor in thy sight, O Lord, let the Lord, I pray thee, go in the midst of us; for it is a stiffnecked people; and pardon our iniquity and our sin, and take us for thine inheritance.

[10]And he said, Behold, I make a covenant: before all thy people I will do marvels, such as have not been wrought in all the earth, nor in any nation; and all the people among which thou art shall see the work of Jehovah; for it is a terrible thing that I do with thee. [11]Observe thou that which I command thee this day: behold, I drive out before thee the Amorite, and the Canaanite, and the Hittite, and the Perizzite, and the Hivite, and the Jebusite. [12]Take heed to thyself, lest thou make a covenant with the inhabitants of the land whither thou goest, lest it be for a snare in the midst of thee: [13]but ye shall break down their altars, and dash in pieces their pillars, and ye shall cut down their Asherim; [14]for thou shalt worship no other god: for Jehovah, whose name is Jealous, is a jealous God: [15]lest thou make a covenant with the inhabitants of the land, and they play the harlot after their gods, and sacrifice unto their gods, and one call thee and thou eat of his sacrifice; [16]and thou take of their daughters unto thy sons, and their daughters play the harlot after their gods, and make thy sons play the harlot after their gods. [17]Thou shalt make thee no molten gods.

[18]The feast of unleavened bread shalt thou keep. Seven days thou shalt eat unleavened bread, as I commanded thee, at the time appointed in the month Abib; for in the month Abib thou camest out from Egypt. [19]All that openeth the womb is mine; and all thy cattle that is male, the firstlings of cow and sheep. [20]And the firstling of an ass thou shalt redeem with a lamb: and if thou wilt not redeem it, then thou shalt break its neck. All the first-born of thy sons thou shalt redeem. And none shall appear before me empty.

[21]Six days thou shalt work, but on the seventh day thou shalt rest: in plowing time and in harvest thou shalt rest. [22]And thou shalt observe the feast of weeks, even of the first-fruits of wheat harvest, and the feast of ingathering at the year's end. [23]Three times in the year shall all thy males appear before the Lord Jehovah, the God of Israel. [24]For I will cast out nations before thee, and enlarge thy borders: neither shall any man desire thy land, when thou goest up to appear before Jehovah thy God three times in the year.

[25]Thou shalt not offer the blood of my sacrifice with leavened bread; neither shall the sacrifice of the feast of the passover be left unto the morning. [26]The first of the first-fruits of thy ground thou shalt bring unto

the house of Jehovah thy God. Thou shalt not boil a kid in its mother's milk. [27]And Jehovah said unto Moses, Write thou these words: for after the tenor of these words I have made a covenant with thee and with Israel. [28]And he was there with Jehovah forty days and forty nights; he did neither eat bread, nor drink water. And he wrote upon the tables the words of the covenant, the ten commandments.

[29]And it came to pass, when Moses came down from mount Sinai with the two tables of the testimony in Moses' hand, when he came down from the mount, that Moses knew not that the skin of his face shone by reason of his speaking with him. [30]And when Aaron and all the children of Israel saw Moses, behold, the skin of his face shone; and they were afraid to come nigh him. [31]And Moses called unto them; and Aaron and all the rulers of the congregation returned unto him: and Moses spake to them. [32]And afterward all the children of Israel came nigh: and he gave them in commandment all that Jehovah had spoken with him in mount Sinai. [33]And when Moses had done speaking with them, he put a veil on his face. [34]But when Moses went in before Jehovah to speak with him, he took the veil off, until he came out; and he came out, and spake unto the children of Israel that which he was commanded. [35]And the children of Israel saw the face of Moses, that the skin of Moses' face shone: and Moses put the veil upon his face again, until he went in to speak with him. . . . . .

[Chapters 35-39 give additional instructions on the tabernacle.]

EXODUS 40

[1]And Jehovah spake unto Moses, saying, [2]On the first day of the first month shalt thou rear up the tabernacle of the tent of meeting. [3]And thou shalt put therein the ark of the testimony, and thou shalt screen the ark with the veil. [4]And thou shalt bring in the table, and set in order the things that are upon it; and thou shalt bring in the candlestick, and light the lamps thereof. [5]And thou shalt set the golden altar for incense before the ark of the testimony, and put the screen of the door to the tabernacle. [6]And thou shalt set the altar of burnt-offering before the door of the tabernacle of the tent of meeting. [7]And thou shalt set the laver between the tent of meeting and the altar, and shalt put water therein. [8]And thou shalt set up the court round about, and hang up the screen of the gate of the court. [9]And thou shalt take the anointing oil, and anoint the tabernacle, and all that is therein, and shalt hallow it, and all the furniture thereof: and it shall be holy. [10]And thou shalt anoint the altar of burnt-offering, and all its vessels, and sanctify the altar: and the altar shall be most holy. [11]And thou shalt anoint the laver and its base, and sanctify it.

¹²And thou shalt bring Aaron and his sons unto the door of the tent of meeting, and shalt wash them with water. ¹³And thou shalt put upon Aaron the holy garments; and thou shalt anoint him, and sanctify him, that he may minister unto me in the priest's office. ¹⁴And thou shalt bring his sons, and put coats upon them; ¹⁵and thou shalt anoint them, as thou didst anoint their father, that they may minister unto me in the priest's office: and their anointing shall be to them for an everlasting priesthood throughout their generations. ¹⁶Thus did Moses: according to all that Jehovah commanded him, so did he.

¹⁷And it came to pass in the first month in the second year, on the first day of the month, that the tabernacle was reared up. ¹⁸And Moses reared up the tabernacle, and laid its sockets, and set up the boards thereof, and put in the bars thereof, and reared up its pillars. ¹⁹And he spread the tent over the tabernacle, and put the covering of the tent above upon it; as Jehovah commanded Moses. ²⁰And he took and put the testimony into the ark, and set the staves on the ark, and put the mercy-seat above upon the ark: ²¹and he brought the ark into the tabernacle, and set up the veil of the screen, and screened the ark of the testimony; as Jehovah commanded Moses. ²²And he put the table in the tent of meeting, upon the side of the tabernacle northward, without the veil. ²³And he set the bread in order upon it before Jehovah; as Jehovah commanded Moses. ²⁴And he put the candlestick in the tent of meeting, over against the table, on the side of the tabernacle southward. ²⁵And he lighted the lamps before Jehovah; as Jehovah commanded Moses. ²⁶And he put the golden altar in the tent of meeting before the veil: ²⁷and he burnt thereon incense of sweet spices; as Jehovah commanded Moses. ²⁸And he put the screen of the door to the tabernacle. ²⁹And he set the altar of burnt-offering at the door of the tabernacle of the tent of meeting, and offered upon it the burnt-offering and the meal-offering; as Jehovah commanded Moses. ³⁰And he set the laver between the tent of meeting and the altar, and put water therein, wherewith to wash.

³¹And Moses and Aaron and his sons washed their hands and their feet thereat; ³²when they went into the tent of meeting, and when they came near unto the altar, they washed; as Jehovah commanded Moses. ³³And he reared up the court round about the tabernacle and the altar, and set up the screen of the gate of the court. So Moses finished the work.

³⁴Then the cloud covered the tent of meeting, and the glory of Jehovah filled the tabernacle. ³⁵And Moses was not able to enter into the tent of meeting, because the cloud abode thereon, and the glory of Jehovah filled the tabernacle. ³⁶And when the cloud was taken up from over the tabernacle, the children of Israel went onward, throughout all their journeys:

[37]but if the cloud was not taken up, then they journeyed not till the day that it was taken up. [38]For the cloud of Jehovah was upon the tabernacle by day, and there was fire therein by night, in the sight of all the house of Israel, throughout all their journeys.

Chapter 2

NUMBERS, THE FOURTH BOOK OF MOSES

NUMBERS 6

[22]And Jehovah spake unto Moses, saying, [23]Speak unto Aaron and unto his sons, saying, On this wise ye shall bless the children of Israel: ye shall say unto them,

[24]Jehovah bless thee, and keep thee:

[25]Jehovah make his face to shine upon thee, and be gracious unto thee:

[26]Jehovah lift up his countenance upon thee, and give thee peace.

[27]So shall they put my name upon the children of Israel; and I will bless them. . . .

NUMBERS 9

[15]And on the day that the tabernacle was reared up the cloud covered the tabernacle, even the tent of the testimony: and at even it was upon the tabernacle as it were the appearance of fire, until morning. [16]So it was alway: the cloud covered it, and the appearance of fire by night. [17]And whenever the cloud was taken up from over the Tent, then after that the children of Israel journeyed: and in the place where the cloud abode, there the children of Israel encamped. [18]At the commandment of Jehovah the children of Israel journeyed, and at the commandment of Jehovah they encamped: as long as the cloud abode upon the tabernacle they remained encamped. [19]And when the cloud tarried upon the tabernacle many days, then the children of Israel kept the charge of Jehovah, and journeyed not. [20]And sometimes the cloud was a few days upon the tabernacle; then according to the commandment of Jehovah they remained encamped, and according to the commandment of Jehovah they journeyed. [21]And sometimes the cloud was from evening until morning; and when the cloud was taken up in the morning, they journeyed: or if it continued by day and

by night, when the cloud was taken up, they journeyed. [22]Whether it were two days, or a month, or a year, that the cloud tarried upon the tabernacle, abiding thereon, the children of Israel remained encamped, and journeyed not; but when it was taken up, they journeyed. [23]At the commandment of Jehovah they encamped, and at the commandment of Jehovah they journeyed: they kept the charge of Jehovah, at the commandment of Jehovah by Moses.

NUMBERS 10

[11]And it came to pass in the second year, in the second month, on the twentieth day of the month, that the cloud was taken up from over the tabernacle of the testimony. [12]And the children of Israel set forward according to their journeys out of the wilderness of Sinai; and the cloud abode in the wilderness of Paran. [13]And they first took their journey according to the commandment of Jehovah by Moses. . . .

[29]And Moses said unto Hobab, the son of Reuel the Midianite, Moses' father-in-law, We are journeying unto the place of which Jehovah said, I will give it you: come thou with us, and we will do thee good; for Jehovah hath spoken good concerning Israel. [30]And he said unto him, I will not go; but I will depart to mine own land, and to my kindred. [31]And he said, Leave us not, I pray thee; forasmuch as thou knowest how we are to encamp in the wilderness, and thou shalt be to us instead of eyes. [32]And it shall be, if thou go with us, yea, it shall be, that what good soever Jehovah shall do unto us, the same will we do unto thee.

[33]And they set forward from the mount of Jehovah three days' journey; and the ark of the covenant of Jehovah went before them three days' journey, to seek out a resting-place for them. [34]And the cloud of Jehovah was over them by day, when they set forward from the camp. [35]And it came to pass, when the ark set forward, that Moses said, Rise up, O Jehovah, and let thine enemies be scattered; and let them that hate thee flee before thee. [36]And when it rested, he said, Return, O Jehovah, unto the ten thousands of the thousands of Israel.

NUMBERS 11

[1]And the people were as murmurers, speaking evil in the ears of Jehovah: and when Jehovah heard it, his anger was kindled; and the fire of Jehovah burnt among them, and devoured in the uttermost part of the camp. [2]And the people cried unto Moses; and Moses prayed unto Jehovah, and the fire abated. [3]And the name of that place was called Taberah, because the fire of Jehovah burnt among them.

⁴And the mixed multitude that was among them lusted exceedingly: and the children of Israel also wept again, and said, Who shall give us flesh to eat? ⁵We remember the fish, which we did eat in Egypt for nought; the cucumbers, and the melons, and the leeks, and the onions, and the garlic: ⁶but now our soul is dried away; there is nothing at all save this manna to look upon. ⁷And the manna was like coriander seed, and the appearance thereof as the appearance of bdellium. ⁸The people went about, and gathered it, and ground it in mills, or beat it in mortars, and boiled it in pots, and made cakes of it: and the taste of it was as the taste of fresh oil. ⁹And when the dew fell upon the camp in the night, the manna fell upon it. ¹⁰And Moses heard the people weeping throughout their families, every man at the door of his tent: and the anger of Jehovah was kindled greatly; and Moses was displeased.

¹¹And Moses said unto Jehovah, Wherefore hast thou dealt ill with thy servant? and wherefore have I not found favor in thy sight, that thou layest the burden of all this people upon me? ¹²Have I conceived all this people? have I brought them forth, that thou shouldest say unto me, Carry them in thy bosom, as a nursing-father carrieth the sucking child, unto the land which thou swarest unto their fathers? ¹³Whence should I have flesh to give unto all this people? for they weep unto me, saying, Give us flesh, that we may eat. ¹⁴I am not able to bear all this people alone, because it is too heavy for me. ¹⁵And if thou deal thus with me, kill me, I pray thee, out of hand, if I have found favor in thy sight; and let me not see my wretchedness.

¹⁶And Jehovah said unto Moses, Gather unto me seventy men of the elders of Israel, whom thou knowest to be the elders of the people, and officers over them; and bring them unto the tent of meeting, that they may stand there with thee. ¹⁷And I will come down and talk with thee there: and I will take of the Spirit which is upon thee, and will put it upon them; and they shall bear the burden of the people with thee, that thou bear it not thyself alone. ¹⁸And say thou unto the people, Sanctify yourselves against tomorrow, and ye shall eat flesh; for ye have wept in the ears of Jehovah, saying, Who shall give us flesh to eat? for it was well with us in Egypt: therefore Jehovah will give you flesh, and ye shall eat. ¹⁹Ye shall not eat one day, nor two days, nor five days, neither ten days, nor twenty days, ²⁰but a whole month, until it come out at your nostrils, and it be loathsome unto you; because that ye have rejected Jehovah who is among you, and have wept before him, saying, Why came we forth out of Egypt?

²¹And Moses said, The people, among whom I am, are six hundred thousand footmen; and thou hast said, I will give them flesh, that they may eat a whole month. ²²Shall flocks and herds be slain for them, to

suffice them? or shall all the fish of the sea be gathered together for them, to suffice them? [23]And Jehovah said unto Moses, Is Jehovah's hand waxed short? now shalt thou see whether my word shall come to pass unto thee or not.

[24]And Moses went out, and told the people the words of Jehovah: and he gathered seventy men of the elders of the people, and set them round about the Tent. [25]And Jehovah came down in the cloud, and spake unto him, and took of the Spirit that was upon him, and put it upon the seventy elders: and it came to pass, that, when the Spirit rested upon them, they prophesied, but they did so no more.

[26]But there remained two men in the camp, the name of the one was Eldad, and the name of the other Medad: and the Spirit rested upon them; and they were of them that were written, but had not gone out unto the Tent; and they prophesied in the camp. [27]And there ran a young man, and told Moses, and said, Eldad and Medad do prophesy in the camp. [28]And Joshua the son of Nun, the minister of Moses, one of his chosen men, answered and said, My lord Moses, forbid them. [29]And Moses said unto him, Art thou jealous for my sake? would that all Jehovah's people were prophets, that Jehovah would put his Spirit upon them! [30]And Moses gat him into the camp, he and the elders of Israel.

[31]And there went forth a wind from Jehovah, and brought quails from the sea, and let them fall by the camp, about a day's journey on this side, and a day's journey on the other side, round about the camp, and about two cubits above the face of the earth. [32]And the people rose up all that day, and all the night, and all the next day, and gathered the quails: he that gathered least gathered ten homers: and they spread them all abroad for themselves round about the camp. [33]While the flesh was yet between their teeth, ere it was chewed, the anger of Jehovah was kindled against the people, and Jehovah smote the people with a very great plague. [34]And the name of that place was called Kibrothhattaavah, because there they buried the people that lusted. [35]From Kibrothhattaavah the people journeyed unto Hazeroth; and they abode at Hazeroth.

NUMBERS 12

[1]And Miriam and Aaron spake against Moses because of the Cushite woman whom he had married; for he had married a Cushite woman. [2]And they said, Hath Jehovah indeed spoken only with Moses? hath he not spoken also with us? And Jehovah heard it. [3]Now the man Moses was very meek, above all the men that were upon the face of the earth.

⁴And Jehovah spake suddenly unto Moses, and unto Aaron, and unto Miriam, Come out ye three unto the tent of meeting. And they three came out. ⁵And Jehovah came down in a pillar of cloud, and stood at the door of the Tent, and called Aaron and Miriam; and they both came forth. ⁶And he said, Hear now my words: if there be a prophet among you, I Jehovah will make myself known unto him in a vision, I will speak with him in a dream. ⁷My servant Moses is not so; he is faithful in all my house: ⁸with him will I speak mouth to mouth, even manifestly, and not in dark speeches; and the form of Jehovah shall he behold: wherefore then were ye not afraid to speak against my servant, against Moses?

⁹And the anger of Jehovah was kindled against them; and he departed. ¹⁰And the cloud removed from over the Tent; and, behold, Miriam was leprous, as white as snow: and Aaron looked upon Miriam, and, behold, she was leprous. ¹¹And Aaron said unto Moses, Oh, my lord, lay not, I pray thee, sin upon us, for that we have done foolishly, and for that we have sinned. ¹²Let her not, I pray, be as one dead, of whom the flesh is half consumed when he cometh out of his mother's womb. ¹³And Moses cried unto Jehovah, saying, Heal her, O God, I beseech thee. ¹⁴And Jehovah said unto Moses, If her father had but spit in her face, should she not be ashamed seven days? let her be shut up without the camp seven days, and after that she shall be brought in again. ¹⁵And Miriam was shut up without the camp seven days: and the people journeyed not till Miriam was brought in again.

¹⁶And afterward the people journeyed from Hazeroth, and encamped in the wilderness of Paran.

NUMBERS 13

¹And Jehovah spake unto Moses, saying, ²Send thou men, that they may spy out the land of Canaan, which I give unto the children of Israel: of every tribe of their fathers shall ye send a man, every one a prince among them. ³And Moses sent them from the wilderness of Paran according to the commandment of Jehovah: all of them men who were heads of the children of Israel. . . .

¹⁷And Moses sent them to spy out the land of Canaan, and said unto them, Get you up this way by the South, and go up into the hill-country: ¹⁸and see the land, what it is; and the people that dwell therein, whether they are strong or weak, whether they are few or many; ¹⁹and what the land is that they dwell in, whether it is good or bad; and what cities they are that they dwell in, whether in camps, or in strongholds; ²⁰and what the land is, whether it is fat or lean, whether

there is wood therein, or not. And be ye of good courage, and bring of the fruit of the land. Now the time was the time of the first-ripe grapes.

²¹So they went up, and spied out the land from the wilderness of Zin unto Rehob, to the entrance of Hamath. ²²And they went up by the South, and came unto Hebron; and Ahiman, Sheshai, and Talmai, the children of Anak, were there. (Now Hebron was built seven years before Zoan in Egypt.) ²³And they came unto the valley of Eshcol, and cut down from thence a branch with one cluster of grapes, and they bare it upon a staff between two; they brought also of the pomegranates, and of the figs. ²⁴That place was called the valley of Eshcol, because of the cluster which the children of Israel cut down from thence.

²⁵And they returned from spying out the land at the end of forty days. ²⁶And they went and came to Moses, and to Aaron, and to all the congregation of the children of Israel, unto the wilderness of Paran, to Kadesh; and brought back word unto them, and unto all the congregation, and showed them the fruit of the land. ²⁷And they told him, and said, We came unto the land whither thou sentest us; and surely it floweth with milk and honey; and this is the fruit of it. ²⁸Howbeit the people that dwell in the land are strong, and the cities are fortified, and very great: and moreover we saw the children of Anak there. ²⁹Amalek dwelleth in the land of the South: and the Hittite, and the Jebusite, and the Amorite, dwell in the hill-country; and the Canaanite dwelleth by the sea, and along by the side of the Jordan.

³⁰And Caleb stilled the people before Moses, and said, Let us go up at once, and possess it; for we are well able to overcome it. ³¹But the men that went up with him said, We are not able to go up against the people; for they are stronger than we. ³²And they brought up an evil report of the land which they had spied out unto the children of Israel, saying, The land, through which we have gone to spy it out, is a land that eateth up the inhabitants thereof; and all the people that we saw in it are men of great stature. ³³And there we saw the Nephilim, the sons of Anak, who come of the Nephilim: and we were in our own sight as grasshoppers, and so we were in their sight.

NUMBERS 14

¹And all the congregation lifted up their voice, and cried; and the people wept that night. ²And all the children of Israel murmured against Moses and against Aaron: and the whole congregation said unto them, Would that we had died in the land of Egypt! or would that we had died in this wilderness! ³And wherefore doth Jehovah bring us unto this land, to fall

by the sword? Our wives and our little ones will be a prey: were it not better for us to return into Egypt?

⁴And they said one to another, Let us make a captain, and let us return into Egypt. ⁵Then Moses and Aaron fell on their faces before all the assembly of the congregation of the children of Israel. ⁶And Joshua the son of Nun and Caleb the son of Jephunneh, who were of them that spied out the land, rent their clothes: ⁷and they spake unto all the congregation of the children of Israel, saying, The land, which we passed through to spy it out, is an exceeding good land. ⁸If Jehovah delight in us, then he will bring us into this land, and give it unto us; a land which floweth with milk and honey. ⁹Only rebel not against Jehovah, neither fear ye the people of the land; for they are bread for us: their defence is removed from over them, and Jehovah is with us: fear them not. ¹⁰But all the congregation bade stone them with stones. And the glory of Jehovah appeared in the tent of meeting unto all the children of Israel.

¹¹And Jehovah said unto Moses, How long will this people despise me? and how long will they not believe in me, for all the signs which I have wrought among them? ¹²I will smite them with the pestilence, and disinherit them, and will make of thee a nation greater and mightier than they.

¹³And Moses said unto Jehovah, Then the Egyptians will hear it; for thou broughtest up this people in thy might from among them; ¹⁴and they will tell it to the inhabitants of this land. They have heard that thou Jehovah art in the midst of this people; for thou Jehovah art seen face to face, and thy cloud standeth over them, and thou goest before them, in a pillar of cloud by day, and in a pillar of fire by night. ¹⁵Now if thou shalt kill this people as one man, then the nations which have heard the fame of thee will speak, saying, ¹⁶Because Jehovah was not able to bring this people into the land which he sware unto them, therefore he hath slain them in the wilderness. ¹⁷And now, I pray thee, let the power of the Lord be great, according as thou hast spoken, saying, ¹⁸Jehovah is slow to anger, and abundant in lovingkindness, forgiving iniquity and transgression; and that will by no means clear the guilty, visiting the iniquity of the fathers upon the children, upon the third and upon the fourth generation. ¹⁹Pardon, I pray thee, the iniquity of this people according unto the greatness of thy lovingkindness, and according as thou hast forgiven this people, from Egypt even until now.

²⁰And Jehovah said, I have pardoned according to thy word: ²¹but in very deed, as I live, and as all the earth shall be filled with the glory of Jehovah; ²²because all those men that have seen my glory, and my signs, which I wrought in Egypt and in the wilderness, yet have tempted me

these ten times, and have not hearkened to my voice; ²³surely they shall not see the land which I sware unto their fathers, neither shall any of them that despised me see it: ²⁴but my servant Caleb, because he had another spirit with him, and hath followed me fully, him will I bring into the land whereinto he went; and his seed shall possess it. ²⁵Now the Amalekite and the Canaanite dwell in the valley: tomorrow turn ye, and get you into the wilderness by the way to the Red Sea.

²⁶And Jehovah spake unto Moses and unto Aaron, saying, ²⁷How long shall I bear with this evil congregation, that murmur against me? I have heard the murmurings of the children of Israel, which they murmur against me. ²⁸Say unto them, As I live, saith Jehovah, surely as ye have spoken in mine ears, so will I do to you: ²⁹your dead bodies shall fall in this wilderness; and all that were numbered of you, according to your whole number, from twenty years old and upward, that have murmured against me, ³⁰surely ye shall not come into the land, concerning which I sware that I would make you dwell therein, save Caleb the son of Jephunneh, and Joshua the son of Nun. ³¹But your little ones, that ye said should be a prey, them will I bring in, and they shall know the land which ye have rejected. ³²But as for you, your dead bodies shall fall in this wilderness. ³³And your children shall be wanderers in the wilderness forty years, and shall bear your whoredoms, until your dead bodies be consumed in the wilderness.

³⁴After the number of the days in which ye spied out the land, even forty days, for every day a year, shall ye bear your iniquities, even forty years, and ye shall know my alienation. ³⁵I, Jehovah, have spoken, surely this will I do unto all this evil congregation, that are gathered together against me: in this wilderness they shall be consumed, and there they shall die.

³⁶And the men, whom Moses sent to spy out the land, who returned, and made all the congregation to murmur against him, by bringing up an evil report against the land, ³⁷even those men that did bring up an evil report of the land, died by the plague before Jehovah. ³⁸But Joshua the son of Nun, and Caleb the son of Jephunneh, remained alive of those men that went to spy out the land.

³⁹And Moses told these words unto all the children of Israel: and the people mourned greatly. ⁴⁰And they rose up early in the morning, and gat them up to the top of the mountain, saying, Lo, we are here, and will go up unto the place which Jehovah hath promised: for we have sinned. ⁴¹And Moses said, Wherefore now do ye transgress the commandment of Jehovah, seeing it shall not prosper? ⁴²Go not up, for Jehovah is not among you; that ye be not smitten down before your enemies. ⁴³For there the Amalekite and the Canaanite are before you, and ye shall fall by the sword: because

ye are turned back from following Jehovah, therefore Jehovah will not be with you. [44]But they presumed to go up to the top of the mountain: nevertheless the ark of the covenant of Jehovah, and Moses, departed not out of the camp. [45]Then the Amalekite came down, and the Canaanite who dwelt in that mountain, and smote them and beat them down, even unto Hormah. . . .

NUMBERS 16

[1]Now Korah, the son of Izhar, the son of Kohath, the son of Levi, with Dathan and Abiram, the sons of Eliab, and On, the son of Peleth, sons of Reuben, took men: [2]and they rose up before Moses, with certain of the children of Israel, two hundred and fifty princes of the congregation, called to the assembly, men of renown; [3]and they assembled themselves together against Moses and against Aaron, and said unto them, Ye take too much upon you, seeing all the congregation are holy, every one of them, and Jehovah is among them: wherefore then lift ye up yourselves above the assembly of Jehovah?

[4]And when Moses heard it, he fell upon his face: [5]and he spake unto Korah and unto all his company, saying, In the morning Jehovah will show who are his, and who is holy, and will cause him to come near unto him: even him whom he shall choose will he cause to come near unto him. [6]This do: take you censers, Korah, and all his company; [7]and put fire in them, and put incense upon them before Jehovah tomorrow: and it shall be that the man whom Jehovah doth choose, he shall be holy: ye take too much upon you, ye sons of Levi.

[8]And Moses said unto Korah, Hear now, ye sons of Levi: [9]seemeth it but a small thing unto you, that the God of Israel hath separated you from the congregation of Israel, to bring you near to himself, to do the service of the tabernacle of Jehovah, and to stand before the congregation to minister unto them; [10]and that he hath brought thee near, and all thy brethren the sons of Levi with thee? and seek ye the priesthood also? [11]Therefore thou and all thy company are gathered together against Jehovah: and Aaron, what is he that ye murmur against him?

[12]And Moses sent to call Dathan and Abiram, the sons of Eliab; and they said, We will not come up: [13]is it a small thing that thou hast brought us up out of a land flowing with milk and honey, to kill us in the wilderness, but thou must needs make thyself also a prince over us? [14]Moreover thou hast not brought us into a land flowing with milk and honey, nor given us inheritance of fields and vineyards: wilt thou put out the eyes of these men? we will not come up.

¹⁵And Moses was very wroth, and said unto Jehovah, Respect not thou their offering: I have not taken one ass from them, neither have I hurt one of them. ¹⁶And Moses said unto Korah, Be thou and all thy company before Jehovah, thou, and they, and Aaron, tomorrow: ¹⁷and take ye every man his censer, and put incense upon them, and bring ye before Jehovah every man his censer, two hundred and fifty censers; thou also, and Aaron, each his censer. ¹⁸And they took every man his censer, and put fire in them, and laid incense thereon, and stood at the door of the tent of meeting with Moses and Aaron. ¹⁹And Korah assembled all the congregation against them unto the door of the tent of meeting: and the glory of Jehovah appeared unto all the congregation.

²⁰And Jehovah spake unto Moses and unto Aaron, saying, ²¹Separate yourselves from among this congregation, that I may consume them in a moment. ²²And they fell upon their faces, and said, O God, the God of the spirits of all flesh, shall one man sin, and wilt thou be wroth with all the congregation? ²³And Jehovah spake unto Moses, saying, ²⁴Speak unto the congregation, saying, Get you up from about the tabernacle of Korah, Dathan, and Abiram.

²⁵And Moses rose up and went unto Dathan and Abiram; and the elders of Israel followed him. ²⁶And he spake unto the congregation, saying, Depart, I pray you, from the tents of these wicked men, and touch nothing of theirs, lest ye be consumed in all their sins. ²⁷So they gat them up from the tabernacle of Korah, Dathan, and Abiram, on every side: and Dathan and Abiram came out, and stood at the door of their tents, and their wives, and their sons, and their little ones.

²⁸And Moses said, Hereby ye shall know that Jehovah hath sent me to do all these works; for I have not done them of mine own mind. ²⁹If these men die the common death of all men, or if they be visited after the visitation of all men; then Jehovah hath not sent me. ³⁰But if Jehovah make a new thing, and the ground open its mouth, and swallow them up, with all that appertain unto them, and they go down alive into Sheol; then ye shall understand that these men have despised Jehovah.

³¹And it came to pass, as he made an end of speaking all these words, that the ground clave asunder that was under them; ³²and the earth opened its mouth, and swallowed them up, and their households, and all the men that appertained unto Korah, and all their goods. ³³So they, and all that appertained to them, went down alive into Sheol: and the earth closed upon them, and they perished from among the assembly. ³⁴And all Israel that were round about them fled at the cry of them; for they said, Lest the earth swallow us up. ³⁵And fire came forth from Jehovah, and devoured the two hundred and fifty men that offered the incense.

³⁶And Jehovah spake unto Moses, saying, ³⁷Speak unto Eleazar the son of Aaron the priest, that he take up the censers out of the burning, and scatter thou the fire yonder; for they are holy, ³⁸even the censers of these sinners against their own lives; and let them be made beaten plates for a covering of the altar: for they offered them before Jehovah; therefore they are holy; and they shall be a sign unto the children of Israel. ³⁹And Eleazar the priest took the brazen censers, which they that were burnt had offered; and they beat them out for a covering of the altar, ⁴⁰to be a memorial unto the children of Israel, to the end that no stranger, that is not of the seed of Aaron, come near to burn incense before Jehovah; that he be not as Korah, and as his company: as Jehovah spake unto him by Moses.

⁴¹But on the morrow all the congregation of the children of Israel murmured against Moses and against Aaron, saying, Ye have killed the people of Jehovah. ⁴²And it came to pass, when the congregation was assembled against Moses and against Aaron, that they looked toward the tent of meeting: and, behold, the cloud covered it, and the glory of Jehovah appeared. ⁴³And Moses and Aaron came to the front of the tent of meeting. ⁴⁴And Jehovah spake unto Moses, saying, ⁴⁵Get you up from among this congregation, that I may consume them in a moment. And they fell upon their faces.

⁴⁶And Moses said unto Aaron, Take thy censer, and put fire therein from off the altar, and lay incense thereon, and carry it quickly unto the congregation, and make atonement for them: for there is wrath gone out from Jehovah; the plague is begun. ⁴⁷And Aaron took as Moses spake, and ran into the midst of the assembly; and, behold, the plague was begun among the people: and he put on the incense, and made atonement for the people. ⁴⁸And he stood between the dead and the living; and the plague was stayed. ⁴⁹Now they that died by the plague were fourteen thousand and seven hundred, besides them that died about the matter of Korah. ⁵⁰And Aaron returned unto Moses unto the door of the tent of meeting: and the plague was stayed.

NUMBERS 17

¹And Jehovah spake unto Moses, saying, ²Speak unto the children of Israel, and take of them rods, one for each fathers' house, of all their princes according to their fathers' houses, twelve rods: write thou every man's name upon his rod. ³And thou shalt write Aaron's name upon the rod of Levi; for there shall be one rod for each head of their fathers' houses. ⁴And thou shalt lay them up in the tent of meeting before the testimony, where I meet with you. ⁵And it shall come to pass, that the rod

of the man whom I shall choose shall bud: and I will make to cease from me the murmurings of the children of Israel, which they murmur against you. [6]And Moses spake unto the children of Israel; and all their princes gave him rods, for each prince one, according to their fathers' houses, even twelve rods: and the rod of Aaron was among their rods. [7]And Moses laid up the rods before Jehovah in the tent of the testimony.

[8]And it came to pass on the morrow, that Moses went into the tent of the testimony; and, behold, the rod of Aaron for the house of Levi was budded, and put forth buds, and produced blossoms, and bare ripe almonds. [9]And Moses brought out all the rods from before Jehovah unto all the children of Israel: and they looked, and took every man his rod. [10]And Jehovah said unto Moses, Put back the rod of Aaron before the testimony, to be kept for a token against the children of rebellion; that thou mayest make an end of their murmurings against me, that they die not. [11]Thus did Moses: as Jehovah commanded him, so did he.

[12]And the children of Israel spake unto Moses, saying, Behold, we perish, we are undone, we are all undone. [13]Every one that cometh near, that cometh near unto the tabernacle of Jehovah, dieth: shall we perish all of us? . . .

NUMBERS 20

[1]And the children of Israel, even the whole congregation, came into the wilderness of Zin in the first month: and the people abode in Kadesh; and Miriam died there, and was buried there. [2]And there was no water for the congregation: and they assembled themselves together against Moses and against Aaron. [3]And the people strove with Moses, and spake, saying, Would that we had died when our brethren died before Jehovah! [4]And why have ye brought the assembly of Jehovah into this wilderness, that we should die there, we and our beasts? [5]And wherefore have ye made us to come up out of Egypt, to bring us in unto this evil place? it is no place of seed, or of figs, or of vines, or of pomegranates; neither is there any water to drink.

[6]And Moses and Aaron went from the presence of the assembly unto the door of the tent of meeting, and fell upon their faces: and the glory of Jehovah appeared unto them. [7]And Jehovah spake unto Moses, saying, [8]Take the rod, and assemble the congregation, thou, and Aaron thy brother, and speak ye unto the rock before their eyes, that it give forth its water; and thou shalt bring forth to them water out of the rock; so thou shalt give the congregation and their cattle drink. [9]And Moses took the rod from before Jehovah, as he commanded him.

[10]And Moses and Aaron gathered the assembly together before the rock, and he said unto them, Hear now, ye rebels; shall we bring you forth water out of this rock? [11]And Moses lifted up his hand, and smote the rock with his rod twice: and water came forth abundantly, and the congregation drank, and their cattle. [12]And Jehovah said unto Moses and Aaron, Because ye believed not in me, to sanctify me in the eyes of the children of Israel, therefore ye shall not bring this assembly into the land which I have given them. [13]These are the waters of Meribah; because the children of Israel strove with Jehovah, and he was sanctified in them.

[14]And Moses sent messengers from Kadesh unto the king of Edom, Thus saith thy brother Israel, Thou knowest all the travail that hath befallen us: [15]how our fathers went down into Egypt, and we dwelt in Egypt a long time; and the Egyptians dealt ill with us, and our fathers: [16]and when we cried unto Jehovah, he heard our voice, and sent an angel, and brought us forth out of Egypt: and, behold, we are in Kadesh, a city in the uttermost of thy border. [17]Let us pass, I pray thee, through thy land: we will not pass through field or through vineyard, neither will we drink of the water of the wells: we will go along the king's highway; we will not turn aside to the right hand nor to the left, until we have passed thy border.

[18]And Edom said unto him, Thou shalt not pass through me, lest I come out with the sword against thee. [19]And the children of Israel said unto him, We will go up by the highway; and if we drink of thy water, I and my cattle, then will I give the price thereof: let me only, without doing anything else, pass through on my feet. [20]And he said, Thou shalt not pass through. And Edom came out against him with much people, and with a strong hand. [21]Thus Edom refused to give Israel passage through his border: wherefore Israel turned away from him.

[22]And they journeyed from Kadesh: and the children of Israel, even the whole congregation, came unto mount Hor. [23]And Jehovah spake unto Moses and Aaron in mount Hor, by the border of the land of Edom, saying, [24]Aaron shall be gathered unto his people; for he shall not enter into the land which I have given unto the children of Israel, because ye rebelled against my word at the waters of Meribah. [25]Take Aaron and Eleazar his son, and bring them up unto mount Hor; [26]and strip Aaron of his garments, and put them upon Eleazar his son: and Aaron shall be gathered unto his people, and shall die there.

[27]And Moses did as Jehovah commanded: and they went up into mount Hor in the sight of all the congregation. [28]And Moses stripped Aaron of his garments, and put them upon Eleazar his son; and Aaron died there on the top of the mount: and Moses and Eleazar came down from the mount. [29]And when all the congregation saw that Aaron was dead, they wept for Aaron thirty days, even all the house of Israel.

NUMBERS 21

¹And the Canaanite, the king of Arad, who dwelt in the South, heard tell that Israel came by the way of Atharim; and he fought against Israel, and took some of them captive. ²And Israel vowed a vow unto Jehovah, and said, If thou wilt indeed deliver this people into my hand, then I will utterly destroy their cities. ³And Jehovah hearkened to the voice of Israel, and delivered up the Canaanites; and they utterly destroyed them and their cities: and the name of the place was called Hormah.

⁴And they journeyed from mount Hor by the way to the Red Sea, to compass the land of Edom: and the soul of the people was much discouraged because of the way. ⁵And the people spake against God, and against Moses, Wherefore have ye brought us up out of Egypt to die in the wilderness? for there is no bread, and there is no water; and our soul loatheth this light bread. ⁶And Jehovah sent fiery serpents among the people, and they bit the people; and much people of Israel died.

⁷And the people came to Moses, and said, We have sinned, because we have spoken against Jehovah, and against thee; pray unto Jehovah, that he take away the serpents from us. And Moses prayed for the people. ⁸And Jehovah said unto Moses, Make thee a fiery serpent, and set it upon a standard: and it shall come to pass, that every one that is bitten, when he seeth it, shall live. ⁹And Moses made a serpent of brass, and set it upon the standard: and it came to pass, that if a serpent had bitten any man, when he looked unto the serpent of brass, he lived. . . .

²¹And Israel sent messengers unto Sihon king of the Amorites, saying, ²²Let me pass through thy land: we will not turn aside into field, or into vineyard; we will not drink of the water of the wells: we will go by the king's highway, until we have passed thy border. ²³And Sihon would not suffer Israel to pass through his border: but Sihon gathered all his people together, and went out against Israel into the wilderness, and came to Jahaz; and he fought against Israel. ²⁴And Israel smote him with the edge of the sword, and possessed his land from the Arnon unto the Jabbok, even unto the children of Ammon; for the border of the children of Ammon was strong. . . .

³¹Thus Israel dwelt in the land of the Amorites. ³²And Moses sent to spy out Jazer; and they took the towns thereof, and drove out the Amorites that were there.

³³And they turned and went up by the way of Bashan: and Og the king of Bashan went out against them, he and all his people, to battle at Edrei. ³⁴And Jehovah said unto Moses, Fear him not: for I have delivered him into thy hand, and all his people, and his land; and thou shalt do to him

as thou didst unto Sihon king of the Amorites, who dwelt at Heshbon. [35]So they smote him, and his sons and all his people, until there was none left him remaining: and they possessed his land. . . .

NUMBERS 27

[12]And Jehovah said unto Moses, Get thee up into this mountain of Abarim, and behold the land which I have given unto the children of Israel. [13]And when thou hast seen it, thou also shalt be gathered unto thy people, as Aaron thy brother was gathered; [14]because ye rebelled against my word in the wilderness of Zin, in the strife of the congregation, to sanctify me at the waters before their eyes. (These are the waters of Meribah of Kadesh in the wilderness of Zin.)

[15]And Moses spake unto Jehovah, saying, [16]Let Jehovah, the God of the spirits of all flesh, appoint a man over the congregation, [17]who may go out before them, and who may come in before them, and who may lead them out, and who may bring them in; that the congregation of Jehovah be not as sheep which have no shepherd.

[18]And Jehovah said unto Moses, Take thee Joshua the son of Nun, a man in whom is the Spirit, and lay thy hand upon him; [19]and set him before Eleazar the priest, and before all the congregation; and give him a charge in their sight. [20]And thou shalt put of thine honor upon him, that all the congregation of the children of Israel may obey. [21]And he shall stand before Eleazar the priest, who shall inquire for him by the judgment of the Urim before Jehovah: at his word shall they go out, and at his word they shall come in, both he, and all the children of Israel with him, even all the congregation.

[22]And Moses did as Jehovah commanded him; and he took Joshua, and set him before Eleazar the priest, and before all the congregation: [23]and he laid his hands upon him, and gave him a charge, as Jehovah spake by Moses. . . .

Chapter 3

DEUTERONOMY, THE FIFTH BOOK OF MOSES

DEUTERONOMY 1

[1]These are the words which Moses spake unto all Israel beyond the Jordan in the wilderness, in the Arabah over against Suph, between Paran, and Tophel, and Laban, and Hazeroth, and Di-zahab. [2]It is eleven days' journey from Horeb by the way of mount Seir unto Kadesh-barnea. [3]And it came to pass in the fortieth year, in the eleventh month, on the first day of the month, that Moses spake unto the children of Israel, according unto all that Jehovah had given him in commandment unto them; [4]after he had smitten Sihon the king of the Amorites, who dwelt in Heshbon, and Og the king of Bashan, who dwelt in Ashtaroth, at Edrei. [5]Beyond the Jordan, in the land of Moab, began Moses to declare this law, saying, [6]Jehovah our God spake unto us in Horeb, saying, Ye have dwelt long enough in this mountain: [7]turn you, and take your journey, and go to the hill-country of the Amorites, and unto all the places nigh thereunto, in the Arabah, in the hill-country, and in the lowland, and in the South, and by the sea-shore, the land of the Canaanites, and Lebanon, as far as the great river, the river Euphrates. [8]Behold, I have set the land before you: go in and possess the land which Jehovah sware unto your fathers, to Abraham, to Isaac, and to Jacob, to give unto them and to their seed after them.

[9]And I spake unto you at that time, saying, I am not able to bear you myself alone: [10]Jehovah your God hath multiplied you, and, behold, ye are this day as the stars of heaven for multitude. [11]Jehovah, the God of your fathers, make you a thousand times as many as ye are, and bless you, as he hath promised you! [12]How can I myself alone bear your cumbrance, and your burden, and your strife? [13]Take you wise men, and understanding, and known, according to your tribes, and I will make them heads over you. [14]And ye answered me, and said, The thing which thou hast spoken is good for us to do.

¹⁵So I took the heads of your tribes, wise men, and known, and made them heads over you, captains of thousands, and captains of hundreds, and captains of fifties, and captains of tens, and officers, according to your tribes. ¹⁶And I charged your judges at that time, saying, Hear the causes between your brethren, and judge righteously between a man and his brother, and the sojourner that is with him. ¹⁷Ye shall not respect persons in judgment; ye shall hear the small and the great alike; ye shall not be afraid of the face of man; for the judgment is God's: and the cause that is too hard for you ye shall bring unto me, and I will hear it. ¹⁸And I commanded you at that time all the things which ye should do.

¹⁹And we journeyed from Horeb, and went through all that great and terrible wilderness which ye saw, by the way to the hill-country of the Amorites, as Jehovah our God commanded us; and we came to Kadesh-barnea. ²⁰And I said unto you, Ye are come unto the hill-country of the Amorites, which Jehovah our God giveth unto us. ²¹Behold, Jehovah thy God hath set the land before thee: go up, take possession, as Jehovah, the God of thy fathers, hath spoken unto thee; fear not, neither be dismayed.

²²And ye came near unto me every one of you, and said, Let us send men before us, that they may search the land for us, and bring us word again of the way by which we must go up, and the cities unto which we shall come. ²³And the thing pleased me well; and I took twelve men of you, one man for every tribe: ²⁴and they turned and went up into the hill-country, and came unto the valley of Eshcol, and spied it out. ²⁵And they took of the fruit of the land in their hands, and brought it down unto us, and brought us word again, and said, It is a good land which Jehovah our God giveth unto us.

²⁶Yet ye would not go up, but rebelled against the commandment of Jehovah your God: ²⁷and ye murmured in your tents, and said, Because Jehovah hated us, he hath brought us forth out of the land of Egypt, to deliver us into the hand of the Amorites, to destroy us. ²⁸Whither are we going up? our brethren have made our heart to melt, saying, The people are greater and taller than we; the cities are great and fortified up to heaven; and moreover we have seen the sons of the Anakim there.

²⁹Then I said unto you, Dread not, neither be afraid of them. ³⁰Jehovah your God who goeth before you, he will fight for you, according to all that he did for you in Egypt before your eyes, ³¹and in the wilderness, where thou hast seen how that Jehovah thy God bare thee, as a man doth bear his son, in all the way that ye went, until ye came unto this place. ³²Yet in this thing ye did not believe Jehovah your God, ³³who went before you in the way, to seek you out a place to pitch your tents in, in fire by night, to show you by what way ye should go, and in the cloud by day.

[34]And Jehovah heard the voice of your words, and was wroth, and sware, saying, [35]Surely there shall not one of these men of this evil generation see the good land, which I sware to give unto your fathers, [36]save Caleb the son of Jephunneh: he shall see it; and to him will I give the land that he hath trodden upon, and to his children, because he hath wholly followed Jehovah. [37]Also Jehovah was angry with me for your sakes, saying, Thou also shalt not go in thither: [38]Joshua the son of Nun, who standeth before thee, he shall go in thither: encourage thou him; for he shall cause Israel to inherit it. [39]Moreover your little ones, that ye said should be a prey, and your children, that this day have no knowledge of good or evil, they shall go in thither, and unto them will I give it, and they shall possess it. [40]But as for you, turn you, and take your journey into the wilderness by the way to the Red Sea.

[41]Then ye answered and said unto me, We have sinned against Jehovah, we will go up and fight, according to all that Jehovah our God commanded us. And ye girded on every man his weapons of war, and were forward to go up into the hill-country. [42]And Jehovah said unto me, Say unto them, Go not up, neither fight; for I am not among you; lest ye be smitten before your enemies.

[43]So I spake unto you, and ye hearkened not; but ye rebelled against the commandment of Jehovah, and were presumptuous, and went up into the hill-country. [44]And the Amorites, that dwelt in that hill-country, came out against you, and chased you, as bees do, and beat you down in Seir, even unto Hormah. [45]And ye returned and wept before Jehovah; but Jehovah hearkened not to your voice, nor gave ear unto you. [46]So ye abode in Kadesh many days, according unto the days that ye abode there.

DEUTERONOMY 2

[1]Then we turned, and took our journey into the wilderness by the way to the Red Sea, as Jehovah spake unto me; and we compassed mount Seir many days. [2]And Jehovah spake unto me, saying, [3]Ye have compassed this mountain long enough: turn you northward. [4]And command thou the people, saying, Ye are to pass through the border of your brethren the children of Esau, that dwell in Seir; and they will be afraid of you: take ye good heed unto yourselves therefore; [5]contend not with them; for I will not give you of their land, no, not so much as for the sole of the foot to tread on; because I have given mount Seir unto Esau for a possession. [6]Ye shall purchase food of them for money, that ye may eat; and ye shall also buy water of them for money, that ye may drink. [7]For Jehovah thy God hath blessed thee in all the work of thy hand; he hath known thy walking

through this great wilderness: these forty years Jehovah thy God hath been with thee; thou hast lacked nothing. [8]So we passed by from our brethren the children of Esau, that dwell in Seir, from the way of the Arabah from Elath and from Ezion-geber.

And we turned and passed by the way of the wilderness of Moab. [9]And Jehovah said unto me, Vex not Moab, neither contend with them in battle; for I will not give thee of his land for a possession; because I have given Ar unto the children of Lot for a possession. [10](The Emim dwelt therein aforetime, a people great, and many, and tall, as the Anakim: [11]these also are accounted Rephaim, as the Anakim; but the Moabites call them Emim. [12]The Horites also dwelt in Seir aforetime, but the children of Esau succeeded them; and they destroyed them from before them, and dwelt in their stead; as Israel did unto the land of his possession, which Jehovah gave unto them.)

[13]Now rise up, and get you over the brook Zered. And we went over the brook Zered. [14]And the days in which we came from Kadesh-barnea, until we were come over the brook Zered, were thirty and eight years; until all the generation of the men of war were consumed from the midst of the camp, as Jehovah sware unto them. [15]Moreover the hand of Jehovah was against them, to destroy them from the midst of the camp, until they were consumed.

[16]So it came to pass, when all the men of war were consumed and dead from among the people, [17]that Jehovah spake unto me, saying, [18]Thou art this day to pass over Ar, the border of Moab: [19]and when thou comest nigh over against the children of Ammon, vex them not, nor contend with them; for I will not give thee of the land of the children of Ammon for a possession; because I have given it unto the children of Lot for a possession.

[20](That also is accounted a land of Rephaim: Rephaim dwelt therein aforetime; but the Ammonites call them Zamzummim, [21]a people great, and many, and tall, as the Anakim; but Jehovah destroyed them before them; and they succeeded them, and dwelt in their stead; [22]as he did for the children of Esau, that dwell in Seir, when he destroyed the Horites from before them; and they succeeded them, and dwelt in their stead even unto this day: [23]and the Avvim, that dwelt in villages as far as Gaza, the Caphtorim, that came forth out of Caphtor, destroyed them, and dwelt in their stead.)

[24]Rise ye up, take your journey, and pass over the valley of the Arnon: behold, I have given into thy hand Sihon the Amorite, king of Heshbon, and his land; begin to possess it, and contend with him in battle. [25]This day will I begin to put the dread of thee and the fear of thee upon the

peoples that are under the whole heaven, who shall hear the report of thee, and shall tremble, and be in anguish because of thee.

[26]And I sent messengers out of the wilderness of Kedemoth unto Sihon king of Heshbon with words of peace, saying, [27]Let me pass through thy land: I will go along by the highway, I will turn neither unto the right hand nor to the left. [28]Thou shalt sell me food for money, that I may eat; and give me water for money, that I may drink: only let me pass through on my feet, [29]as the children of Esau that dwell in Seir, and the Moabites that dwell in Ar, did unto me; until I shall pass over the Jordan into the land which Jehovah our God giveth us.

[30]But Sihon king of Heshbon would not let us pass by him; for Jehovah thy God hardened his spirit, and made his heart obstinate, that he might deliver him into thy hand, as at this day. [31]And Jehovah said unto me, Behold, I have begun to deliver up Sihon and his land before thee: begin to possess, that thou mayest inherit his land. [32]Then Sihon came out against us, he and all his people, unto battle at Jahaz. [33]And Jehovah our God delivered him up before us; and we smote him, and his sons, and all his people. [34]And we took all his cities at that time, and utterly destroyed every inhabited city, with the women and the little ones; we left none remaining: [35]only the cattle we took for a prey unto ourselves, with the spoil of the cities which we had taken. [36]From Aroer, which is on the edge of the valley of the Arnon, and from the city that is in the valley, even unto Gilead, there was not a city too high for us; Jehovah our God delivered up all before us: [37]only to the land of the children of Ammon thou camest not near; all the side of the river Jabbok, and the cities of the hill-country, and wheresoever Jehovah our God forbade us.

DEUTERONOMY 3

[1]Then we turned, and went up the way to Bashan: and Og the king of Bashan came out against us, he and all his people, unto battle at Edrei. [2]And Jehovah said unto me, Fear him not; for I have delivered him, and all his people, and his land, into thy hand; and thou shalt do unto him as thou didst unto Sihon king of the Amorites, who dwelt at Heshbon. [3]So Jehovah our God delivered into our hand Og also, the king of Bashan, and all his people: and we smote him until none was left to him remaining. [4]And we took all his cities at that time; there was not a city which we took not from them; threescore cities, all the region of Argob, the kingdom of Og in Bashan. [5]All these were cities fortified with high walls, gates, and bars; besides the unwalled towns a great many. [6]And we utterly destroyed them, as we did unto Sihon king of Heshbon, utterly

destroying every inhabited city, with the women and the little ones. ⁷But all the cattle, and the spoil of the cities, we took for a prey unto ourselves.

⁸And we took the land at that time out of the hand of the two kings of the Amorites that were beyond the Jordan, from the valley of the Arnon unto mount Hermon; ⁹(which Hermon the Sidonians call Sirion, and the Amorites call it Senir;) ¹⁰all the cities of the plain, and all Gilead, and all Bashan, unto Salecah and Edrei, cities of the kingdom of Og in Bashan. ¹¹(For only Og king of Bashan remained of the remnant of the Rephaim; behold, his bedstead was a bedstead of iron; is it not in Rabbah of the children of Ammon? nine cubits was the length thereof, and four cubits the breadth of it, after the cubit of a man.)

¹²And this land we took in possession at that time: from Aroer, which is by the valley of the Arnon, and half the hill-country of Gilead, and the cities thereof, gave I unto the Reubenites and to the Gadites: ¹³and the rest of Gilead, and all Bashan, the kingdom of Og, gave I unto the half-tribe of Manasseh; all the region of Argob, even all Bashan. (The same is called the land of Rephaim. ¹⁴Jair the son of Manasseh took all the region of Argob, unto the border of the Geshurites and the Maacathites, and called them, even Bashan, after his own name, Havvoth-jair, unto this day.)

¹⁵And I gave Gilead unto Machir. ¹⁶And unto the Reubenites and unto the Gadites I gave from Gilead even unto the valley of the Arnon, the middle of the valley, and the border thereof, even unto the river Jabbok, which is the border of the children of Ammon; ¹⁷the Arabah also, and the Jordan and the border thereof, from Chinnereth even unto the sea of the Arabah, the Salt Sea, under the slopes of Pisgah eastward.

¹⁸And I commanded you at that time, saying, Jehovah your God hath given you this land to possess it: ye shall pass over armed before your brethren the children of Israel, all the men of valor. ¹⁹But your wives, and your little ones, and your cattle, (I know that ye have much cattle,) shall abide in your cities which I have given you, ²⁰until Jehovah give rest unto your brethren, as unto you, and they also possess the land which Jehovah your God giveth them beyond the Jordan: then shall ye return every man unto his possession, which I have given you. ²¹And I commanded Joshua at that time, saying, Thine eyes have seen all that Jehovah your God hath done unto these two kings: so shall Jehovah do unto all the kingdoms whither thou goest over. ²²Ye shall not fear them; for Jehovah your God, he it is that fighteth for you.

²³And I besought Jehovah at that time, saying, ²⁴O Lord Jehovah, thou hast begun to show thy servant thy greatness, and thy strong hand: for what god is there in heaven or in earth, that can do according to thy works,

and according to thy mighty acts? [25]Let me go over, I pray thee, and see the good land that is beyond the Jordan, that goodly mountain, and Lebanon.

[26]But Jehovah was wroth with me for your sakes, and hearkened not unto me; and Jehovah said unto me, Let it suffice thee; speak no more unto me of this matter. [27]Get thee up unto the top of Pisgah, and lift up thine eyes westward, and northward, and southward, and eastward, and behold with thine eyes: for thou shalt not go over this Jordan. [28]But charge Joshua, and encourage him, and strengthen him; for he shall go over before this people, and he shall cause them to inherit the land which thou shalt see. [29]So we abode in the valley over against Beth-peor.

DEUTERONOMY 4

[1]And now, O Israel, hearken unto the statutes and unto the ordinances, which I teach you, to do them; that ye may live, and go in and possess the land which Jehovah, the God of your fathers, giveth you. [2]Ye shall not add unto the word which I command you, neither shall ye diminish from it, that ye may keep the commandments of Jehovah your God which I command you. [3]Your eyes have seen what Jehovah did because of Baal-peor; for all the men that followed Baal-peor, Jehovah thy God hath destroyed them from the midst of thee. [4]But ye that did cleave unto Jehovah your God are alive every one of you this day.

[5]Behold, I have taught you statutes and ordinances, even as Jehovah my God commanded me, that ye should do so in the midst of the land whither ye go in to possess it. [6]Keep therefore and do them; for this is your wisdom and your understanding in the sight of the peoples, that shall hear all these statutes, and say, Surely this great nation is a wise and understanding people. [7]For what great nation is there, that hath a god so nigh unto them, as Jehovah our God is whensoever we call upon him? [8]And what great nation is there, that hath statutes and ordinances so righteous as all this law, which I set before you this day?

[9]Only take heed to thyself, and keep thy soul diligently, lest thou forget the things which thine eyes saw, and lest they depart from thy heart all the days of thy life; but make them known unto thy children and thy children's children; [10]the day that thou stoodest before Jehovah thy God in Horeb, when Jehovah said unto me, Assemble me the people, and I will make them hear my words, that they may learn to fear me all the days that they live upon the earth, and that they may teach their children.

[11]And ye came near and stood under the mountain; and the mountain burned with fire unto the heart of heaven, with darkness, cloud, and thick darkness. [12]And Jehovah spake unto you out of the midst of the

fire: ye heard the voice of words, but ye saw no form; only ye heard a voice. [13]And he declared unto you his covenant, which he commanded you to perform, even the ten commandments; and he wrote them upon two tables of stone. [14]And Jehovah commanded me at that time to teach you statutes and ordinances, that ye might do them in the land whither ye go over to possess it.

[15]Take ye therefore good heed unto yourselves; for ye saw no manner of form on the day that Jehovah spake unto you in Horeb out of the midst of the fire. [16]Lest ye corrupt yourselves, and make you a graven image in the form of any figure, the likeness of male or female, [17]the likeness of any beast that is on the earth, the likeness of any winged bird that flieth in the heavens, [18]the likeness of anything that creepeth on the ground, the likeness of any fish that is in the water under the earth; [19]and lest thou lift up thine eyes unto heaven, and when thou seest the sun and the moon and the stars, even all the host of heaven, thou be drawn away and worship them, and serve them, which Jehovah thy God hath allotted unto all the peoples under the whole heaven.

[20]But Jehovah hath taken you, and brought you forth out of the iron furnace, out of Egypt, to be unto him a people of inheritance, as at this day. [21]Furthermore Jehovah was angry with me for your sakes, and sware that I should not go over the Jordan, and that I should not go in unto that good land, which Jehovah thy God giveth thee for an inheritance: [22]but I must die in this land, I must not go over the Jordan; but ye shall go over, and possess that good land. [23]Take heed unto yourselves, lest ye forget the covenant of Jehovah your God, which he made with you, and make you a graven image in the form of anything which Jehovah thy God hath forbidden thee. [24]For Jehovah thy God is a devouring fire, a jealous God.

[25]When thou shalt beget children, and children's children, and ye shall have been long in the land, and shall corrupt yourselves, and make a graven image in the form of anything, and shall do that which is evil in the sight of Jehovah thy God, to provoke him to anger; [26]I call heaven and earth to witness against you this day, that ye shall soon utterly perish from off the land whereunto ye go over the Jordan to possess it; ye shall not prolong your days upon it, but shall utterly be destroyed. [27]And Jehovah will scatter you among the peoples, and ye shall be left few in number among the nations, whither Jehovah shall lead you away. [28]And there ye shall serve gods, the work of men's hands, wood and stone, which neither see, nor hear, nor eat, nor smell.

[29]But from thence ye shall seek Jehovah thy God, and thou shalt find him, when thou searchest after him with all thy heart and with all thy soul. [30]When thou art in tribulation, and all these things are come upon

thee, in the latter days thou shalt return to Jehovah thy God, and hearken unto his voice: [31]for Jehovah thy God is a merciful God; he will not fail thee, neither destroy thee, nor forget the covenant of thy fathers which he sware unto them.

[32]For ask now of the days that are past, which were before thee, since the day that God created man upon the earth, and from the one end of heaven unto the other, whether there hath been any such thing as this great thing is, or hath been heard like it? [33]Did ever a people hear the voice of God speaking out of the midst of the fire, as thou hast heard, and live? [34]Or hath God assayed to go and take him a nation from the midst of another nation, by trials, by signs, and by wonders, and by war, and by a mighty hand, and by an outstretched arm, and by great terrors, according to all that Jehovah your God did for you in Egypt before your eyes? [35]Unto thee it was showed, that thou mightest know that Jehovah he is God; there is none else besides him. [36]Out of heaven he made thee to hear his voice, that he might instruct thee: and upon earth he made thee to see his great fire; and thou heardest his words out of the midst of the fire. [37]And because he loved thy fathers, therefore he chose their seed after them, and brought thee out with his presence, with his great power, out of Egypt; [38]to drive out nations from before thee greater and mightier than thou, to bring thee in, to give thee their land for an inheritance, as at this day.

[39]Know therefore this day, and lay it to thy heart, that Jehovah he is God in heaven above and upon the earth beneath; there is none else. [40]And thou shalt keep his statutes, and his commandments, which I command thee this day, that it may go well with thee, and with thy children after thee, and that thou mayest prolong thy days in the land, which Jehovah thy God giveth thee, for ever.

[41]Then Moses set apart three cities beyond the Jordan toward the sunrising; [42]that the manslayer might flee thither, that slayeth his neighbor unawares, and hated him not in time past; and that fleeing unto one of these cities he might live: [43]namely, Bezer in the wilderness, in the plain country, for the Reubenites; and Ramoth in Gilead, for the Gadites; and Golan in Bashan, for the Manassites.

[44]And this is the law which Moses set before the children of Israel: [45]these are the testimonies, and the statutes, and the ordinances, which Moses spake unto the children of Israel, when they came forth out of Egypt, [46]beyond the Jordan, in the valley over against Beth-peor, in the land of Sihon king of the Amorites, who dwelt at Heshbon, whom Moses and the children of Israel smote, when they came forth out of Egypt. [47]And they took his land in possession, and the land of Og king of Bashan, the two kings of the Amorites, who were beyond the Jordan

toward the sunrising; [48]from Aroer, which is on the edge of the valley of the Arnon, even unto mount Sion (the same is Hermon), [49]and all the Arabah beyond the Jordan eastward, even unto the sea of the Arabah, under the slopes of Pisgah. . . .

[Chapters 5-28 review the Ten Commandments and other laws Jehovah gave the Israelites.]

DEUTERONOMY 29

[1]These are the words of the covenant which Jehovah commanded Moses to make with the children of Israel in the land of Moab, besides the covenant which he made with them in Horeb.

[2]And Moses called unto all Israel, and said unto them, Ye have seen all that Jehovah did before your eyes in the land of Egypt unto Pharaoh, and unto all his servants, and unto all his land; [3]the great trials which thine eyes saw, the signs, and those great wonders: [4]but Jehovah hath not given you a heart to know, and eyes to see, and ears to hear, unto this day. [5]And I have led you forty years in the wilderness: your clothes are not waxed old upon you, and thy shoe is not waxed old upon thy foot. [6]Ye have not eaten bread, neither have ye drunk wine or strong drink; that ye may know that I am Jehovah your God. [7]And when ye came unto this place, Sihon the king of Heshbon, and Og the king of Bashan, came out against us unto battle, and we smote them: [8]and we took their land, and gave it for an inheritance unto the Reubenites, and to the Gadites, and to the half-tribe of the Manassites. [9]Keep therefore the words of this covenant, and do them, that ye may prosper in all that ye do.

[10]Ye stand this day all of you before Jehovah your God; your heads, your tribes, your elders, and your officers, even all the men of Israel, [11]your little ones, your wives, and thy sojourner that is in the midst of thy camps, from the hewer of thy wood unto the drawer of thy water; [12]that thou mayest enter into the covenant of Jehovah thy God, and into his oath, which Jehovah thy God maketh with thee this day; [13]that he may establish thee this day unto himself for a people, and that he may be unto thee a God, as he spake unto thee, and as he sware unto thy fathers, to Abraham, to Isaac, and to Jacob.

[14]Neither with you only do I make this covenant and this oath, [15]but with him that standeth here with us this day before Jehovah our God, and also with him that is not here with us this day [16](for ye know how we dwelt in the land of Egypt, and how we came through the midst of the nations through which ye passed; [17]and ye have seen their abominations, and their idols, wood and stone, silver and gold, which were among them); [18]lest

there should be among you man, or woman, or family, or tribe, whose heart turneth away this day from Jehovah our God, to go to serve the gods of those nations; lest there should be among you a root that beareth gall and wormwood; [19]and it come to pass, when he heareth the words of this curse, that he bless himself in his heart, saying, I shall have peace, though I walk in the stubbornness of my heart, to destroy the moist with the dry. [20]Jehovah will not pardon him, but then the anger of Jehovah and his jealousy will smoke against that man, and all the curse that is written in this book shall lie upon him, and Jehovah will blot out his name from under heaven. [21]And Jehovah will set him apart unto evil out of all the tribes of Israel, according to all the curses of the covenant that is written in this book of the law.

[22]And the generation to come, your children that shall rise up after you, and the foreigner that shall come from a far land, shall say, when they see the plagues of that land, and the sicknesses wherewith Jehovah hath made it sick; [23]and that the whole land thereof is brimstone, and salt, and a burning, that it is not sown, nor beareth, nor any grass groweth therein, like the overthrow of Sodom and Gomorrah, Admah and Zeboiim, which Jehovah overthrew in his anger, and in his wrath: [24]even all the nations shall say, Wherefore hath Jehovah done thus unto this land? what meaneth the heat of this great anger?

[25]Then men shall say, Because they forsook the covenant of Jehovah, the God of their fathers, which he made with them when he brought them forth out of the land of Egypt, [26]and went and served other gods, and worshipped them, gods that they knew not, and that he had not given unto them: [27]therefore the anger of Jehovah was kindled against this land, to bring upon it all the curse that is written in this book; [28]and Jehovah rooted them out of their land in anger, and in wrath, and in great indignation, and cast them into another land, as at this day. [29]The secret things belong unto Jehovah our God; but the things that are revealed belong unto us and to our children for ever, that we may do all the words of this law.

DEUTERONOMY 30

[1]And it shall come to pass, when all these things are come upon thee, the blessing and the curse, which I have set before thee, and thou shalt call them to mind among all the nations, whither Jehovah thy God hath driven thee, [2]and shalt return unto Jehovah thy God, and shalt obey his voice according to all that I command thee this day, thou and thy children, with all thy heart, and with all thy soul; [3]that then Jehovah thy God will turn thy captivity, and have compassion upon thee, and will return and gather thee

from all the peoples, whither Jehovah thy God hath scattered thee. [4]If any of thine outcasts be in the uttermost parts of heaven, from thence will Jehovah thy God gather thee, and from thence will he fetch thee: [5]and Jehovah thy God will bring thee into the land which thy fathers possessed, and thou shalt possess it; and he will do thee good, and multiply thee above thy fathers. [6]And Jehovah thy God will circumcise thy heart, and the heart of thy seed, to love Jehovah thy God with all thy heart, and with all thy soul, that thou mayest live. [7]And Jehovah thy God will put all these curses upon thine enemies, and on them that hate thee, that persecuted thee. [8]And thou shalt return and obey the voice of Jehovah, and do all his commandments which I command thee this day. [9]And Jehovah thy God will make thee plenteous in all the work of thy hand, in the fruit of thy body, and in the fruit of thy cattle, and in the fruit of thy ground, for good: for Jehovah will again rejoice over thee for good, as he rejoiced over thy fathers; [10]if thou shalt obey the voice of Jehovah thy God, to keep his commandments and his statutes which are written in this book of the law; if thou turn unto Jehovah thy God with all thy heart, and with all thy soul.

[11]For this commandment which I command thee this day, it is not too hard for thee, neither is it far off. [12]It is not in heaven, that thou shouldest say, Who shall go up for us to heaven, and bring it unto us, and make us to hear it, that we may do it? [13]Neither is it beyond the sea, that thou shouldest say, Who shall go over the sea for us, and bring it unto us, and make us to hear it, that we may do it? [14]But the word is very nigh unto thee, in thy mouth, and in thy heart, that thou mayest do it.

[15]See, I have set before thee this day life and good, and death and evil; [16]in that I command thee this day to love Jehovah thy God, to walk in his ways, and to keep his commandments and his statutes and his ordinances, that thou mayest live and multiply, and that Jehovah thy God may bless thee in the land whither thou goest in to possess it. [17]But if thy heart turn away, and thou wilt not hear, but shalt be drawn away, and worship other gods, and serve them; [18]I denounce unto you this day, that ye shall surely perish; ye shall not prolong your days in the land, whither thou passest over the Jordan to go in to possess it. [19]I call heaven and earth to witness against you this day, that I have set before thee life and death, the blessing and the curse: therefore choose life, that thou mayest live, thou and thy seed; [20]to love Jehovah thy God, to obey his voice, and to cleave unto him; for he is thy life, and the length of thy days; that thou mayest dwell in the land which Jehovah sware unto thy fathers, to Abraham, to Isaac, and to Jacob, to give them.

DEUTERONOMY 31

¹And Moses went and spake these words unto all Israel. ²And he said unto them, I am a hundred and twenty years old this day; I can no more go out and come in: and Jehovah hath said unto me, Thou shalt not go over this Jordan. ³Jehovah thy God, he will go over before thee; he will destroy these nations from before thee, and thou shalt dispossess them: and Joshua, he shall go over before thee, as Jehovah hath spoken. ⁴And Jehovah will do unto them as he did to Sihon and to Og, the kings of the Amorites, and unto their land; whom he destroyed. ⁵And Jehovah will deliver them up before you, and ye shall do unto them according unto all the commandment which I have commanded you. ⁶Be strong and of good courage, fear not, nor be affrighted at them: for Jehovah thy God, he it is that doth go with thee; he will not fail thee, nor forsake thee.

⁷And Moses called unto Joshua, and said unto him in the sight of all Israel, Be strong and of good courage: for thou shalt go with this people into the land which Jehovah hath sworn unto their fathers to give them; and thou shalt cause them to inherit it. ⁸And Jehovah, he it is that doth go before thee; he will be with thee, he will not fail thee, neither forsake thee: fear not, neither be dismayed.

⁹And Moses wrote this law, and delivered it unto the priests the sons of Levi, that bare the ark of the covenant of Jehovah, and unto all the elders of Israel. ¹⁰And Moses commanded them, saying, At the end of every seven years, in the set time of the year of release, in the feast of tabernacles, ¹¹when all Israel is come to appear before Jehovah thy God in the place which he shall choose, thou shalt read this law before all Israel in their hearing. ¹²Assemble the people, the men and the women and the little ones, and thy sojourner that is within thy gates, that they may hear, and that they may learn, and fear Jehovah your God, and observe to do all the words of this law; ¹³and that their children, who have not known, may hear, and learn to fear Jehovah your God, as long as ye live in the land whither ye go over the Jordan to possess it.

¹⁴And Jehovah said unto Moses, Behold, thy days approach that thou must die: call Joshua, and present yourselves in the tent of meeting, that I may give him a charge. And Moses and Joshua went, and presented themselves in the tent of meeting. ¹⁵And Jehovah appeared in the Tent in a pillar of cloud: and the pillar of cloud stood over the door of the Tent. ¹⁶And Jehovah said unto Moses, Behold, thou shalt sleep with thy fathers; and this people will rise up, and play the harlot after the strange gods of the land, whither they go to be among them, and will forsake me, and break my covenant which I have made with them. ¹⁷Then my anger

shall be kindled against them in that day, and I will forsake them, and I will hide my face from them, and they shall be devoured, and many evils and troubles shall come upon them; so that they will say in that day, Are not these evils come upon us because our God is not among us? [18]And I will surely hide my face in that day for all the evil which they shall have wrought, in that they are turned unto other gods.

[19]Now therefore write ye this song for you, and teach thou it the children of Israel: put it in their mouths, that this song may be a witness for me against the children of Israel. [20]For when I shall have brought them into the land which I sware unto their fathers, flowing with milk and honey, and they shall have eaten and filled themselves, and waxed fat; then will they turn unto other gods, and serve them, and despise me, and break my covenant. [21]And it shall come to pass, when many evils and troubles are come upon them, that this song shall testify before them as a witness; for it shall not be forgotten out of the mouths of their seed: for I know their imagination which they frame this day, before I have brought them into the land which I sware. [22]So Moses wrote this song the same day, and taught it the children of Israel. [23]And he gave Joshua the son of Nun a charge, and said, Be strong and of good courage; for thou shalt bring the children of Israel into the land which I sware unto them: and I will be with thee.

[24]And it came to pass, when Moses had made an end of writing the words of this law in a book, until they were finished, [25]that Moses commanded the Levites, that bare the ark of the covenant of Jehovah, saying, [26]Take this book of the law, and put it by the side of the ark of the covenant of Jehovah your God, that it may be there for a witness against thee. [27]For I know thy rebellion, and thy stiff neck: behold, while I am yet alive with you this day, ye have been rebellious against Jehovah; and how much more after my death? [28]Assemble unto me all the elders of your tribes, and your officers, that I may speak these words in their ears, and call heaven and earth to witness against them. [29]For I know that after my death ye will utterly corrupt yourselves, and turn aside from the way which I have commanded you; and evil will befall you in the latter days; because ye will do that which is evil in the sight of Jehovah, to provoke him to anger through the work of your hands.

[30]And Moses spake in the ears of all the assembly of Israel the words of this song, until they were finished.

DEUTERONOMY 32

[1]*Give ear, ye heavens, and I will speak;*
And let the earth hear the words of my mouth.

²*My doctrine shall drop as the rain;*
My speech shall distil as the dew,
As the small rain upon the tender grass,
And as the showers upon the herb.
³*For I will proclaim the name of Jehovah:*
Ascribe ye greatness unto our God.
⁴*The Rock, his work is perfect;*
For all his ways are justice:
A God of faithfulness and without iniquity,
Just and right is he.
⁵*They have dealt corruptly with him,*
they are not his children, it is their blemish;
They are a perverse and crooked generation.
⁶*Do ye thus requite Jehovah,*
O foolish people and unwise?
Is not he thy father that hath bought thee?
He hath made thee, and established thee.
⁷*Remember the days of old,*
Consider the years of many generations:
Ask thy father, and he will show thee;
Thine elders, and they will tell thee.
⁸*When the Most High gave to the nations their*
inheritance,
When he separated the children of men,
He set the bounds of the peoples
According to the number of the children of Israel.
⁹*For Jehovah's portion is his people;*
Jacob is the lot of his inheritance.
¹⁰*He found him in a desert land,*
And in the waste howling wilderness;
He compassed him about, he cared for him,
He kept him as the apple of his eye.
¹¹*As an eagle that stirreth up her nest,*
That fluttereth over her young,
He spread abroad his wings, he took them,
He bare them on his pinions.
¹²*Jehovah alone did lead him,*
And there was no foreign god with him.
¹³*He made him ride on the high places of the earth,*
And he did eat the increase of the field;
And he made him to suck honey out of the rock,

And oil out of the flinty rock;
[14]Butter of the herd, and milk of the flock,
With fat of lambs,
And rams of the breed of Bashan, and goats,
With the finest of the wheat;
And of the blood of the grape thou drankest wine.
[15]But Jeshurun waxed fat, and kicked:
Thou art waxed fat, thou art grown thick,
        thou art become sleek;
Then he forsook God who made him,
And lightly esteemed the Rock of his salvation.
[16]They moved him to jealousy with strange gods;
With abominations provoked they him to anger.
[17]They sacrificed unto demons, which were no God,
To gods that they knew not,
To new gods that came up of late,
Which your fathers dreaded not.
[18]Of the Rock that begat thee thou art unmindful,
And hast forgotten God that gave thee birth.
[19]And Jehovah saw it, and abhorred them,
Because of the provocation of his sons and his daughters.
[20]And he said, I will hide my face from them,
I will see what their end shall be:
For they are a very perverse generation,
Children in whom is no faithfulness.
[21]They have moved me to jealousy with that which is
        not God;
They have provoked me to anger with their vanities:
And I will move them to jealousy with those that are not
        a people;
I will provoke them to anger with a foolish nation.
[22]For a fire is kindled in mine anger,
And burneth unto the lowest Sheol,
And devoureth the earth with its increase,
And setteth on fire the foundations of the mountains.
[23]I will heap evils upon them;
I will spend mine arrows upon them:
[24]They shall be wasted with hunger, and devoured with
        burning heat
And bitter destruction;
And the teeth of beasts will I send upon them,

With the poison of crawling things of the dust.
²⁵Without shall the sword bereave,
And in the chambers terror;
It shall destroy both young man and virgin,
The suckling with the man of gray hairs.
²⁶I said, I would scatter them afar,
I would make the remembrance of them to cease from
        among men;
²⁷Were it not that I feared the provocation of the enemy,
Lest their adversaries should judge amiss,
Lest they should say, Our hand is exalted,
And Jehovah hath not done all this.
²⁸For they are a nation void of counsel,
And there is no understanding in them.
²⁹Oh that they were wise, that they understood this,
That they would consider their latter end!
³⁰How should one chase a thousand,
And two put ten thousand to flight,
Except their Rock had sold them,
And Jehovah had delivered them up?
³¹For their rock is not as our Rock,
Even our enemies themselves being judges.
³²For their vine is of the vine of Sodom,
And of the fields of Gomorrah:
Their grapes are grapes of gall,
Their clusters are bitter:
³³Their wine is the poison of serpents,
And the cruel venom of asps.
³⁴Is not this laid up in store with me,
Sealed up among my treasures?
³⁵Vengeance is mine, and recompense,
At the time when their foot shall slide:
For the day of their calamity is at hand,
And the things that are to come upon them
        shall make haste.
³⁶For Jehovah will judge his people,
And repent himself for his servants;
When he seeth that their power is gone,
And there is none remaining, shut up or left at large.
³⁷And he will say, Where are their gods,
The rock in which they took refuge;

38Which did eat the fat of their sacrifices,
And drank the wine of their drink-offering?
Let them rise up and help you,
Let them be your protection.
39See now that I, even I, am he,
And there is no god with me:
I kill, and I make alive;
I wound, and I heal;
And there is none that can deliver out of my hand.
40For I lift up my hand to heaven,
And say, As I live for ever,
41If I whet my glittering sword,
And my hand take hold on judgment;
I will render vengeance to mine adversaries,
And will recompense them that hate me.
42I will make mine arrows drunk with blood,
And my sword shall devour flesh;
With the blood of the slain and the captives,
From the head of the leaders of the enemy.
43Rejoice, O ye nations, with his people:
For he will avenge the blood of his servants,
And will render vengeance to his adversaries,
And will make expiation for his land, for his people.

44And Moses came and spake all the words of this song in the ears of the people, he, and Hoshea the son of Nun. 45And Moses made an end of speaking all these words to all Israel; 46And he said unto them, Set your heart unto all the words which I testify unto you this day, which ye shall command your children to observe to do, even all the words of this law. 47For it is no vain thing for you; because it is your life, and through this thing ye shall prolong your days in the land, whither ye go over the Jordan to possess it.

48And Jehovah spake unto Moses that selfsame day, saying, 49Get thee up into this mountain of Abarim, unto mount Nebo, which is in the land of Moab, that is over against Jericho; and behold the land of Canaan, which I give unto the children of Israel for a possession; 50and die in the mount whither thou goest up, and be gathered unto thy people, as Aaron thy brother died in mount Hor, and was gathered unto his people: 51because ye trespassed against me in the midst of the children of Israel at the waters of Meribah of Kadesh, in the wilderness of Zin; because ye sanctified me not in the midst of the children of Israel. 52For thou shalt see the land before thee; but thou shalt not go thither into the land which I give the children of Israel.

DEUTERONOMY 33

¹And this is the blessing, wherewith Moses the man of God blessed the children of Israel before his death. ²And he said,

> *Jehovah came from Sinai,*
> *And rose from Seir unto them;*
> *He shined forth from mount Paran,*
> *And he came from the ten thousands of holy ones:*
> *At his right hand was a fiery law for them.*
> ³*Yea, he loveth the people;*
> *All his saints are in thy hand:*
> *And they sat down at thy feet;*
> *Every one shall receive of thy words.*
> ⁴*Moses commanded us a law,*
> *An inheritance for the assembly of Jacob.*
> ⁵*And he was king in Jeshurun,*
> *When the heads of the people were gathered,*
> *All the tribes of Israel together.*
> ⁶*Let Reuben live, and not die;*
> *Nor let his men be few.*
> ⁷*And this is the blessing of Judah: and he said,*
> *Hear, Jehovah, the voice of Judah,*
> *And bring him in unto his people.*
> *With his hands he contended for himself;*
> *And thou shalt be a help against his adversaries.*
> ⁸*And of Levi he said,*
> *Thy Thummim and thy Urim are with thy godly one,*
> *Whom thou didst prove at Massah,*
> *With whom thou didst strive at the waters of Meribah;*
> ⁹*Who said of his father, and of his mother,*
> *I have not seen him;*
> *Neither did he acknowledge his brethren,*
> *Nor knew he his own children:*
> *For they have observed thy word,*
> *And keep thy covenant.*
> ¹⁰*They shall teach Jacob thine ordinances,*
> *And Israel thy law:*

They shall put incense before thee,
And whole burnt-offering upon thine altar.
¹¹Bless, Jehovah, his substance,
And accept the work of his hands:
Smite through the loins of them that rise up against him,
And of them that hate him, that they rise not again.
¹²Of Benjamin he said,
The beloved of Jehovah shall dwell in safety by him;
He covereth him all the day long,
And he dwelleth between his shoulders.
¹³And of Joseph he said,
Blessed of Jehovah be his land,
For the precious things of heaven, for the dew,
And for the deep that coucheth beneath,
¹⁴And for the precious things of the fruits of the sun,
And for the precious things of the growth of the moons,
¹⁵And for the chief things of the ancient mountains,
And for the precious things of the everlasting hills,
¹⁶And for the precious things of the earth
                and the fulness thereof,
And the good will of him that dwelt in the bush.
Let the blessing come upon the head of Joseph,
And upon the crown of the head of him that was separate
                from his brethren.
¹⁷The firstling of his herd, majesty is his;
And his horns are the horns of the wild-ox:
With them he shall push the peoples all of them,
                even the ends of the earth:
And they are the ten thousands of Ephraim,
And they are the thousands of Manasseh.
¹⁸And of Zebulun he said,
Rejoice, Zebulun, in thy going out;
And, Issachar, in thy tents.
¹⁹They shall call the peoples unto the mountain;
There shall they offer sacrifices of righteousness:
For they shall suck the abundance of the seas,
And the hidden treasures of the sand.
²⁰And of Gad he said,
Blessed be he that enlargeth Gad:
He dwelleth as a lioness,
And teareth the arm, yea, the crown of the head.

[21] And he provided the first part for himself,
For there was the lawgiver's portion reserved;
And he came with the heads of the people;
He executed the righteousness of Jehovah,
And his ordinances with Israel.
[22] And of Dan he said,
Dan is a lion's whelp,
That leapeth forth from Bashan.
[23] And of Naphtali he said,
O Naphtali, satisfied with favor,
And full with the blessing of Jehovah,
Possess thou the west and the south.
[24] And of Asher he said,
Blessed be Asher with children;
Let him be acceptable unto his brethren,
And let him dip his foot in oil.
[25] Thy bars shall be iron and brass;
And as thy days, so shall thy strength be.
[26] There is none like unto God, O Jeshurun,
Who rideth upon the heavens for thy help,
And in his excellency on the skies.
[27] The eternal God is thy dwelling-place,
And underneath are the everlasting arms.
And he thrust out the enemy from before thee,
And said, Destroy.
[28] And Israel dwelleth in safety,
The fountain of Jacob alone,
In a land of grain and new wine;
Yea, his heavens drop down dew.
[29] Happy art thou, O Israel:
Who is like unto thee, a people saved by Jehovah,
The shield of thy help,
And the sword of thy excellency!
And thine enemies shall submit themselves unto thee;
And thou shalt tread upon their high places.

DEUTERONOMY 34

[1] And Moses went up from the plains of Moab unto mount Nebo, to the top of Pisgah, that is over against Jericho. And Jehovah showed him all the

land of Gilead, unto Dan, [2]and all Naphtali, and the land of Ephraim and Manasseh, and all the land of Judah, unto the hinder sea, [3]and the South, and the Plain of the valley of Jericho the city of palm-trees, unto Zoar. [4]And Jehovah said unto him, This is the land which I sware unto Abraham, unto Isaac, and unto Jacob, saying, I will give it unto thy seed: I have caused thee to see it with thine eyes, but thou shalt not go over thither.

[5]So Moses the servant of Jehovah died there in the land of Moab, according to the word of Jehovah. [6]And he buried him in the valley in the land of Moab over against Beth-peor: but no man knoweth of his sepulchre unto this day. [7]And Moses was a hundred and twenty years old when he died: his eye was not dim, nor his natural force abated. [8]And the children of Israel wept for Moses in the plains of Moab thirty days: so the days of weeping in the mourning for Moses were ended.

[9]And Joshua the son of Nun was full of the spirit of wisdom; for Moses had laid his hands upon him: and the children of Israel hearkened unto him, and did as Jehovah commanded Moses. [10]And there hath not arisen a prophet since in Israel like unto Moses, whom Jehovah knew face to face, [11]in all the signs and the wonders, which Jehovah sent him to do in the land of Egypt, to Pharaoh, and to all his servants, and to all his land, [12]and in all the mighty hand, and in all the great terror, which Moses wrought in the sight of all Israel.

Chapter 4

JOSHUA

JOSHUA 1

[1]Now it came to pass after the death of Moses the servant of Jehovah, that Jehovah spake unto Joshua the son of Nun, Moses' minister, saying, [2]Moses my servant is dead; now therefore arise, go over this Jordan, thou, and all this people, unto the land which I do give to them, even to the children of Israel. [3]Every place that the sole of your foot shall tread upon, to you have I given it, as I spake unto Moses. [4]From the wilderness, and this Lebanon, even unto the great river, the river Euphrates, all the land of the Hittites, and unto the great sea toward the going down of the sun, shall be your border. [5]There shall not any man be able to stand before thee all the days of thy life. As I was with Moses, so I will be with thee; I will not fail thee, nor forsake thee. [6]Be strong and of good courage; for thou shalt cause this people to inherit the land which I sware unto their fathers to give them. [7]Only be strong and very courageous, to observe to do according to all the law, which Moses my servant commanded thee: turn not from it to the right hand or to the left, that thou mayest have good success whithersoever thou goest. [8]This book of the law shall not depart out of thy mouth, but thou shalt meditate thereon day and night, that thou mayest observe to do according to all that is written therein: for then thou shalt make thy way prosperous, and then thou shalt have good success. [9]Have not I commanded thee? Be strong and of good courage; be not affrighted, neither be thou dismayed: for Jehovah thy God is with thee whithersoever thou goest.

[10]Then Joshua commanded the officers of the people, saying, [11]Pass through the midst of the camp, and command the people, saying, Prepare you victuals; for within three days ye are to pass over this Jordan, to go in to possess the land, which Jehovah your God giveth you to possess it.

¹²And to the Reubenites, and to the Gadites, and to the half-tribe of Manasseh, spake Joshua, saying, ¹³Remember the word which Moses the servant of Jehovah commanded you, saying, Jehovah your God giveth you rest, and will give you this land. ¹⁴Your wives, your little ones, and your cattle, shall abide in the land which Moses gave you beyond the Jordan; but ye shall pass over before your brethren armed, all the mighty men of valor, and shall help them; ¹⁵until Jehovah have given your brethren rest, as he hath given you, and they also have possessed the land which Jehovah your God giveth them: then ye shall return unto the land of your possession, and possess it, which Moses the servant of Jehovah gave you beyond the Jordan toward the sunrising.

¹⁶And they answered Joshua, saying, All that thou hast commanded us we will do, and whithersoever thou sendest us we will go. ¹⁷According as we hearkened unto Moses in all things, so will we hearken unto thee: only Jehovah thy God be with thee, as he was with Moses. ¹⁸Whosoever he be that shall rebel against thy commandment, and shall not hearken unto thy words in all that thou commandest him, he shall be put to death: only be strong and of good courage. . . .

JOSHUA 3

¹And Joshua rose up early in the morning; and they removed from Shittim, and came to the Jordan, he and all the children of Israel; and they lodged there before they passed over. ²And it came to pass after three days, that the officers went through the midst of the camp; ³and they commanded the people, saying, When ye see the ark of the covenant of Jehovah your God, and the priests the Levites bearing it, then ye shall remove from your place, and go after it. ⁴Yet there shall be a space between you and it, about two thousand cubits by measure: come not near unto it, that ye may know the way by which ye must go; for ye have not passed this way heretofore. ⁵And Joshua said unto the people, Sanctify yourselves; for tomorrow Jehovah will do wonders among you. ⁶And Joshua spake unto the priests, saying, Take up the ark of the covenant, and pass over before the people. And they took up the ark of the covenant, and went before the people.

⁷And Jehovah said unto Joshua, This day will I begin to magnify thee in the sight of all Israel, that they may know that, as I was with Moses, so I will be with thee. ⁸And thou shalt command the priests that bear the ark of the covenant, saying, When ye are come to the brink of the waters of the Jordan, ye shall stand still in the Jordan. ⁹And Joshua said unto the children of Israel, Come hither, and hear the words of Jehovah your

God. [10]And Joshua said, Hereby ye shall know that the living God is among you, and that he will without fail drive out from before you the Canaanite, and the Hittite, and the Hivite, and the Perizzite, and the Girgashite, and the Amorite, and the Jebusite. [11]Behold, the ark of the covenant of the Lord of all the earth passeth over before you into the Jordan. [12]Now therefore take you twelve men out of the tribes of Israel, for every tribe a man. [13]And it shall come to pass, when the soles of the feet of the priests that bear the ark of Jehovah, the Lord of all the earth, shall rest in the waters of the Jordan, that the waters of the Jordan shall be cut off, even the waters that come down from above; and they shall stand in one heap.

[14]And it came to pass, when the people removed from their tents, to pass over the Jordan, the priests that bare the ark of the covenant being before the people; [15]and when they that bare the ark were come unto the Jordan, and the feet of the priests that bare the ark were dipped in the brink of the water (for the Jordan overfloweth all its banks all the time of harvest,) [16]that the waters which came down from above stood, and rose up in one heap, a great way off, at Adam, the city that is beside Zarethan; and those that went down toward the sea of the Arabah, even the Salt Sea, were wholly cut off: and the people passed over right against Jericho. [17]And the priests that bare the ark of the covenant of Jehovah stood firm on dry ground in the midst of the Jordan; and all Israel passed over on dry ground, until all the nation were passed clean over the Jordan.

JOSHUA 4

[1]And it came to pass, when all the nation were clean passed over the Jordan, that Jehovah spake unto Joshua, saying, [2]Take you twelve men out of the people, out of every tribe a man, [3]and command ye them, saying, Take you hence out of the midst of the Jordan, out of the place where the priests' feet stood firm, twelve stones, and carry them over with you, and lay them down in the lodging-place, where ye shall lodge this night. [4]Then Joshua called the twelve men, whom he had prepared of the children of Israel, out of every tribe a man: [5]and Joshua said unto them, Pass over before the ark of Jehovah your God into the midst of the Jordan, and take you up every man of you a stone upon his shoulder, according unto the number of the tribes of the children of Israel; [6]that this may be a sign among you, that, when your children ask in time to come, saying, What mean ye by these stones? [7]then ye shall say unto them, Because the waters of the Jordan were cut off before the ark of the covenant of Jehovah; when it passed over the Jordan, the waters of the Jordan were cut off: and these stones shall be for a memorial unto the children of Israel for ever.

⁸And the children of Israel did so as Joshua commanded, and took up twelve stones out of the midst of the Jordan, as Jehovah spake unto Joshua, according to the number of the tribes of the children of Israel; and they carried them over with them unto the place where they lodged, and laid them down there. ⁹And Joshua set up twelve stones in the midst of the Jordan, in the place where the feet of the priests that bare the ark of the covenant stood: and they are there unto this day. ¹⁰For the priests that bare the ark stood in the midst of the Jordan, until everything was finished that Jehovah commanded Joshua to speak unto the people, according to all that Moses commanded Joshua: and the people hasted and passed over.

¹¹And it came to pass, when all the people were clean passed over, that the ark of Jehovah passed over, and the priests, in the presence of the people. ¹²And the children of Reuben, and the children of Gad, and the half-tribe of Manasseh, passed over armed before the children of Israel, as Moses spake unto them: ¹³about forty thousand ready armed for war passed over before Jehovah unto battle, to the plains of Jericho. ¹⁴On that day Jehovah magnified Joshua in the sight of all Israel; and they feared him, as they feared Moses, all the days of his life.

¹⁵And Jehovah spake unto Joshua, saying, ¹⁶Command the priests that bear the ark of the testimony, that they come up out of the Jordan. ¹⁷Joshua therefore commanded the priests, saying, Come ye up out of the Jordan. ¹⁸And it came to pass, when the priests that bare the ark of the covenant of Jehovah were come up out of the midst of the Jordan, and the soles of the priests' feet were lifted up unto the dry ground, that the waters of the Jordan returned unto their place, and went over all its banks, as aforetime.

¹⁹And the people came up out of the Jordan on the tenth day of the first month, and encamped in Gilgal, on the east border of Jericho. ²⁰And those twelve stones, which they took out of the Jordan, did Joshua set up in Gilgal. ²¹And he spake unto the children of Israel, saying, When your children shall ask their fathers in time to come, saying, What mean these stones? ²²Then ye shall let your children know, saying, Israel came over this Jordan on dry land. ²³For Jehovah your God dried up the waters of the Jordan from before you, until ye were passed over, as Jehovah your God did to the Red Sea, which he dried up from before us, until we were passed over; ²⁴that all the peoples of the earth may know the hand of Jehovah, that it is mighty; that ye may fear Jehovah your God for ever.

Part II

WRITINGS FROM JOSEPHUS'S
Antiquities of the Jews

Josephus was born Joseph ben Mattathias in 37 C.E. in Jerusalem of a priestly and royal family. He excelled in his studies of Jewish law and studied with the Sadducees, Pharisees, and the Essenes, eventually aligning himself with the Pharisees. In 62 C.E. he went to Rome to free some imprisoned priests. After accomplishing this mission through the intercession of Nero's wife, Poppaea, he returned to Jerusalem in 65 C.E. to find the country in revolt against Rome.

Although Josephus had deep misgivings about the revolt, it became inevitable, due to reasons he discusses in his history, primarily the abuses of the Romans; this spurred the growth of fanatical Messianic Jewish movements which believed that the world was coming to an end shortly. In 66 C.E. the Masada was seized by the Zealots and the Romans were on the march; Josephus was appointed the commander of Galilee.

Josephus had to fight a defensive war against overwhelming force while refereeing internecine squabbles in the Jewish ranks. In 67 C.E. Josephus and other rebels were cornered in a cave during the siege of Jotapata and took a suicide pact. However, Josephus survived, and was taken hostage by the Romans, led by Vespasian.

Josephus shrewdly reinterpreted the Messianic prophecies. He predicted that Vespasian would become the ruler of the "entire world." Josephus joined the Romans, for which he was branded a traitor. He acted as consultant to the Romans and a go-between with the revolutionaries. Unable to convince the rebels to surrender, Josephus ended up watching the second destruction of the Temple and the defeat of the Jewish nation.

His prophecy became true in 68 C.E. when Nero committed suicide and Vespasian became Caesar. As a result, Josephus was freed; he moved to Rome and became a Roman citizen, taking the Vespasian family name Flavius. Vespasian commissioned Josephus to write a history of the war, which he finished in 78 C.E., the *Jewish War*. His second major work, the *Antiquities of the Jews,* was completed in 93 C.E. He wrote *Against*

Apion in about 96-100 C.E. and *The Life of Josephus*, his autobiography, about 100. He died shortly after.

Despite his ambivalent role, Josephus was an eyewitness to history, and his writings are considered authoritative. These texts are key to understanding a pivotal point in world history, which has tragic repercussions even to this day.

—J.B.H.

Note from publisher: This volume extracts those sections of Josephus's *Antiquities of the Jews* that pertain to Moses and the exodus of Israel, including a portion of Book 2 (corresponding to chapter 1 below), all of Book 3 (chapter 2 below), and a portion of Book 4 (chapter 3 below). To accommodate the format of this book, divisions in Josephus's work that were called chapters are here designated as subsections of chapters; to enable readers to reference Josephus' work as needed, the original chapter numbers are indicated as appropriate. Part and chapter headings have also been simplified in this volume. This edition of *Antiquities of the Jews* was translated by William Whiston.

Chapter 1

THE EXODUS OUT OF EGYPT

1: THE DEATH OF JACOB AND JOSEPH
(originally chapter 8)

1. Now when Jacob had lived seventeen years in Egypt, he fell into a disease, and died in the presence of his sons; but not till he made his prayers for their enjoying prosperity, and till he had foretold to them prophetically how every one of them was to dwell in the land of Canaan. But this happened many years afterward. He also enlarged upon the praises of Joseph how he had not remembered the evil doings of his brethren to their disadvantage; nay, on the contrary, was kind to them, bestowing upon them so many benefits, as seldom are bestowed on men's own benefactors. He then commanded his own sons that they should admit Joseph's sons, Ephraim and Manasses, into their number, and divide the land of Canaan in common with them; concerning whom we shall treat hereafter. However, he made it his request that he might be buried at Hebron. So he died, when he had lived full a hundred and fifty years, three only abated, having not been behind any of his ancestors in piety towards God, and having such a recompense for it, as it was fit those should have who were so good as these were. But Joseph, by the king's permission, carried his father's dead body to Hebron, and there buried it, at a great expense. Now his brethren were at first unwilling to return back with him, because they were afraid lest, now their father was dead, he should punish them for their secret practices against him; since he was now gone, for whose sake he had been so gracious to them. But he persuaded them to fear no harm, and to entertain no suspicions of him: so he brought them along with him, and gave them great possessions, and never left off his particular concern for them.

2. Joseph also died when he had lived a hundred and ten years; having been a man of admirable virtue, and conducting all his affairs by the

rules of reason; and used his authority with moderation, which was the cause of his so great felicity among the Egyptians, even when he came from another country, and that in such ill circumstances also, as we have already described. At length his brethren died, after they had lived happily in Egypt. Now the posterity and sons of these men, after some time, carried their bodies, and buried them at Hebron: but as to the bones of Joseph, they carried them into the land of Canaan afterward, when the Hebrews went out of Egypt, for so had Joseph made them promise him upon oath. But what became of every one of these men, and by what toils they got the possession of the land of Canaan, shall be shown hereafter, when I have first explained upon what account it was that they left Egypt.

2: THE AFFLICTIONS THAT BEFELL THE HEBREWS IN EGYPT, DURING FOUR HUNDRED YEARS
(originally chapter 9)

1. Now it happened that the Egyptians grew delicate and lazy, as to pains-taking, and gave themselves up to other pleasures, and in particular to the love of gain. They also became very ill-affected towards the Hebrews, as touched with envy at their prosperity; for when they saw how the nation of the Israelites flourished, and were become eminent already in plenty of wealth, which they had acquired by their virtue and natural love of labor, they thought their increase was to their own detriment. And having, in length of time, forgotten the benefits they had received from Joseph, particularly the crown being now come into another family, they became very abusive to the Israelites, and contrived many ways of afflicting them; for they enjoined them to cut a great number of channels for the river, and to build walls for their cities and ramparts, that they might restrain the river, and hinder its waters from stagnating, upon its running over its own banks: they set them also to build pyramids, and by all this wore them out; and forced them to learn all sorts of mechanical arts, and to accustom themselves to hard labor. And four hundred years did they spend under these afflictions; for they strove one against the other which should get the mastery, the Egyptians desiring to destroy the Israelites by these labors, and the Israelites desiring to hold out to the end under them.

2. While the affairs of the Hebrews were in this condition, there was this occasion offered itself to the Egyptians, which made them more solicitous for the extinction of our nation. One of those sacred scribes,[1] who are very

---

1. Instead of this single priest or prophet of the Egyptians, without a name in Josephus, the Targum of Jonathan names the two famous antagonists of Moses, Jannes and Jambres. Nor is it at all unlikely that it might be one of these who foreboded so much misery to the Egyptians, and so much happiness to the Israelites, from the rearing of Moses.

sagacious in foretelling future events truly, told the king, that about this time there would a child be born to the Israelites, who, if he were reared, would bring the Egyptian dominion low, and would raise the Israelites; that he would excel all men in virtue, and obtain a glory that would be remembered through all ages. Which thing was so feared by the king, that, according to this man's opinion, he commanded that they should cast every male child, which was born to the Israelites, into the river, and destroy it; that besides this, the Egyptian midwives[2] should watch the labors of the Hebrew women, and observe what is born, for those were the women who were enjoined to do the office of midwives to them; and by reason of their relation to the king, would not transgress his commands. He enjoined also, that if any parents should disobey him, and venture to save their male children alive, they and their families should be destroyed. This was a severe affliction indeed to those that suffered it, not only as they were deprived of their sons, and while they were the parents themselves, they were obliged to be subservient to the destruction of their own children, but as it was to be supposed to tend to the extirpation of their nation, while upon the destruction of their children, and their own gradual dissolution, the calamity would become very hard and inconsolable to them. And this was the ill state they were in. But no one can be too hard for the purpose of God, though he contrive ten thousand subtle devices for that end; for this child, whom the sacred scribe foretold, was brought up and concealed from the observers appointed by the king; and he that foretold him did not mistake in the consequences of his preservation, which were brought to pass after the manner following:—

3. A man whose name was Amram, one of the nobler sort of the Hebrews, was afraid for his whole nation, lest it should fail, by the want of young men to be brought up hereafter, and was very uneasy at it, his wife being then with child, and he knew not what to do. Hereupon he betook himself to prayer to God; and entreated him to have compassion on those men who had nowise transgressed the laws of his worship, and to afford them deliverance from the miseries they at that time endured, and to render abortive their enemies' hopes of the destruction of their nation. Accordingly God had mercy on him, and was moved by his supplication. He stood by

---

2. Josephus is clear that these midwives were Egyptians, and not Israelites, as in our other copies: which is very probable, it being not easily to be supposed that Pharaoh could trust the Israelite midwives to execute so barbarous a command against their own nation. (Consult, therefore, and correct hence our ordinary copies, Exodus 1:15, 22.) And, indeed, Josephus seems to have had much completer copies of the Pentateuch, or other authentic records now lost, about the birth and actions of Moses, than either our Hebrew, Samaritan, or Greek Bibles afford us, which enabled him to be so large and particular about him.

him in his sleep, and exhorted him not to despair of his future favors. He said further, that he did not forget their piety towards him, and would always reward them for it, as he had formerly granted his favor to their forefathers, and made them increase from a few to so great a multitude. He put him in mind, that when Abraham was come alone out of Mesopotamia into Canaan, he had been made happy, not only in other respects, but that when his wife was at first barren, she was afterwards by him enabled to conceive seed, and bare him sons. That he left to Ismael and to his posterity the country of Arabia; as also to his sons by Ketura, Troglodytis; and to Isaac, Canaan. That by my assistance, said he, he did great exploits in war, which, unless you be yourselves impious, you must still remember. As for Jacob, he became well known to strangers also, by the greatness of that prosperity in which he lived, and left to his sons, who came into Egypt with no more than seventy souls, while you are now become above six hundred thousand. Know therefore that I shall provide for you all in common what is for your good, and particularly for thyself what shall make thee famous; for that child, out of dread of whose nativity the Egyptians have doomed the Israelite children to destruction, shall be this child of thine, and shall be concealed from those who watch to destroy him: and when he is brought up in a surprising way, he shall deliver the Hebrew nation from the distress they are under from the Egyptians. His memory shall be famous while the world lasts; and this not only among the Hebrews, but foreigners also:—all which shall be the effect of my favor to thee, and to thy posterity. He shall also have such a brother, that he shall himself obtain my priesthood, and his posterity shall have it after him to the end of the world.

4. When the vision had informed him of these things, Amram awaked and told it to Jochebed who was his wife. And now the fear increased upon them on account of the prediction in Amram's dream; for they were under concern, not only for the child, but on account of the great happiness that was to come to him also. However, the mother's labor was such as afforded a confirmation to what was foretold by God; for it was not known to those that watched her, by the easiness of her pains, and because the throes of her delivery did not fall upon her with violence. And now they nourished the child at home privately for three months; but after that time Amram, fearing he should be discovered, and, by falling under the king's displeasure, both he and his child should perish, and so he should make the promise of God of none effect, he determined rather to trust the safety and care of the child to God, than to depend on his own concealment of him, which he looked upon as a thing uncertain, and whereby both the child, so privately to be nourished, and himself should be in imminent danger; but he believed that God would some way for certain procure

the safety of the child, in order to secure the truth of his own predictions. When they had thus determined, they made an ark of bulrushes, after the manner of a cradle, and of a bigness sufficient for an infant to be laid in, without being too straitened: they then daubed it over with slime, which would naturally keep out the water from entering between the bulrushes, and put the infant into it, and setting it afloat upon the river, they left its preservation to God; so the river received the child, and carried him along. But Miriam, the child's sister, passed along upon the bank over against him, as her mother had bid her, to see whither the ark would be carried, where God demonstrated that human wisdom was nothing, but that the Supreme Being is able to do whatsoever he pleases: that those who, in order to their own security, condemn others to destruction, and use great endeavors about it, fail of their purpose; but that others are in a surprising manner preserved, and obtain a prosperous condition almost from the very midst of their calamities; those, I mean, whose dangers arise by the appointment of God. And, indeed, such a providence was exercised in the case of this child, as showed the power of God.

5. Thermuthis was the king's daughter. She was now diverting herself by the banks of the river; and seeing a cradle borne along by the current, she sent some that could swim, and bid them bring the cradle to her. When those that were sent on this errand came to her with the cradle, and she saw the little child, she was greatly in love with it, on account of its largeness and beauty; for God had taken such great care in the formation of Moses, that he caused him to be thought worthy of bringing up, and providing for, by all those that had taken the most fatal resolutions, on account of the dread of his nativity, for the destruction of the rest of the Hebrew nation. Thermuthis bid them bring her a woman that might afford her breast to the child; yet would not the child admit of her breast, but turned away from it, and did the like to many other women. Now Miriam was by when this happened, not to appear to be there on purpose, but only as staying to see the child; and she said, "It is in vain that thou, O queen, callest for these women for the nourishing of the child, who are no way of kin to it; but still, if thou wilt order one of the Hebrew women to be brought, perhaps it may admit the breast of one of its own nation." Now since she seemed to speak well, Thermuthis bid her procure such a one, and to bring one of those Hebrew women that gave suck. So when she had such authority given her, she came back and brought the mother, who was known to nobody there. And now the child gladly admitted the breast, and seemed to stick close to it; and so it was, that, at the queen's desire, the nursing of the child was entirely intrusted to the mother.

6. Hereupon it was that Thermuthis imposed this name *Mouses* upon him, from what had happened when he was put into the river; for the Egyptians call water by the name of *Mo,* and such as are saved out of it, by the name of *Uses:* so by putting these two words together, they imposed this name upon him. And he was, by the confession of all, according to God's prediction, as well for his greatness of mind as for his contempt of difficulties, the best of all the Hebrews, for Abraham was his ancestor of the seventh generation. For Moses was the son of Amram, who was the son of Caath, whose father Levi was the son of Jacob, who was the son of Isaac, who was the son of Abraham. Now Moses's understanding became superior to his age, nay, far beyond that standard; and when he was taught, he discovered greater quickness of apprehension than was usual at his age, and his actions at that time promised greater, when he should come to the age of a man. God did also give him that tallness, when he was but three years old, as was wonderful. And as for his beauty, there was nobody so unpolite as, when they saw Moses, they were not greatly surprised at the beauty of his countenance; nay, it happened frequently, that those that met him as he was carried along the road, were obliged to turn again upon seeing the child; that they left what they were about, and stood still a great while to look on him; for the beauty of the child was so remarkable and natural to him on many accounts, that it detained the spectators, and made them stay longer to look upon him.

7. Thermuthis therefore perceiving him to be so remarkable a child, adopted him for her son, having no child of her own. And when one time she had carried Moses to her father, she showed him to him, and said she thought to make him her successor, if it should please God she should have no legitimate child of her own; and said to him, "I have brought you up a child who is of a divine form,[3] and of a generous mind; and as I have received him from the bounty of the river, in a wonderful manner, I thought proper to adopt him my son, and the heir of thy kingdom." And when she had said this, she put the infant into her father's hands: so he took him, and hugged him to his breast; and on his daughter's account, in a pleasant way, put his diadem upon his head; but Moses threw it down to the ground, and, in a puerile mood, he wreathed it round, and trod upon it with his feet, which seemed to bring along with it an evil presage concerning the kingdom of Egypt. But when the sacred scribe saw this, (he was the same person who foretold that his nativity would bring the

---

3. What Josephus here says of the beauty of Moses, that he was of a divine form, is very like what St. Stephen says of the same beauty; that Moses was beautiful in the sight of God (Acts 7:20).

dominion of that kingdom low,) he made a violent attempt to kill him; and crying out in a frightful manner, he said, "This, O king! this child is he of whom God foretold, that if we kill him we shall be in no danger; he himself affords an attestation to the prediction of the same thing, by his trampling upon thy government, and treading upon thy diadem. Take him, therefore, out of the way, and deliver the Egyptians from the fear they are in about him; and deprive the Hebrews of the hope they have of being encouraged by him." But Thermuthis prevented him, and snatched the child away. And the king was not hasty to slay him, God himself, whose providence protected Moses, inclining the king to spare him. He was, therefore, educated with great care. So the Hebrews depended on him, and were of good hopes great things would be done by him; but the Egyptians were suspicious of what would follow such his education. Yet because, if Moses had been slain, there was no one, either akin or adopted, that had any oracle on his side for pretending to the crown of Egypt, and likely to be of greater advantage to them, they abstained from killing him.

3: HOW MOSES MADE WAR WITH THE ETHIOPIANS
(originally chapter 10)

1. Moses, therefore, when he was born, and brought up in the foregoing manner, and came to the age of maturity, made his virtue manifest to the Egyptians; and showed that he was born for the bringing them down, and raising the Israelites. And the occasion he laid hold of was this:—The Ethiopians, who are next neighbors to the Egyptians, made an inroad into their country, which they seized upon, and carried off the effects of the Egyptians, who, in their rage, fought against them, and revenged the affronts they had received from them; but being overcome in battle, some of them were slain, and the rest ran away in a shameful manner, and by that means saved themselves; whereupon the Ethiopians followed after them in the pursuit, and thinking that it would be a mark of cowardice if they did not subdue all Egypt, they went on to subdue the rest with greater vehemence; and when they had tasted the sweets of the country, they never left off the prosecution of the war: and as the nearest parts had not courage enough at first to fight with them, they proceeded as far as Memphis, and the sea itself, while not one of the cities was able to oppose them. The Egyptians, under this sad oppression, betook themselves to their oracles and prophecies; and when God had given them this counsel, to make use of Moses the Hebrew, and take his assistance, the king commanded his

daughter to produce him, that he might be the general of their army.[4]
Upon which, when she had made him swear he would do him no harm,
she delivered him to the king, and supposed his assistance would be of
great advantage to them. She withal reproached the priest, who, when
they had before admonished the Egyptians to kill him, was not ashamed
now to own their want of his help.

2. So Moses, at the persuasion both of Thermuthis and the king himself,
cheerfully undertook the business: and the sacred scribes of both nations
were glad; those of the Egyptians, that they should at once overcome
their enemies by his valor, and that by the same piece of management
Moses would be slain; but those of the Hebrews, that they should escape
from the Egyptians, because Moses was to be their general. But Moses
prevented the enemies, and took and led his army before those enemies
were apprised of his attacking them; for he did not march by the river,
but by land, where he gave a wonderful demonstration of his sagacity; for
when the ground was difficult to be passed over, because of the multitude
of serpents, (which it produces in vast numbers, and, indeed, is singular
in some of those productions, which other countries do not breed, and
yet such as are worse than others in power and mischief, and an unusual
fierceness of sight, some of which ascend out of the ground unseen, and
also fly in the air, and so come upon men at unawares, and do them a
mischief,) Moses invented a wonderful stratagem to preserve the army
safe, and without hurt; for he made baskets, like unto arks, of sedge, and
filled them with ibes,[5] and carried them along with them; which animal
is the greatest enemy to serpents imaginable, for they fly from them when
they come near them; and as they fly they are caught and devoured by
them, as if it were done by the harts; but the ibes are tame creatures, and
only enemies to the serpentine kind: but about these ibes I say no more
at present, since the Greeks themselves are not unacquainted with this
sort of bird. As soon, therefore, as Moses was come to the land which was
the breeder of these serpents, he let loose the ibes, and by their means

---

4. This history of Moses, as general of the Egyptians against the Ethiopians, is wholly
omitted in our Bibles; but is thus by Irenaeus, from Josephus, and that soon after his own
age:—"Josephus says, that when Moses was nourished in the palace, he was appointed
general of the army against the Ethiopians, and conquered them, when he married that king's
daughter; because, out of her affection for him, she delivered the city up to him." (See the
Fragments of Irenaeus, ap. edit., Grab, p. 472.) Nor perhaps did St. Stephen refer to anything
else when he said of Moses, before he was sent by God to the Israelites, that he was not only
learned in all the wisdom of the Egyptians, but was also mighty in words and in deeds (Acts
7:22).

5. Pliny speaks of these birds called ibes; and says, "The Egyptians invoked them against
the serpents" (*Hist. Nat.* B. X. chapter 28).

repelled the serpentine kind, and used them for his assistants before the army came upon that ground. When he had therefore proceeded thus on his journey, he came upon the Ethiopians before they expected him; and, joining battle with them, he beat them, and deprived them of the hopes they had of success against the Egyptians, and went on in overthrowing their cities, and indeed made a great slaughter of these Ethiopians. Now when the Egyptian army had once tasted of this prosperous success, by the means of Moses, they did not slacken their diligence, insomuch that the Ethiopians were in danger of being reduced to slavery, and all sorts of destruction; and at length they retired to Saba, which was a royal city of Ethiopia, which Cambyses afterwards named Mero, after the name of his own sister. The place was to be besieged with very great difficulty, since it was both encompassed by the Nile quite round, and the other rivers, Astapus and Astaboras, made it a very difficult thing for such as attempted to pass over them; for the city was situate in a retired place, and was inhabited after the manner of an island, being encompassed with a strong wall, and having the rivers to guard them from their enemies, and having great ramparts between the wall and the rivers, insomuch, that when the waters come with the greatest violence, it can never be drowned; which ramparts make it next to impossible for even such as are gotten over the rivers to take the city. However, while Moses was uneasy at the army's lying idle, (for the enemies durst not come to a battle,) this accident happened:—Tharbis was the daughter of the king of the Ethiopians: she happened to see Moses as he led the army near the walls, and fought with great courage; and admiring the subtilty of his undertakings, and believing him to be the author of the Egyptians' success, when they had before despaired of recovering their liberty, and to be the occasion of the great danger the Ethiopians were in, when they had before boasted of their great achievements, she fell deeply in love with him; and upon the prevalency of that passion, sent to him the most faithful of all her servants to discourse with him about their marriage. He thereupon accepted the offer, on condition she would procure the delivering up of the city; and gave her the assurance of an oath to take her to his wife; and that when he had once taken possession of the city, he would not break his oath to her. No sooner was the agreement made, but it took effect immediately; and when Moses had cut off the Ethiopians, he gave thanks to God, and consummated his marriage, and led the Egyptians back to their own land.

4: HOW MOSES FLED OUT OF EGYPT INTO MIDIAN
(originally chapter 11)

1. Now the Egyptians, after they had been preserved by Moses, entertained a hatred to him, and were very eager in compassing their designs against him, as suspecting that he would take occasion, from his good success, to raise a sedition, and bring innovations into Egypt; and told the king he ought to be slain. The king had also some intentions of himself to the same purpose, and this as well out of envy at his glorious expedition at the head of his army, as out of fear of being brought low by him and being instigated by the sacred scribes, he was ready to undertake to kill Moses: but when he had learned beforehand what plots there were against him, he went away privately; and because the public roads were watched, he took his flight through the deserts, and where his enemies could not suspect he would travel; and, though he was destitute of food, he went on, and despised that difficulty courageously; and when he came to the city Midian, which lay upon the Red Sea, and was so denominated from one of Abraham's sons by Keturah, he sat upon a certain well, and rested himself there after his laborious journey, and the affliction he had been in. It was not far from the city, and the time of the day was noon, where he had an occasion offered him by the custom of the country of doing what recommended his virtue, and afforded him an opportunity of bettering his circumstances.

2. For that country having but little water, the shepherds used to seize on the wells before others came, lest their flocks should want water, and lest it should be spent by others before they came. There were now come, therefore, to this well seven sisters that were virgins, the daughters of Raguel, a priest, and one thought worthy by the people of the country of great honor. These virgins, who took care of their father's flocks, which sort of work it was customary and very familiar for women to do in the country of the Troglodytes, they came first of all, and drew water out of the well in a quantity sufficient for their flocks, into troughs, which were made for the reception of that water; but when the shepherds came upon the maidens, and drove them away, that they might have the command of the water themselves, Moses, thinking it would be a terrible reproach upon him if he overlooked the young women under unjust oppression, and should suffer the violence of the men to prevail over the right of the maidens, he drove away the men, who had a mind to more than their share, and afforded a proper assistance to the women; who, when they had received such a benefit from him, came to their father, and told him how they had been affronted by the shepherds, and assisted by a stranger, and entreated that

he would not let this generous action be done in vain, nor go without a reward. Now the father took it well from his daughters that they were so desirous to reward their benefactor; and bid them bring Moses into his presence, that he might be rewarded as he deserved. And when Moses came, he told him what testimony his daughters bare to him, that he had assisted them; and that, as he admired him for his virtue, he said that Moses had bestowed such his assistance on persons not insensible of benefits, but where they were both able and willing to return the kindness, and even to exceed the measure of his generosity. So he made him his son, and gave him one of his daughters in marriage; and appointed him to be the guardian and superintendent over his cattle; for of old, all the wealth of the barbarians was in those cattle.

5: THE BURNING BUSH AND THE ROD OF MOSES
(originally chapter 12)

1. Now Moses, when he had obtained the favor of Jethro, for that was one of the names of Raguel, staid there and fed his flock; but some time afterward, taking his station at the mountain called Sinai, he drove his flocks thither to feed them. Now this is the highest of all the mountains thereabout, and the best for pasturage, the herbage being there good; and it had not been before fed upon, because of the opinion men had that God dwelt there, the shepherds not daring to ascend up to it; and here it was that a wonderful prodigy happened to Moses; for a fire fed upon a thorn bush, yet did the green leaves and the flowers continue untouched, and the fire did not at all consume the fruit branches, although the flame was great and fierce. Moses was affrighted at this strange sight, as it was to him; but he was still more astonished when the fire uttered a voice, and called to him by name, and spake words to him, by which it signified how bold he had been in venturing to come into a place whither no man had ever come before, because the place was divine; and advised him to remove a great way off from the flame, and to be contented with what he had seen; and though he were himself a good man, and the offspring of great men, yet that he should not pry any further; and he foretold to him, that he should have glory and honor among men, by the blessing of God upon him. He also commanded him to go away thence with confidence to Egypt, in order to his being the commander and conductor of the body of the Hebrews, and to his delivering his own people from the injuries they suffered there: "For," said God, "they shall inhabit this happy land which your forefather Abraham inhabited, and shall have the enjoyment of all good things." But still he enjoined them, when he brought the Hebrews out of the land of

Egypt, to come to that place, and to offer sacrifices of thanksgiving there. Such were the divine oracles which were delivered out of the fire.

2. But Moses was astonished at what he saw, and much more at what he heard; and he said, "I think it would be an instance of too great madness, O Lord, for one of that regard I bear to thee, to distrust thy power, since I myself adore it, and know that it has been made manifest to my progenitors: but I am still in doubt how I, who am a private man, and one of no abilities, should either persuade my own countrymen to leave the country they now inhabit, and to follow me to a land whither I lead them; or, if they should be persuaded, how can I force Pharaoh to permit them to depart, since they augment their own wealth and prosperity by the labors and works they put upon them?"

3. But God persuaded him to be courageous on all occasions, and promised to be with him, and to assist him in his words, when he was to persuade men; and in his deeds, when he was to perform wonders. He bid him also to take a signal of the truth of what he said, by throwing his rod upon the ground, which, when he had done, it crept along, and was become a serpent, and rolled itself round in its folds, and erected its head, as ready to revenge itself on such as should assault it; after which it become a rod again as it was before. After this God bid Moses to put his right hand into his bosom: he obeyed, and when he took it out it was white, and in color like to chalk, but afterward it returned to its wonted color again. He also, upon God's command, took some of the water that was near him, and poured it upon the ground, and saw the color was that of blood. Upon the wonder that Moses showed at these signs, God exhorted him to be of good courage, and to be assured that he would be the greatest support to him; and bid him make use of those signs, in order to obtain belief among all men, that "thou art sent by me, and dost all things according to my commands. Accordingly I enjoin thee to make no more delays, but to make haste to Egypt, and to travel night and day, and not to draw out the time, and so make the slavery of the Hebrews and their sufferings to last the longer."

4. Moses having now seen and heard these wonders that assured him of the truth of these promises of God, had no room left him to disbelieve them: he entreated him to grant him that power when he should be in Egypt; and besought him to vouchsafe him the knowledge of his own name; and since he had heard and seen him, that he would also tell him his name, that when he offered sacrifice he might invoke him by such his name in his oblations. Whereupon God declared to him his holy name, which had never been discovered to men before; concerning which it is

not lawful for me to say any more.[6] Now these signs accompanied Moses, not then only, but always when he prayed for them: of all which signs he attributed the firmest assent to the fire in the bush; and believing that God would be a gracious supporter to him, he hoped he should be able to deliver his own nation, and bring calamities on the Egyptians.

6: HOW MOSES AND AARON RETURNED INTO EGYPT TO PHARAOH (originally chapter 13)

1. So Moses, when he understood that the Pharaoh, in whose reign he fled away, was dead, asked leave of Raguel to go to Egypt, for the benefit of his own people. And he took with him Zipporah, the daughter of Raguel, whom he had married, and the children he had by her, Gersom and Eleazer, and made haste into Egypt. Now the former of those names, Gersom, in the Hebrew tongue, signifies *that he was in a strange land;* and Eleazer, *that, by the assistance of the God of his fathers, he had escaped from the Egyptians.* Now when they were near the borders, Aaron his brother, by the command of God, met him, to whom he declared what had befallen him at the mountain, and the commands that God had given him. But as they were going forward, the chief men among the Hebrews, having learned that they were coming, met them: to whom Moses declared the signs he had seen; and while they could not believe them, he made them see them, So they took courage at these surprising and unexpected sights, and hoped well of their entire deliverance, as believing now that God took care of their preservation.

2. Since then Moses found that the Hebrews would be obedient to whatsoever he should direct, as they promised to be, and were in love with liberty, he came to the king, who had indeed but lately received the government, and told him how much he had done for the good of the Egyptians, when they were despised by the Ethiopians, and their country laid waste by them; and how he had been the commander of their forces, and had labored for them, as if they had been his own people and he informed him in what danger he had been during that expedition, without

---

6. This superstitious fear of discovering the name with four letters, which of late we have been used falsely to pronounce Jehovah, but seems to have been originally pronounced Jahoh, or Jao, is never, I think, heard of till this passage of Josephus; and this superstition, in not pronouncing that name, has continued among the Rabbinical Jews to this day (though whether the Samaritans and Caraites observed it so early, does not appear). Josephus also durst not set down the very words of the ten commandments, as we shall see hereafter in book 3, chapter 5, section 4, which superstitious silence I think has yet not been continued even by the Rabbins. It is, however, no doubt but both these cautious concealments were taught Josephus by the Pharisees, a body of men at once very wicked and very superstitious.

having any proper returns made him as he had deserved. He also informed him distinctly what things happened to him at Mount Sinai; and what God said to him; and the signs that were done by God, in order to assure him of the authority of those commands which he had given him. He also exhorted him not to disbelieve what he told him, nor to oppose the will of God.

3. But when the king derided Moses; he made him in earnest see the signs that were done at Mount Sinai. Yet was the king very angry with him and called him an ill man, who had formerly run away from his Egyptian slavery, and came now back with deceitful tricks, and wonders, and magical arts, to astonish him. And when he had said this, he commanded the priests to let him see the same wonderful sights; as knowing that the Egyptians were skillful in this kind of learning, and that he was not the only person who knew them, and pretended them to be divine; as also he told him, that when he brought such wonderful sights before him, he would only be believed by the unlearned. Now when the priests threw down their rods, they became serpents. But Moses was not daunted at it; and said, "O king, I do not myself despise the wisdom of the Egyptians, but I say that what I do is so much superior to what these do by magic arts and tricks, as Divine power exceeds the power of man: but I will demonstrate that what I do is not done by craft, or counterfeiting what is not really true, but that they appear by the providence and power of God." And when he had said this, he cast his rod down upon the ground, and commanded it to turn itself into a serpent. It obeyed him, and went all round, and devoured the rods of the Egyptians, which seemed to be dragons, until it had consumed them all. It then returned to its own form, and Moses took it into his hand again.

4. However, the king was no more moved when was done than before; and being very angry, he said that he should gain nothing by this his cunning and shrewdness against the Egyptians;—and he commanded him that was the chief taskmaster over the Hebrews, to give them no relaxation from their labors, but to compel them to submit to greater oppressions than before; and though he allowed them chaff before for making their bricks, he would allow it them no longer, but he made them to work hard at brick-making in the day-time, and to gather chaff in the night. Now when their labor was thus doubled upon them, they laid the blame upon Moses, because their labor and their misery were on his account become more severe to them. But Moses did not let his courage sink for the king's threatenings; nor did he abate of his zeal on account of the Hebrews' complaints; but he supported himself, and set his soul resolutely against them both, and used his own utmost diligence to procure liberty to his countrymen. So he went to the king, and persuaded him to let the Hebrews go to Mount Sinai, and there to sacrifice to God, because God

had enjoined them so to do. He persuaded him also not to counterwork the designs of God, but to esteem his favor above all things, and to permit them to depart, lest, before he be aware, he lay an obstruction in the way of the Divine commands, and so occasion his own suffering such punishments as it was probable anyone that counterworked the Divine commands should undergo, since the severest afflictions arise from every object to those that provoke the Divine wrath against them; for such as these have neither the earth nor the air for their friends; nor are the fruits of the womb according to nature, but everything is unfriendly and adverse towards them. He said further, that the Egyptians should know this by sad experience; and that besides, the Hebrew people should go out of their country without their consent.

7: THE TEN PLAGUES WHICH CAME UPON THE EGYPTIANS (originally chapter 14)

1. But when the king despised the words of Moses, and had no regard at all to them, grievous plagues seized the Egyptians; every one of which I will describe, both because no such plagues did ever happen to any other nation as the Egyptians now felt, and because I would demonstrate that Moses did not fail in any one thing that he foretold them; and because it is for the good of mankind, that they may learn this caution.—Not to do anything that may displease God, lest he be provoked to wrath, and avenge their iniquities upon them. For the Egyptian river ran with bloody water at the command of God, insomuch that it could not be drunk, and they had no other spring of water neither; for the water was not only of the color of blood, but it brought upon those that ventured to drink of it, great pains and bitter torment. Such was the river to the Egyptians; but it was sweet and fit for drinking to the Hebrews, and no way different from what it naturally used to be. As the king therefore knew not what to do in these surprising circumstances, and was in fear for the Egyptians, he gave the Hebrews leave to go away; but when the plague ceased, he changed his mind again, end would not suffer them to go.

2. But when God saw that he was ungrateful, and upon the ceasing of this calamity would not grow wiser, he sent another plague upon the Egyptians:—An innumerable multitude of frogs consumed the fruit of the ground; the river was also full of them, insomuch that those who drew water had it spoiled by the blood of these animals, as they died in, and were destroyed by, the water; and the country was full of filthy slime, as they were born, and as they died: they also spoiled their vessels in their houses which they used, and were found among what they eat and what

they drank, and came in great numbers upon their beds. There was also an ungrateful smell, and a stink arose from them, as they were born, and as they died therein. Now, when the Egyptians were under the oppression of these miseries, the king ordered Moses to take the Hebrews with him, and be gone. Upon which the whole multitude of the frogs vanished away; and both the land and the river returned to their former natures. But as soon as Pharaoh saw the land freed from this plague, he forgot the cause of it, and retained the Hebrews; and, as though he had a mind to try the nature of more such judgments, he would not yet suffer Moses and his people to depart, having granted that liberty rather out of fear than out of any good consideration.

3. Accordingly, God punished his falseness with another plague, added to the former; for there arose out of the bodies of the Egyptians an innumerable quantity of lice, by which, wicked as they were, they miserably perished, as not able to destroy this sort of vermin either with washes or with ointments. At which terrible judgment the king of Egypt was in disorder, upon the fear into which he reasoned himself, lest his people should be destroyed, and that the manner of this death was also reproachful, so that he was forced in part to recover himself from his wicked temper to a sounder mind, for he gave leave for the Hebrews themselves to depart. But when the plague thereupon ceased, he thought it proper to require that they should leave their children and wives behind them, as pledges of their return; whereby he provoked God to be more vehemently angry at him, as if he thought to impose on his providence, and as if it were only Moses, and not God, who punished the Egyptians for the sake of the Hebrews: for he filled that country full of various sorts of pestilential creatures, with their various properties, such indeed as had never come into the sight of men before, by whose means the men perished themselves, and the land was destitute of husbandmen for its cultivation; but if anything escaped destruction from them, it was killed by a distemper which the men underwent also.

4. But when Pharaoh did not even then yield to the will of God, but, while he gave leave to the husbands to take their wives with them, yet insisted that the children should be left behind, God presently resolved to punish his wickedness with several sorts of calamities, and those worse than the foregoing, which yet had so generally afflicted them; for their bodies had terrible boils, breaking forth with blains, while they were already inwardly consumed; and a great part of the Egyptians perished in this manner. But when the king was not brought to reason by this plague, hail was sent down from heaven; and such hail it was, as the climate of Egypt had never suffered before, nor was it like to that which falls in other

climates in winter time, but was larger than that which falls in the middle of spring to those that dwell in the northern and north-western regions. This hail broke down their boughs laden with fruit. After this a tribe of locusts consumed the seed which was not hurt by the hail; so that to the Egyptians all hopes of the future fruits of the ground were entirely lost.

5. One would think the forementioned calamities might have been sufficient for one that was only foolish, without wickedness, to make him wise, and to make him sensible what was for his advantage. But Pharaoh, led not so much by his folly as by his wickedness, even when he saw the cause of his miseries, he still contested with God, and willfully deserted the cause of virtue; so he bid Moses take the Hebrews away, with their wives and children, but to leave their cattle behind, since their own cattle were destroyed. But when Moses said that what he desired was unjust, since they were obliged to offer sacrifices to God of those cattle; and the time being prolonged on this account, a thick darkness, without the least light, spread itself over the Egyptians, whereby their sight being obstructed, and their breathing hindered by the thickness of the air, they died miserably, and under a terror lest they should be swallowed up by the dark cloud. Beside this, when the darkness, after three days and as many nights, was dissipated, and when Pharaoh did not still repent and let the Hebrews go, Moses came to him and said, "How long wilt thou be disobedient to the command of God? for he enjoins thee to let the Hebrews go; nor is there any other way of being freed from the calamities you are under, unless you do so." But the king was angry at what he said, and threatened to cut off his head if he came any more to trouble him about these matters. Hereupon Moses said he would not speak to him any more about them, for that he himself, together with the principal men among the Egyptians, should desire the Hebrews to go away. So when Moses had said this, he went his way.

6. But when God had signified, that with one plague he would compel the Egyptians to let Hebrews go, he commanded Moses to tell the people that they should have a sacrifice ready, and they should prepare themselves on the tenth day of the month Xanthicus, against the fourteenth, (which month is called by the Egyptians Pharmuth, Nisan by the Hebrews; but the Macedonians call it Xanthicus,) and that he should carry the Hebrews with all they had. Accordingly, he having got the Hebrews ready for their departure, and having sorted the people into tribes, he kept them together in one place: but when the fourteenth day was come, and all were ready to depart, they offered the sacrifice, and purified their houses with the blood, using bunches of hyssop for that purpose; and when they had supped, they burnt the remainder of the flesh, as just ready to depart. Whence it

is that we do still offer this sacrifice in like manner to this day, and call this festival *Pascha* which signifies *the feast of the passover;* because on that day God passed us over, and sent the plague upon the Egyptians; for the destruction of the first-born came upon the Egyptians that night, so that many of the Egyptians who lived near the king's palace, persuaded Pharaoh to let the Hebrews go. Accordingly he called for Moses, and bid them be gone; as supposing, that if once the Hebrews were gone out of the country, Egypt should be freed from its miseries. They also honored the Hebrews with gifts;[7] some, in order to get them to depart quickly, and others on account of their neighborhood, and the friendship they had with them.

8: HOW THE HEBREWS LEFT EGYPT
(originally chapter 15)

1. So the Hebrews went out of Egypt, while the Egyptians wept, and repented that they had treated them so hardly.—Now they took their journey by Letopolis, a place at that time deserted, but where Babylon was built afterwards, when Cambyses laid Egypt waste: but as they went away hastily, on the third day they came to a place called Beelzephon, on the Red Sea; and when they had no food out of the land, because it was a desert, they eat of loaves kneaded of flour, only warmed by a gentle heat; and this food they made use of for thirty days; for what they brought with them out of Egypt would not suffice them any longer time; and this only while they dispensed it to each person, to use so much only as would serve for necessity, but not for satiety. Whence it is that, in memory of the want we were then in, we keep a feast for eight days, which is called *the feast of unleavened bread.* Now the entire multitude of those that went out, including the women and children, was not easy to be numbered, but those that were of an age fit for war, were six hundred thousand.

2. They left Egypt in the month Xanthicus, on the fifteenth day of the lunar month; four hundred and thirty years after our forefather Abraham came into Canaan, but two hundred and fifteen years only after Jacob

---

7. These large presents made to the Israelites, of vessels of and vessels of gold, and raiment, were, as Josephus truly calls them, gifts really given them; not lent them, as our English falsely renders them. They were spoils required, not of them (Genesis 15:14; Exodus 3:22; 11:2; Psalm 105:37), as the same version falsely renders the Hebrew word here use (Exodus 12:35, 36). God had ordered the Jews to demand these as their pay and reward, during their long and bitter slavery in Egypt, as atonement for the lives of the Egyptians, and as the condition of the Jews' departure, and of the Egyptians' deliverance from these terrible judgments, which, had they not now ceased, they had soon been all dead men, as they themselves confess (Exodus 12:33). Nor was there any sense in borrowing or lending, when the Israelites were finally departing out of the land forever.

removed into Egypt.[8] It was the eightieth year of the age of Moses, and of that of Aaron three more. They also carried out the bones of Joseph with them, as he had charged his sons to do.

3. But the Egyptians soon repented that the Hebrews were gone; and the king also was mightily concerned that this had been procured by the magic arts of Moses; so they resolved to go after them. Accordingly they took their weapons, and other warlike furniture, and pursued after them, in order to bring them back, if once they overtook them, because they would now have no pretense to pray to God against them, since they had already been permitted to go out; and they thought they should easily overcome them, as they had no armor, and would be weary with their journey; so they made haste in their pursuit, and asked of everyone they met which way they were gone. And indeed that land was difficult to be traveled over, not only by armies, but by single persons. Now Moses led the Hebrews this way, that in case the Egyptians should repent and be desirous to pursue after them, they might undergo the punishment of their wickedness, and of the breach of those promises they had made to them. As also he led them this way on account of the Philistines, who had quarreled with them, and hated them of old, that by all means they might not know of their departure, for their country is near to that of Egypt; and thence it was that Moses led them not along the road that tended to the land of the Philistines, but he was desirous that they should go through the desert, that so after a long journey, and after many afflictions, they might enter upon the land of Canaan. Another reason of this was, that God commanded him to bring the people to Mount Sinai, that there they might offer him sacrifices. Now when the Egyptians had overtaken the Hebrews, they prepared to fight them, and by their multitude they drove them into a narrow place; for the number that pursued after them was six hundred chariots, with fifty thousand horsemen, and two hundred thousand foot-men, all armed. They also seized on the passages by which they imagined the Hebrews might fly, shutting them up between inaccessible precipices and the sea; for there was [on each side] a [ridge of] mountains that terminated at the sea, which were impassable by reason of their roughness, and obstructed their flight; wherefore they there pressed upon the Hebrews with their army, where [the ridges of] the mountains were closed with the sea; which army

---

8. Why our Masorete copy so groundlessly abridges this account in Exodus 12:40, as to ascribe 430 years to the sole peregrination of the Israelites in Egypt, when it is clear even by that Masorete chronology elsewhere, as well as from the express text itself, in the Samaritan, Septuagint, and Josephus, that they sojourned in Egypt but half that time,—and that by consequence, the other half of their peregrination was in the land of Canaan, before they came into Egypt,—is hard to say.

they placed at the chops of the mountains, that so they might deprive them of any passage into the plain.

4. When the Hebrews, therefore, were neither able to bear up, being thus, as it were, besieged, because they wanted provisions, nor saw any possible way of escaping; and if they should have thought of fighting, they had no weapons; they expected a universal destruction, unless they delivered themselves up to the Egyptians. So they laid the blame on Moses, and forgot all the signs that had been wrought by God for the recovery of their freedom; and this so far, that their incredulity prompted them to throw stones at the prophet, while he encouraged them and promised them deliverance; and they resolved that they would deliver themselves up to the Egyptians. So there was sorrow and lamentation among the women and children, who had nothing but destruction before their eyes, while they were encompassed with mountains, the sea, and their enemies, and discerned no way of flying from them.

5. But Moses, though the multitude looked fiercely at him, did not, however, give over the care of them, but despised all dangers, out of his trust in God, who, as he had afforded them the several steps already taken for the recovery of their liberty, which he had foretold them, would not now suffer them to be subdued by their enemies, to be either made slaves or be slain by them; and, standing in midst of them, he said, "It is not just of us to distrust even men, when they have hitherto well managed our affairs, as if they would not be the same hereafter; but it is no better than madness, at this time to despair of the providence of God, by whose power all those things have been performed he promised, when you expected no such things: I mean all that I have been concerned in for deliverance and escape from slavery. Nay, when we are in the utmost distress, as you see we ought rather to hope that God will succor us, by whose operation it is that we are now this narrow place, that he may out of such difficulties as are otherwise insurmountable and out of which neither you nor your enemies expect you can be delivered, and may at once demonstrate his own power and his providence over us. Nor does God use to give his help in small difficulties to those whom he favors, but in such cases where no one can see how any hope in man can better their condition. Depend, therefore, upon such a Protector as is able to make small things great, and to show that this mighty force against you is nothing but weakness, and be not affrighted at the Egyptian army, nor do you despair of being preserved, because the sea before, and the mountains behind, afford you no opportunity for flying, for even these mountains, if God so please, may be made plain ground for you, and the sea become dry land."

9: HOW THE SEA WAS DIVIDED ASUNDER FOR THE HEBREWS (originally chapter 16)

1. When Moses had said this, he led them to the sea, while the Egyptians looked on; for they were within sight. Now these were so distressed by the toil of their pursuit, that they thought proper to put off fighting till the next day. But when Moses was come to the sea-shore, he took his rod, and made supplication to God, and called upon him to be their helper and assistant; and said "Thou art not ignorant, O Lord, that it is beyond human strength and human contrivance to avoid the difficulties we are now under; but it must be thy work altogether to procure deliverance to this army, which has left Egypt at thy appointment. We despair of any other assistance or contrivance, and have recourse only to that hope we have in thee; and if there be any method that can promise us an escape by thy providence, we look up to thee for it. And let it come quickly, and manifest thy power to us; and do thou raise up this people unto good courage and hope of deliverance, who are deeply sunk into a disconsolate state of mind. We are in a helpless place, but still it is a place that thou possessest; still the sea is thine, the mountains also that enclose us are thine; so that these mountains will open themselves if thou commandest them, and the sea also, if thou commandest it, will become dry land. Nay, we might escape by a flight through the air, if thou shouldst determine we should have that way of salvation."

2. When Moses had thus addressed himself to God, he smote the sea with his rod, which parted asunder at the stroke, and receiving those waters into itself, left the ground dry, as a road and a place of flight for the Hebrews. Now when Moses saw this appearance of God, and that the sea went out of its own place, and left dry land, he went first of all into it, and bid the Hebrews to follow him along that divine road, and to rejoice at the danger their enemies that followed them were in; and gave thanks to God for this so surprising a deliverance which appeared from him.

3. Now, while these Hebrews made no stay, but went on earnestly, as led by God's presence with them, the Egyptians supposed first that they were distracted, and were going rashly upon manifest destruction. But when they saw that they were going a great way without any harm, and that no obstacle or difficulty fell in their journey, they made haste to pursue them, hoping that the sea would be calm for them also. They put their horse foremost, and went down themselves into the sea. Now the Hebrews, while these were putting on their armor, and therein spending their time, were beforehand with them, and escaped them, and got first over to the land on the other side without any hurt. Whence the others were encouraged,

and more courageously pursued them, as hoping no harm would come to them neither: but the Egyptians were not aware that they went into a road made for the Hebrews, and not for others; that this road was made for the deliverance of those in danger, but not for those that were earnest to make use of it for the others' destruction. As soon, therefore, as ever the whole Egyptian army was within it, the sea flowed to its own place, and came down with a torrent raised by storms of wind,[9] and encompassed the Egyptians. Showers of rain also came down from the sky, and dreadful thunders and lightning, with flashes of fire. Thunderbolts also were darted upon them. Nor was there anything which used to be sent by God upon men, as indications of his wrath, which did not happen at this time, for a dark and dismal night oppressed them. And thus did all these men perish, so that there was not one man left to be a messenger of this calamity to the rest of the Egyptians.

4. But the Hebrews were not able to contain themselves for joy at their wonderful deliverance, and destruction of their enemies; now indeed supposing themselves firmly delivered, when those that would have forced them into slavery were destroyed, and when they found they had God so evidently for their protector. And now these Hebrews having escaped the danger they were in, after this manner, and besides that, seeing their enemies punished in such a way as is never recorded of any other men whomsoever, were all the night employed in singing of hymns, and in mirth.[10] Moses also composed a song unto God, containing his praises,

---

9. These storms of wind, thunder, and lightning, at this drowning of Pharaoh's army, [are] almost wanting in our copies of Exodus, but fully extant in that of David, Psalm 77:16-18.

10. What some have here objected against this passage of the Israelites over the Red Sea, in this one night, from the common maps, viz., that this sea being here about thirty miles broad, so great an army could not pass over it in so short a time, is a great mistake. Mons. Thevenot, an authentic eyewitness, informs us that this sea, for about five days' journey, is nowhere more than about eight or nine miles over-cross, and in one place but four or five miles, according to De Lisle's map, which is made from the best travelers themselves, and not copied from others. What has been further objected against this passage of the Israelites, and drowning of the Egyptians, being miraculous also, viz., that Moses might carry the Israelites over at a low tide without any miracle, while yet the Egyptians, not knowing the tide so well as he, might be drowned upon the return of the tide, is a strange story indeed! That Moses, who never had lived here, should know the quantity and time of the flux and reflux of the Red Sea better than the Egyptians themselves in its neighborhood! Yet does Artapanus, an ancient heathen historian, inform us, that this was what the more ignorant Memphites, who lived at a great distance, pretended, though he confesses, that the more learned Heliopolitans, who lived much nearer, owned the destruction of the Egyptians, and the deliverance of the Israelites, to have been miraculous: and De Castro, a mathematician, who surveyed this sea with great exactness, informs us, that there is no great flux or reflux in this part of the Red Sea, to give a color to this hypothesis; nay, that at the elevation of the tide there is little above half the height of a man. . . . So vain and groundless are these and the like evasions and subterfuges of our modern sceptics and unbelievers, and so

and a thanksgiving for his kindness, in hexameter verse.[11]

5. As for myself, I have delivered every part of this history as I found it in the sacred books; nor let anyone wonder at the strangeness of the narration if a way were discovered to those men of old time, who were free from the wickedness of the modern ages, whether it happened by the will of God or whether it happened of its own accord;—while, for the sake of those that accompanied Alexander, king of Macedonia, who yet lived, comparatively but a little while ago, the Pamphylian Sea retired and afforded them a passage through itself, had no other way to go; I mean, when it was the will of God to destroy the monarchy of the Persians: and this is confessed to be true by all that have written about the actions of Alexander. But as to these events, let everyone determine as he pleases.

6. On the next day Moses gathered together the weapons of the Egyptians, which were brought to the camp of the Hebrews by the current of the sea, and the force of the winds resisting it; and he conjectured that this also happened by Divine Providence, that so they might not be destitute of weapons. So when he had ordered the Hebrews to arm themselves with them, he led them to Mount Sinai, in order to offer sacrifice to God, and to render oblations for the salvation of the multitude, as he was charged to do beforehand.

---

certainly do thorough inquiries and authentic evidence disprove and confute such evasions and subterfuges upon all occasions.

11. What that hexameter verse, in which Moses's triumphant song is here said to be written, distinctly means, our present ignorance of the old Hebrew metre or measure will not let us determine. Nor does it appear to me certain that even Josephus himself had a distinct notion of it.

Chapter 2

THE EXODUS OUT OF EGYPT TO THE REJECTION OF THAT GENERATION

1: HOW MOSES LED THE PEOPLE TO MOUNT SINAI; BUT NOT TILL THEY HAD SUFFERED MUCH IN THEIR JOURNEY

1. When the Hebrews had obtained such a wonderful deliverance, the country was a great trouble to them, for it was entirely a desert, and without sustenance for them; and also had exceeding little water, so that it not only was not at all sufficient for the men, but not enough to feed any of the cattle, for it was parched up, and had no moisture that might afford nutriment to the vegetables; so they were forced to travel over this country, as having no other country but this to travel in. They had indeed carried water along with them from the land over which they had traveled before, as their conductor had bidden them; but when that was spent, they were obliged to draw water out of wells, with pain, by reason of the hardness of the soil. Moreover, what water they found was bitter, and not fit for drinking, and this in small quantities also; and as they thus traveled, they came late in the evening to a place called Marah,[1] which had that name from the badness of its water, for *Mar* denotes *bitterness*. Thither they came afflicted both by the tediousness of their journey, and by their want of food, for it entirely failed them at that time. Now here was a well, which made them choose to stay in the place, which, although it were not sufficient to satisfy so great an army, did yet afford them some comfort, as found in such desert places; for they heard from those who had been

---

1. Dr. Bernard takes notice here, that this place Mar, where the waters were bitter, is called by the Syrians and Arabians Mariri, and by the Syrians sometimes Morath, all derived from the Hebrew Mar. He also takes notice, that it is called The Bitter Fountain by Pliny himself; which waters remain there to this day, and are still bitter, as Thevenot assures us and that there are also abundance of palm-trees. (See his *Travels*, part 1, chapter 26, p. 166.)

to search, that there was nothing to be found, if they traveled on farther. Yet was this water bitter, and not fit for men to drink; and not only so, but it was intolerable even to the cattle themselves.

2. When Moses saw how much the people were cast down, and that the occasion of it could not be contradicted, for the people were not in the nature of a complete army of men, who might oppose a manly fortitude to the necessity that distressed them; the multitude of the children, and of the women also, being of too weak capacities to be persuaded by reason, blunted the courage of the men themselves,—he was therefore in great difficulties, and made everybody's calamity his own; for they ran all of them to him, and begged of him; the women begged for their infants, and the men for the women, that he would not overlook them, but procure some way or other for their deliverance. He therefore betook himself to prayer to God, that he would change the water from its present badness, and make it fit for drinking. And when God had granted him that favor, he took the top of a stick that lay down at his feet, and divided it in the middle, and made the section lengthways. He then let it down into the well, and persuaded the Hebrews that God had hearkened to his prayers, and had promised to render the water such as they desired it to be, in case they would be subservient to him in what he should enjoin them to do, and this not after a remiss or negligent manner. And when they asked what they were to do in order to have the water changed for the better, he bid the strongest men among them that stood there, to draw up water and told them, that when the greatest part was drawn up, the remainder would be fit to drink. So they labored at it till the water was so agitated and purged as to be fit to drink.

3. And now removing from thence they came to Elim; which place looked well at a distance, for there was a grove of palm-trees; but when they came near to it, it appeared to be a bad place, for the palm-trees were no more than seventy; and they were ill-grown and creeping trees, by the want of water, for the country about was all parched, and no moisture sufficient to water them, and make them hopeful and useful, was derived to them from the fountains, which were in number twelve: they were rather a few moist places than springs, which not breaking out of the ground, nor running over, could not sufficiently water the trees. And when they dug into the sand, they met with no water; and if they took a few drops of it into their hands, they found it to be useless, on account of its mud. The trees were too weak to bear fruit, for want of being sufficiently cherished and enlivened by the water. So they laid the blame on their conductor, and made heavy complaints against him; and said that this their miserable state, and the experience they had of adversity, were owing

to him; for that they had then journeyed an entire thirty days, and had spent all the provisions they had brought with them; and meeting with no relief, they were in a very desponding condition. And by fixing their attention upon nothing but their present misfortunes, they were hindered from remembering what deliverances they had received from God, and those by the virtue and wisdom of Moses also; so they were very angry at their conductor, and were zealous in their attempt to stone him, as the direct occasion of their present miseries.

4. But as for Moses himself, while the multitude were irritated and bitterly set against him, he cheerfully relied upon God, and upon his consciousness of the care he had taken of these his own people; and he came into the midst of them, even while they clamored against him, and had stones in their hands in order to dispatch him. Now he was of an agreeable presence, and very able to persuade the people by his speeches; accordingly he began to mitigate their anger, and exhorted them not to be over-mindful of their present adversities, lest they should thereby suffer the benefits that had formerly been bestowed on them to slip out of their memories; and he desired them by no means, on account of their present uneasiness, to cast those great and wonderful favors and gifts, which they had obtained of God, out of their minds, but to expect deliverance out of those their present troubles which they could not free themselves from, and this by the means of that Divine Providence which watched over them. Seeing it is probable that God tries their virtue, and exercises their patience by these adversities, that it may appear what fortitude they have, and what memory they retain of his former wonderful works in their favor, and whether they will not think of them upon occasion of the miseries they now feel. He told them, it appeared they were not really good men, either in patience, or in remembering what had been successfully done for them, sometimes by contemning God and his commands, when by those commands they left the land of Egypt; and sometimes by behaving themselves ill towards him who was the servant of God, and this when he had never deceived them, either in what he said, or had ordered them to do by God's command. He also put them in mind of all that had passed; how the Egyptians were destroyed when they attempted to detain them, contrary to the command of God; and after what manner the very same river was to the others bloody, and not fit for drinking, but was to them sweet, and fit for drinking; and how they went a new road through the sea, which fled a long way from them, by which very means they were themselves preserved, but saw their enemies destroyed; and that when they were in want of weapons, God gave them plenty of them;—and so he recounted all the particular instances, how when they were, in appearance,

just going to be destroyed, God had saved them in a surprising manner; and that he had still the same power; and that they ought not even now to despair of his providence over them; and accordingly he exhorted them to continue quiet, and to consider that help would not come too late, though it come not immediately, if it be present with them before they suffer any great misfortune; that they ought to reason thus: that God delays to assist them, not because he has no regard to them, but because he will first try their fortitude, and the pleasure they take in their freedom, that he may learn whether you have souls great enough to bear want of food, and scarcity of water, on its account; or whether you rather love to be slaves, as cattle are slaves to such as own them, and feed them liberally, but only in order to make them more useful in their service. That as for himself, he shall not be so much concerned for his own preservation; for if he die unjustly, he shall not reckon it any affliction, but that he is concerned for them, lest, by casting stones at him, they should be thought to condemn God himself.

5. By this means Moses pacified the people, and restrained them from stoning him, and brought them to repent of what they were going to do. And because he thought the necessity they were under made their passion less unjustifiable, he thought he ought to apply himself to God by prayer and supplication; and going up to an eminence, he requested of God for some succor for the people, and some way of deliverance from the want they were in, because in him, and in him alone, was their hope of salvation; and he desired that he would forgive what necessity had forced the people to do, since such was the nature of mankind, hard to please, and very complaining under adversities. Accordingly God promised he would take care of them, and afford them the succor they were desirous of. Now when Moses had heard this from God, he came down to the multitude. But as soon as they saw him joyful at the promises he had received from God, they changed their sad countenances into gladness. So he placed himself in the midst of them, and told them he came to bring them from God a deliverance from their present distresses. Accordingly a little after came a vast number of quails, which is a bird more plentiful in this Arabian Gulf than anywhere else, flying over the sea, and hovered over them, till wearied with their laborious flight, and, indeed, as usual, flying very near to the earth, they fell down upon the Hebrews, who caught them, and satisfied their hunger with them, and supposed that this was the method whereby God meant to supply them with food. Upon which Moses returned thanks to God for affording them his assistance so suddenly, and sooner than he had promised them.

6. But presently after this first supply of food, he sent them a second; for as Moses was lifting up his hands in prayer, a dew fell down; and Moses, when he found it stick to his hands, supposed this was also come for food from God to them. He tasted it; and perceiving that the people knew not what it was, and thought it snowed, and that it was what usually fell at that time of the year, he informed them that this dew did not fall from heaven after the manner they imagined, but came for their preservation and sustenance. So he tasted it, and gave them some of it, that they might be satisfied about what he told them. They also imitated their conductor, and were pleased with the food, for it was like honey in sweetness and pleasant taste, but like in its body to bdellium, one of the sweet spices, and in bigness equal to coriander seed. And very earnest they were in gathering it; but they were enjoined to gather it equally[2]—the measure of an omer for each one every day, because this food should not come in too small a quantity, lest the weaker might not be able to get their share, by reason of the overbearing of the strong in collecting it. However, these strong men, when they had gathered more than the measure appointed for them, had no more than others, but only tired themselves more in gathering it, for they found no more than an omer apiece; and the advantage they got by what was superfluous was none at all, it corrupting, both by the worms breeding in it, and by its bitterness. So divine and wonderful a food was this! It also supplied the want of other sorts of food to those that fed on it. And even now, in all that place, this manna comes down in rain,[3] according to what Moses then obtained of God, to send it to the people for their sustenance. Now the Hebrews call this food *manna:* for the particle *man,* in our language, is the asking of a question, *What is this?* So the Hebrews were very joyful at what was sent them from heaven.

---

2. It seems to me, from what Moses (Exodus 16:18), St. Paul (2 Corinthians 8:15), and Josephus here say, compared together, that the quantity of manna that fell daily, and did not putrefy, was just so much as came to an omer apiece, through the whole host of Israel, and no more.

3. This supposal, that the sweet honey-dew or manna, so celebrated in ancient and modern authors, as falling usually in Arabia, was of the very same sort with this manna sent to the Israelites, savors more of Gentilism than of Judaism or Christianity. It is not improbable that some ancient Gentile author, read by Josephus, so thought; nor would he here contradict him; though just before . . . he seems directly to allow that it had not been seen before. However, this food from heaven is here described to be like snow; and in Artapanus, a heathen writer, it is compared to meal, color like to snow, rained down by God. . . . But as to the derivation of the word manna, whether from man, which Josephus says then signified What is it, or from mannah, to divide, i.e., a dividend or portion allotted to everyone, it is uncertain; I incline to the latter derivation. This manna is called angels' food (Psalm 78:26), and by our Savior (John 6:31), etc., as well as by Josephus here and elsewhere (book 3, chapter 5, section 3), said to be sent the Jews from heaven.

Now they made use of this food for forty years, or as long as they were in the wilderness.

7. As soon as they were removed thence, they came to Rephidim, being distressed to the last degree by thirst; and while in the foregoing days they had lit on a few small fountains, but now found the earth entirely destitute of water, they were in an evil case. They again turned their anger against Moses; but he at first avoided the fury of the multitude, and then betook himself to prayer to God, beseeching him, that as he had given them food when they were in the greatest want of it, so he would give them drink, since the favor of giving them food was of no value to them while they had nothing to drink. And God did not long delay to give it them, but promised Moses that he would procure them a fountain, and plenty of water, from a place they did not expect any. So he commanded him to smite the rock which they saw lying there,[4] with his rod, and out of it to receive plenty of what they wanted; for he had taken care that drink should come to them without any labor or pains-taking. When Moses had received this command from God, he came to the people, who waited for him, and looked upon him, for they saw already that he was coming apace from his eminence. As soon as he was come, he told them that God would deliver them from their present distress, and had granted them an unexpected favor; and informed them, that a river should run for their sakes out of the rock. But they were amazed at that hearing, supposing they were of necessity to cut the rock in pieces, now they were distressed by their thirst and by their journey; while Moses only smiting the rock with his rod, opened a passage, and out of it burst water, and that in great abundance, and very clear. But they were astonished at this wonderful effect; and, as it were, quenched their thirst by the very sight of it. So they drank this pleasant, this sweet water; and such it seemed to be, as might well be expected where God was the donor. They were also in admiration how Moses was honored by God; and they made grateful returns of sacrifices to God for his providence towards them. Now that Scripture, which is laid up in the temple,[5] informs us how God foretold to Moses that water should should in this manner be derived out of the rock.

---

4. This rock is there at this day, as the travelers agree; and must be the same that was there in the days of Moses, as being too large to be brought thither by our modern carriages.

5. Note here, that the small book of the principal laws of Moses is ever said to be laid up in the holy house itself; but the larger Pentateuch, as here, somewhere within the limits of the temple and its courts only.

2: HOW THE AMALEKITES AND THE NEIGHBOURING NATIONS, MADE WAR WITH THE HEBREWS AND WERE BEATEN

1. The name of the Hebrews began already to be everywhere renowned, and rumors about them ran abroad. This made the inhabitants of those countries to be in no small fear. Accordingly they sent ambassadors to one another, and exhorted one another to defend themselves, and to endeavor to destroy these men. Those that induced the rest to do so, were such as inhabited Gobolitis and Petra. They were called *Amalekites,* and were the most warlike of the nations that lived thereabout; and whose kings exhorted one another, and their neighbors, to go to this war against the Hebrews; telling them that an army of strangers, and such a one as had run away from slavery under the Egyptians, lay in wait to ruin them; which army they were not, in common prudence and regard to their own safety, to overlook, but to crush them before they gather strength, and come to be in prosperity: and perhaps attack them first in a hostile manner, as presuming upon our indolence in not attacking them before; and that we ought to avenge ourselves of them for what they have done in the wilderness, but that this cannot be so well done when they have once laid their hands on our cities and our goods: that those who endeavor to crush a power in its first rise, are wiser than those that endeavor to put a stop to its progress when it is become formidable; for these last seem to be angry only at the flourishing of others, but the former do not leave any room for their enemies to become troublesome to them. After they had sent such embassages to the neighboring nations, and among one another, they resolved to attack the Hebrews in battle.

2. These proceedings of the people of those countries occasioned perplexity and trouble to Moses, who expected no such warlike preparations. And when these nations were ready to fight, and the multitude of the Hebrews were obliged to try the fortune of war, they were in a mighty disorder, and in want of all necessaries, and yet were to make war with men who were thoroughly well prepared for it. Then therefore it was that Moses began to encourage them, and to exhort them to have a good heart, and rely on God's assistance by which they had been state of freedom and to hope for victory over those who were ready to fight with them, in order to deprive them of that blessing: that they were to suppose their own army to be numerous, wanting nothing, neither weapons, nor money, nor provisions, nor such other conveniences as, when men are in possession of, they fight undauntedly; and that they are to judge themselves to have all these advantages in the Divine assistance. They are also to suppose the enemy's army to be small, unarmed, weak, and such as want those

conveniences which they know must be wanted, when it is God's will that they shall be beaten; and how valuable God's assistance is, they had experienced in abundance of trials; and those such as were more terrible than war, for that is only against men; but these were against famine and thirst, things indeed that are in their own nature insuperable; as also against mountains, and that sea which afforded them no way for escaping; yet had all these difficulties been conquered by God's gracious kindness to them. So he exhorted them to be courageous at this time, and to look upon their entire prosperity to depend on the present conquest of their enemies.

3. And with these words did Moses encourage the multitude, who then called together the princes of their tribes, and their chief men, both separately and conjointly. The young men he charged to obey their elders, and the elders to hearken to their leader. So the people were elevated in their minds, and ready to try their fortune in battle, and hoped to be thereby at length delivered from all their miseries: nay, they desired that Moses would immediately lead them against their enemies without the least delay, that no backwardness might be a hindrance to their present resolution. So Moses sorted all that were fit for war into different troops, and set Joshua, the son of Nun, of the tribe of Ephraim, over them; one that was of great courage, and patient to undergo labors; of great abilities to understand, and to speak what was proper; and very serious in the worship of God; and indeed made like another Moses, a teacher of piety towards God. He also appointed a small party of the armed men to be near the water, and to take care of the children, and the women, and of the entire camp. So that whole night they prepared themselves for the battle; they took their weapons, if any of them had such as were well made, and attended to their commanders as ready to rush forth to the battle as soon as Moses should give the word of command. Moses also kept awake, teaching Joshua after what manner he should order his camp. But when the day began, Moses called for Joshua again, and exhorted him to approve himself in deeds such as one of his reputation made men expect from him; and to gain glory by the present expedition, in the opinion of those under him, for his exploits in this battle. He also gave a particular exhortation to the principal men of the Hebrews, and encouraged the whole army as it stood armed before him. And when he had thus animated the army, both by his words and works, and prepared everything, he retired to a mountain, and committed the army to God and to Joshua.

4. So the armies joined battle; and it came to a close fight, hand to hand, both sides showing great alacrity, and encouraging one another. And

indeed while Moses stretched out his hand towards heaven[6] the Hebrews were too hard for the Amalekites: but Moses not being able to sustain his hands thus stretched out, (for as often as he let down his hands, so often were his own people worsted,) he bade his brother Aaron, and Hur their sister Miriam's husband, to stand on each side of him, and take hold of his hands, and not permit his weariness to prevent it, but to assist him in the extension of his hands. When this was done, the Hebrews conquered the Amalekites by main force; and indeed they had all perished, unless the approach of the night had obliged the Hebrews to desist from killing any more. So our forefathers obtained a most signal and most seasonable victory; for they not only overcame those that fought against them, but terrified also the neighboring nations, and got great and splendid advantages, which they obtained of their enemies by their hard pains in this battle: for when they had taken the enemy's camp, they got ready booty for the public, and for their own private families, whereas till then they had not any sort of plenty, of even necessary food. The forementioned battle, when they had once got it, was also the occasion of their prosperity, not only for the present, but for the future ages also; for they not only made slaves of the bodies of their enemies, but subdued their minds also, and after this battle, became terrible to all that dwelt round about them. Moreover, they acquired a vast quantity of riches; for a great deal of silver and gold was left in the enemy's camp; as also brazen vessels, which they made common use of in their families; many utensils also that were embroidered there were of both sorts, that is, of what were weaved, and what were the ornaments of their armor, and other things that served for use in the family, and for the furniture of their rooms; they got also the prey of their cattle, and of whatsoever uses to follow camps, when they remove from one place to another. So the Hebrews now valued themselves upon their courage, and claimed great merit for their valor; and they perpetually inured themselves to take pains, by which they deemed every difficulty might be surmounted. Such were the consequences of this battle.

---

6. This eminent circumstance, that while Moses's hands were lift up towards heaven, the Israelites prevailed, and while they were let down towards the earth, the Amalekites prevailed, seems to me the earliest intimation we have of the proper posture, used of old, in solemn prayer, which was the stretching out of the hands [and eyes] towards heaven, as other passages of the Old and New Testament inform us. Nay, by the way, this posture seemed to have continued in the Christian church, till the clergy, instead of learning their prayers by heart, read them out of a book, which is in a great measure inconsistent with such an elevated posture, and which seems to me to have been only a later practice, introduced under the corrupt state of the church; though the constant use of divine forms of prayer, praise, and thanksgiving, appears to me to have been the practice of God's people, patriarchs, Jews, and Christians, in all the past ages.

5. On the next day, Moses stripped the dead bodies of their enemies, and gathered together the armor of those that were fled, and gave rewards to such as had signalized themselves in the action; and highly commended Joshua, their general, who was attested to by all the army, on account of the great actions he had done. Nor was any one of the Hebrews slain; but the slain of the enemy's army were too many to be enumerated. So Moses offered sacrifices of thanksgiving to God, and built an altar, which he named *The Lord the Conqueror.* He also foretold that the Amalekites should utterly be destroyed; and that hereafter none of them should remain, because they fought against the Hebrews, and this when they were in the wilderness, and in their distress also. Moreover, he refreshed the army with feasting. And thus did they fight this first battle with those that ventured to oppose them, after they were gone out of Egypt. But when Moses had celebrated this festival for the victory, he permitted the Hebrews to rest for a few days, and then he brought them out after the fight, in order of battle; for they had now many soldiers in light armor. And going gradually on, he came to Mount Sinai, in three months' time after they were removed out of Egypt; at which mountain, as we have before related, the vision of the bush, and the other wonderful appearances, had happened.

3: THAT MOSES KINDLY RECEIVED HIS FATHER-IN-LAW, JETHRO, WHEN HE CAME TO HIM TO MOUNT SINAI

Now when Raguel, Moses's father-in-law, understood in what a prosperous condition his affairs were, he willingly came to meet him. And Moses and his children, and pleased himself with his coming. And when he had offered sacrifice, he made a feast for the multitude, near the Bush he had formerly seen; which multitude, every one according to their families, partook of the feast. But Aaron and his family took Raguel, and sang hymns to God, as to Him who had been the author procurer of their deliverance and their freedom. They also praised their conductor, as him by whose virtue it was that all things had succeeded with them. Raguel also, in his eucharistical oration to Moses, made great encomiums upon the whole multitude; and he could not but admire Moses for his fortitude, and that humanity he had shewn in the delivery of his friends.

4: HOW RAGUEL (JETHRO) SUGGESTED TO MOSES TO SET HIS PEOPLE IN ORDER

1. The next day, as Raguel saw Moses in the midst of a crowd of business (for he determined the differences of those that referred them to him,

every one still going to him, and supposing that they should then only obtain justice, if he were the arbitrator; and those that lost their causes thought it no harm, while they thought they lost them justly, and not by partiality). Raguel however said nothing to him at that time, as not desirous to be any hindrance to such as had a mind to make use of the virtue of their conductor. But afterward he took him to himself, and when he had him alone, he instructed him in what he ought to do; and advised him to leave the trouble of lesser causes to others, but himself to take care of the greater, and of the people's safety, for that certain others of the Hebrews might be found that were fit to determine causes, but that nobody but a Moses could take of the safety of so many ten thousands. "Be therefore," says he, "insensible of thine own virtue, and what thou hast done by ministering under God to the people's preservation. Permit, therefore, the determination of common causes to be done by others, but do thou reserve thyself to the attendance on God only, and look out for methods of preserving the multitude from their present distress. Make use of the method I suggest to you, as to human affairs; and take a review of the army, and appoint chosen rulers over tens of thousands, and then over thousands; then divide them into five hundreds, and again into hundreds, and into fifties; and set rulers over each of them, who may distinguish them into thirties, and keep them in order; and at last number them by twenties and by tens: and let there be one commander over each number, to be denominated from the number of those over whom they are rulers, but such as the whole multitude have tried, and do approve of, as being good and righteous men;[7] and let those rulers decide the controversies they have one with another. But if any great cause arise, let them bring the cognizance of it before the rulers of a higher dignity; but if any great difficulty arise that is too hard for even their determination, let them send it to thee. By these means two advantages will be gained; the Hebrews will have justice done them, and thou wilt be able to attend constantly on God, and procure him to be more favorable to the people."

2. This was the admonition of Raguel; and Moses received his advice very kindly, and acted according to his suggestion. Nor did he conceal the invention of this method, nor pretend to it himself, but informed the multitude who it was that invented it: nay, he has named Raguel in the books he wrote, as the person who invented this ordering of the people, as thinking it right to give a true testimony to worthy persons, although

---

7. This manner of electing the judges and officers of the Israelites by the testimonies and suffrages of the people, before they were ordained by God, or by Moses, deserves to be carefully noted, because it was the pattern of the like manner of the choice and ordination of bishops, presbyters, and deacons, in the Christian church.

he might have gotten reputation by ascribing to himself the inventions of other men; whence we may learn the virtuous disposition of Moses: but of such his disposition, we shall have proper occasion to speak in other places of these books.

5: HOW MOSES ASCENDED UP TO MOUNT SINAI, AND RECEIVED LAWS FROM GOD, AND DELIVERED THEM TO THE HEBREWS

1. Now Moses called the multitude together, and told them that he was going from them unto mount Sinai to converse with God; to receive from him, and to bring back with him, a certain oracle; but he enjoined them to pitch their tents near the mountain, and prefer the habitation that was nearest to God, before one more remote. When he had said this, he ascended up to Mount Sinai, which is the highest of all the mountains that are in that country[8] and is not only very difficult to be ascended by men, on account of its vast altitude, but because of the sharpness of its precipices also; nay, indeed, it cannot be looked at without pain of the eyes: and besides this, it was terrible and inaccessible, on account of the rumor that passed about, that God dwelt there. But the Hebrews removed their tents as Moses had bidden them, and took possession of the lowest parts of the mountain; and were elevated in their minds, in expectation that Moses would return from God with promises of the good things he had proposed to them. So they feasted and waited for their conductor, and kept themselves pure as in other respects, and not accompanying with their wives for three days, as he had before ordered them to do. And they prayed to God that he would favorably receive Moses in his conversing with him, and bestow some such gift upon them by which they might live well. They also lived more plentifully as to their diet; and put on their wives and children more ornamental and decent clothing than they usually wore.

2. So they passed two days in this way of feasting; but on the third day, before the sun was up, a cloud spread itself over the whole camp of the Hebrews, such a one as none had before seen, and encompassed the place where they had pitched their tents; and while all the rest of the air

---

8. Since this mountain, Sinai, is here said to be the highest of all the mountains that are in that country, it must be that now called St. Katherine's, which is one-third higher than that within a mile of it, now called Sinai, as Thevenot informs us (*Travels*, part 1, chapter 23. p. 168). The other name of it, Horeb, is never used by Josephus, and perhaps was its name among the Egyptians only, whence the Israelites were lately come, as Sinai was its name among the Arabians, Canaanites, and other nations. Accordingly when (1 Kings 9:8) the scripture says that Elijah came to Horeb, the mount of God, Josephus justly says (book 8, chapter 13, section 7), that he came to the mountain called Sinai: and Jerome . . . says, that he took this mountain to have two names, Sinai and Choreb (*De Nomin. Heb.*, p. 427).

was clear, there came strong winds, that raised up large showers of rain, which became a mighty tempest. There was also such lightning, as was terrible to those that saw it; and thunder, with its thunderbolts, were sent down, and declared God to be there present in a gracious way to such as Moses desired he should be gracious. Now, as to these matters, every one of my readers may think as he pleases; but I am under a necessity of relating this history as it is described in the sacred books. This sight, and the amazing sound that came to their ears, disturbed the Hebrews to a prodigious degree, for they were not such as they were accustomed to; and then the rumor that was spread abroad, how God frequented that mountain, greatly astonished their minds, so they sorrowfully contained themselves within their tents, as both supposing Moses to be destroyed by the Divine wrath, and expecting the like destruction for themselves.

3. When they were under these apprehensions, Moses appeared as joyful and greatly exalted. When they saw him, they were freed from their fear, and admitted of more comfortable hopes as to what was to come. The air also was become clear and pure of its former disorders, upon the appearance of Moses; whereupon he called together the people to a congregation, in order to their hearing what God would say to them: and when they were gathered together, he stood on an eminence whence they might all hear him, and said, "God has received me graciously, O Hebrews, as he has formerly done; and has suggested a happy method of living for you, and an order of political government, and is now present in the camp: I therefore charge you, for his sake and the sake of his works, and what we have done by his means, that you do not put a low value on what I am going to say, because the commands have been given by me that now deliver them to you, nor because it is the tongue of a man that delivers them to you; but if you have a due regard to the great importance of the things themselves, you will understand the greatness of Him whose institutions they are, and who has not disdained to communicate them to me for our common advantage; for it is not to be supposed that the author of these institutions is barely Moses, the son of Amram and Jochebed, but He who obliged the Nile to run bloody for your sakes, and tamed the haughtiness of the Egyptians by various sorts of judgments; he who provided a way through the sea for us; he who contrived a method of sending us food from heaven, when we were distressed for want of it; he who made the water to issue out of a rock, when we had very little of it before; he by whose means Adam was made to partake of the fruits both of the land and of the sea; he by whose means Noah escaped the deluge; he by whose means our forefather Abraham, of a wandering pilgrim, was made the heir of the land of Canaan; he by whose means Isaac was born

of parents that were very old; he by whose means Jacob was adorned with twelve virtuous sons; he by whose means Joseph became a potent lord over the Egyptians; he it is who conveys these instructions to you by me as his interpreter. And let them be to you venerable, and contended for more earnestly by you than your own children and your own wives; for if you will follow them, you will lead a happy life you will enjoy the land fruitful, the sea calm, and the fruit of the womb born complete, as nature requires; you will be also terrible to your enemies for I have been admitted into the presence of God and been made a hearer of his incorruptible voice so great is his concern for your nation, and its duration."

4. When he had said this, he brought the people, with their wives and children, so near the mountain, that they might hear God himself speaking to them about the precepts which they were to practice; that the energy of what should be spoken might not be hurt by its utterance by that tongue of a man, which could but imperfectly deliver it to their understanding. And they all heard a voice that came to all of them from above, insomuch that no one of these words escaped them, which Moses wrote on two tables; which it is not lawful for us to set down directly, but their import we will declare.

5. The first commandment teaches us that there is but one God, and that we ought to worship him only. The second commands us not to make the image of any living creature to worship it. The third, that we must not swear by God in a false matter. The fourth, that we must keep the seventh day, by resting from all sorts of work. The fifth, that we must honor our parents. The sixth, that we must abstain from murder. The seventh, that we must not commit adultery. The eighth, that we must not be guilty of theft. The ninth, that we must not bear false witness. The tenth, that we must not admit of the desire of anything that is another's.

6. Now when the multitude had heard God himself giving those precepts which Moses had discoursed of, they rejoiced at what was said; and the congregation was dissolved: but on the following days they came to his tent, and desired him to bring them, besides, other laws from God. Accordingly he appointed such laws, and afterwards informed them in what manner they should act in all cases; which laws I shall make mention of in their proper time; but I shall reserve most of those laws for another work, and make there a distinct explication of them.

7. When matters were brought to this state, Moses went up again to Mount Sinai, of which he had told them beforehand. He made his ascent in their sight; and while he stayed there so long a time, (for he was absent from them forty days,) fear seized upon the Hebrews, lest Moses should have come to any harm; nor was there anything else so sad, and that

so much troubled them, as this supposal that Moses was perished. Now there was a variety in their sentiments about it; some saying that he was fallen among wild beasts; and those that were of this opinion were chiefly such as were ill-disposed to him; but others said that he was departed, and gone to God; but the wiser sort were led by their reason to embrace neither of those opinions with any satisfaction, thinking, that as it was a thing that sometimes happens to men to fall among wild beasts and perish that way, so it was probable enough that he might depart and go to God, on account of his virtue; they therefore were quiet, and expected the event: yet were they exceeding sorry upon the supposal that they were deprived of a governor and a protector, such a one indeed as they could never recover again; nor would this suspicion give them leave to expect any comfortable event about this man, nor could they prevent their trouble and melancholy upon this occasion. However, the camp durst not remove all this while, because Moses had bidden them afore to stay there.

8. But when the forty days, and as many nights, were over, Moses came down, having tasted nothing of food usually appointed for the nourishment of men. His appearance filled the army with gladness, and he declared to them what care God had of them, and by what manner of conduct of their lives they might live happily; telling them, that during these days of his absence he had suggested to him also that he would have a tabernacle built for him, into which he would descend when he came to them, and how we should carry it about with us when we remove from this place; and that there would be no longer any occasion for going up to Mount Sinai, but that he would himself come and pitch his tabernacle amongst us, and be present at our prayers; as also, that the tabernacle should be of such measures and construction as he had shown him, and that you are to fall to the work, and prosecute it diligently. When he had said this, he showed them the two tables, with the ten commandments engraven upon them, five upon each table; and the writing was by the hand of God.

6: THE TABERNACLE WHICH MOSES BUILT IN THE WILDERNESS FOR THE HONOR OF GOD

1. Hereupon the Israelites rejoiced at what they had seen and heard of their conductor, and were not wanting in diligence according to their ability; for they brought silver, and gold, and brass, and of the best sorts of wood, and such as would not at all decay by putrefaction; camels' hair also, and sheep-skins, some of them dyed of a blue color, and some of a scarlet; some brought the flower for the purple color, and others for white, with wool dyed by the flowers aforementioned; and fine linen and

precious stones, which those that use costly ornaments set in ouches of gold; they brought also a great quantity of spices; for of these materials did Moses build the tabernacle, which did not at all differ from a movable and ambulatory temple. Now when these things were brought together with great diligence, (for everyone was ambitious to further the work even beyond their ability,) he set architects over the works, and this by the command of God; and indeed the very same which the people themselves would have chosen, had the election been allowed to them. Now their names are set down in writing in the sacred books; and they were these: Besaleel, the son of Uri, of the tribe of Judah, the grandson of Miriam, the sister of their conductor and Aholiab, file son of Ahisamach, of the tribe of Dan. Now the people went on with what they had undertaken with so great alacrity, that Moses was obliged to restrain them, by making proclamation, that what had been brought was sufficient, as the artificers had informed him; so they fell to work upon the building of the tabernacle. Moses also informed them, according to the direction of God, both what the measures were to be, and its largeness; and how many vessels it ought to contain for the use of the sacrifices. The women also were ambitious to do their parts, about the garments of the priests, and about other things that would be wanted in this work, both for ornament and for the divine service itself.

2. Now when all things were prepared, the gold, and the silver, and the brass, and what was woven, Moses, when he had appointed beforehand that there should be a festival, and that sacrifices should be offered according to everyone's ability, reared up the tabernacle and when he had measured the open court, fifty cubits broad and a hundred long, he set up brazen pillars, five cubits high, twenty on each of the longer sides, and ten pillars for the breadth behind; every one of the pillars also had a ring. Their chapiters were of silver, but their bases were of brass: they resembled the sharp ends of spears, and were of brass, fixed into the ground. Cords were also put through the rings, and were tied at their farther ends to brass nails of a cubit long, which, at every pillar, were driven into the floor, and would keep the tabernacle from being shaken by the violence of winds; but a curtain of fine soft linen went round all the pillars, and hung down in a flowing and loose manner from their chapiters, and enclosed the whole space, and seemed not at all unlike to a wall about it. And this was the structure of three of the sides of this enclosure; but as for the fourth side, which was fifty cubits in extent, and was the front of the whole, twenty cubits of it were for the opening of the gates, wherein stood two pillars on each side, after the resemblance of open gates. These were made wholly of silver, and polished, and that all over, excepting the bases, which were of brass. Now on each side of

the gates there stood three pillars, which were inserted into the concave bases of the gates, and were suited to them; and round them was drawn a curtain of fine linen; but to the gates themselves, which were twenty cubits in extent, and five in height, the curtain was composed of purple, and scarlet, and blue, and fine linen, and embroidered with many and divers sorts of figures, excepting the figures of animals. Within these gates was the brazen laver for purification, having a basin beneath of the like matter, whence the priests might wash their hands and sprinkle their feet; and this was the ornamental construction of the enclosure about the court of the tabernacle, which was exposed to the open air.

3. As to the tabernacle itself, Moses placed it in the middle of that court, with its front to the east, that, when the sun arose, it might send its first rays upon it. Its length, when it was set up, was thirty cubits, and its breadth was twelve [ten] cubits. The one of its walls was on the south, and the other was exposed to the north, and on the back part of it remained the west. It was necessary that its height should be equal to its breadth [ten cubits]. There were also pillars made of wood, twenty on each side; they were wrought into a quadrangular figure, in breadth a cubit and a half, but the thickness was four fingers: they had thin plates of gold affixed to them on both sides, inwardly and outwardly: they had each of them two tenons belonging to them, inserted into their bases, and these were of silver, in each of which bases there was a socket to receive the tenon; but the pillars on the west wall were six. Now all these tenons and sockets accurately fitted one another, insomuch that the joints were invisible, and both seemed to be one entire and united wall. It was also covered with gold, both within and without. The number of pillars was equal on the opposite sides, and there were on each part twenty, and every one of them had the third part of a span in thickness; so that the number of thirty cubits were fully made up between them; but as to the wall behind, where the six pillars made up together only nine cubits, they made two other pillars, and cut them out of one cubit, which they placed in the corners, and made them equally fine with the other. Now every one of the pillars had rings of gold affixed to their fronts outward, as if they had taken root in the pillars, and stood one row over against another round about, through which were inserted bars gilt over with gold, each of them five cubits long, and these bound together the pillars, the head of one bar running into another, after the nature of one tenon inserted into another; but for the wall behind, there was but one row of bars that went through all the pillars, into which row ran the ends of the bars on each side of the longer walls; the male with its female being so fastened in their joints, that they held the whole firmly together; and for this reason was all this joined so fast together, that

the tabernacle might not be shaken, either by the winds, or by any other means, but that it might preserve itself quiet and immovable continually.

4. As for the inside, Moses parted its length into three partitions. At the distance of ten cubits from the most secret end, Moses placed four pillars, the workmanship of which was the very same with that of the rest; and they stood upon the like bases with them, each a small matter distant from his fellow. Now the room within those pillars was the most holy place; but the rest of the room was the tabernacle, which was open for the priests. However, this proportion of the measures of the tabernacle proved to be an imitation of the system of the world; for that third part thereof which was within the four pillars, to which the priests were not admitted, is, as it were, a heaven peculiar to God. But the space of the twenty cubits, is, as it were, sea and land, on which men live, and so this part is peculiar to the priests only. But at the front, where the entrance was made, they placed pillars of gold, that stood on bases of brass, in number seven; but then they spread over the tabernacle veils of fine linen and purple, and blue, and scarlet colors, embroidered. The first veil was ten cubits every way, and this they spread over the pillars which parted the temple, and kept the most holy place concealed within; and this veil was that which made this part not visible to any. Now the whole temple was called *The Holy Place:* but that part which was within the four pillars, and to which none were admitted, was called *The Holy of Holies.* This veil was very ornamental, and embroidered with all sorts of flowers which the earth produces; and there were interwoven into it all sorts of variety that might be an ornament, excepting the forms of animals. Another veil there was which covered the five pillars that were at the entrance. It was like the former in its magnitude, and texture, and color; and at the corner of every pillar a ring retained it from the top downwards half the depth of the pillars, the other half affording an entrance for the priests, who crept under it. Over this there was a veil of linen, of the same largeness with the former: it was to be drawn this way or that way by cords, the rings of which, fixed to the texture of the veil, and to the cords also, were subservient to the drawing and undrawing of the veil, and to the fastening it at the corner, that then it might be no hindrance to the view of the sanctuary, especially on solemn days; but that on other days, and especially when the weather was inclined to snow, it might be expanded, and afford a covering to the veil of divers colors. Whence that custom of ours is derived, of having a fine linen veil, after the temple has been built, to be drawn over the entrances. But the ten other curtains were four cubits in breadth, and twenty-eight in length; and had golden clasps, in order to join the one curtain to the other, which was done so exactly that they

seemed to be one entire curtain. These were spread over the temple, and covered all the top and parts of the walls, on the sides and behind, so far as within one cubit of the ground. There were other curtains of the same breadth with these, but one more in number, and longer, for they were thirty cubits long; but these were woven of hair, with the like subtilty as those of wool were made, and were extended loosely down to the ground, appearing like a triangular front and elevation at the gates, the eleventh curtain being used for this very purpose. There were also other curtains made of skins above these, which afforded covering and protection to those that were woven both in hot weather and when it rained. And great was the surprise of those who viewed these curtains at a distance, for they seemed not at all to differ from the color of the sky. But those that were made of hair and of skins, reached down in the same manner as did the veil at the gates, and kept off the heat of the sun, and what injury the rains might do. And after this manner was the tabernacle reared.

5. There was also an ark made, sacred to God, of wood that was naturally strong, and could not be corrupted. This was called *Eron* in our own language. Its construction was thus: its length was five spans, but its breadth and height was each of them three spans. It was covered all over with gold, both within and without, so that the wooden part was not seen. It had also a cover united to it, by golden hinges, after a wonderful manner; which cover was every way evenly fitted to it, and had no eminences to hinder its exact conjunction. There were also two golden rings belonging to each of the longer boards, and passing through the entire wood, and through them gilt bars passed along each board, that it might thereby be moved and carried about, as occasion should require; for it was not drawn in a cart by beasts of burden, but borne on the shoulders of the priests. Upon this its cover were two images, which the Hebrews call *Cherubims;* they are flying creatures, but their form is not like to that of any of the creatures which men have seen, though Moses said he had seen such beings near the throne of God. In this ark he put the two tables whereon the ten commandments were written, five upon each table, and two and a half upon each side of them; and this ark he placed in the most holy place.

6. But in the holy place he placed a table, like those at Delphi. Its length was two cubits, and its breadth one cubit, and its height three spans. It had feet also, the lower half of which were complete feet, resembling those which the Dorians put to their bedsteads; but the upper parts towards the table were wrought into a square form. The table had a hollow towards every side, having a ledge of four fingers' depth, that went round about like a spiral, both on the upper and lower part of the body of the work. Upon every one of the feet was there also inserted a ring, not far from the

cover, through which went bars of wood beneath, but gilded, to be taken out upon occasion, there being a cavity where it was joined to the rings; for they were not entire rings; but before they came quite round they ended in acute points, the one of which was inserted into the prominent part of the table, and the other into the foot; and by these it was carried when they journeyed: Upon this table, which was placed on the north side of the temple, not far from the most holy place, were laid twelve unleavened loaves of bread, six upon each heap, one above another: they were made of two tenth-deals of the purest flour, which tenth-deal [an omer] is a measure of the Hebrews, containing seven Athenian *cotyloe;* and above those loaves were put two vials full of frankincense. Now after seven days other loaves were brought in their stead, on the day which is by us called the *Sabbath;* for we call the seventh day the *Sabbath.* But for the occasion of this intention of placing loaves here, we will speak to it in another place.

7. Over against this table, near the southern wall, was set a candlestick of cast gold, hollow within, being of the weight of one hundred pounds, which the Hebrews call *Chinchares;* if it be turned into the Greek language, it denotes a *talent.* It was made with its knops, and lilies, and pomegranates, and bowls (which ornaments amounted to seventy in all); by which means the shaft elevated itself on high from a single base, and spread itself into as many branches as there are planets, including the sun among them. It terminated in seven heads, in one row, all standing parallel to one another; and these branches carried seven lamps, one by one, in imitation of the number of the planets. These lamps looked to the east and to the south, the candlestick being situated obliquely.

8. Now between this candlestick and the table, which, as we said, were within the sanctuary, was the altar of incense, made of wood indeed, but of the same wood of which the foregoing vessels were made, such as was not liable to corruption; it was entirely crusted over with a golden plate. Its breadth on each side was a cubit, but the altitude double. Upon it was a grate of gold, that was extant above the altar, which had a golden crown encompassing it round about, whereto belonged rings and bars, by which the priests carried it when they journeyed. Before this tabernacle there was reared a brazen altar, but it was within made of wood, five cubits by measure on each side, but its height was but three, in like manner adorned with brass plates as bright as gold. It had also a brazen hearth of network; for the ground underneath received the fire from the hearth, because it had no basis to receive it. Hard by this altar lay the basins, and the vials, and the censers, and the caldrons, made of gold; but the other vessels, made for the use of the sacrifices, were all of brass. And such was the construction of the tabernacle; and these were the vessels thereto belonging.

7: THE GARMENTS OF THE PRIESTS, AND OF THE HIGH PRIEST

1. There were peculiar garments appointed for the priests, and for all the rest, which they call *Cohanoeoe* [priestly] garments, as also for the high priests, which they call *Cahanoeoe Rabbae,* and denote the high priest's garments. Such was therefore the habit of the rest. But when the priest approaches the sacrifices, he purifies himself with the purification which the law prescribes; and, in the first place, he puts on that which is called *Machanase,* which means somewhat that is fast tied. It is a girdle, composed of fine twined linen, and is put about the privy parts, the feet being to be inserted into them in the nature of breeches, but above half of it is cut off, and it ends at the thighs, and is there tied fast.

2. Over this he wore a linen vestment, made of fine flax doubled: it is called *Chethone,* and denotes *linen,* for we call linen by the name of *Chethone.* This vestment reaches down to the feet, and sits close to the body; and has sleeves that are tied fast to the arms: it is girded to the breast a little above the elbows, by a girdle often going round, four fingers broad, but so loosely woven, that you would think it were the skin of a serpent. It is embroidered with flowers of scarlet, and purple, and blue, and fine twined linen, but the warp was nothing but fine linen. The beginning of its circumvolution is at the breast; and when it has gone often round, it is there tied, and hangs loosely there down to the ankles: I mean this, all the time the priest is not about any laborious service, for in this position it appears in the most agreeable manner to the spectators; but when he is obliged to assist at the offering sacrifices, and to do the appointed service, that he may not be hindered in his operations by its motion, he throws it to the left, and bears it on his shoulder. Moses indeed calls this belt *Albaneth;* but we have learned from the Babylonians to call it *Emia,* for so it is by them called. This vestment has no loose or hollow parts anywhere in it, but only a narrow aperture about the neck; and it is tied with certain strings hanging down from the edge over the breast and back, and is fastened above each shoulder: it is called *Massabazanes.*

3. Upon his head he wears a cap, not brought to a conic form nor encircling the whole head, but still covering more than the half of it, which is called *Masnaemphthes;* and its make is such that it seems to be a crown, being made of thick swathes, but the contexture is of linen; and it is doubled round many times, and sewed together; besides which, a piece of fine linen covers the whole cap from the upper part, and reaches down to the forehead, and hides the seams of the swathes, which would otherwise appear indecently: this adheres closely upon the solid part of the head, and is thereto so firmly fixed, that it may not fall off during the

sacred service about the sacrifices. So we have now shown you what is the habit of the generality of the priests.

4. The high priest is indeed adorned with the same garments that we have described, without abating one; only over these he puts on a vestment of a blue color. This also is a long robe, reaching to his feet, [in our language it is called *Meeir,*] and is tied round with a girdle, embroidered with the same colors and flowers as the former, with a mixture of gold interwoven. To the bottom of which garment are hung fringes, in color like pomegranates, with golden bells[9] by a curious and beautiful contrivance; so that between two bells hangs a pomegranate, and between two pomegranates a bell. Now this vesture was not composed of two pieces, nor was it sewed together upon the shoulders and the sides, but it was one long vestment so woven as to have an aperture for the neck; not an oblique one, but parted all along the breast and the back. A border also was sewed to it, lest the aperture should look too indecently: it was also parted where the hands were to come out.

5. Besides these, the high priest put on a third garment, which was called the *Ephod,* which resembles the Epomis of the Greeks. Its make was after this manner: it was woven to the depth of a cubit, of several colors, with gold intermixed, and embroidered, but it left the middle of the breast uncovered: it was made with sleeves also; nor did it appear to be at all differently made from a short coat. But in the void place of this garment there was inserted a piece of the bigness of a span, embroidered with gold, and the other colors of the ephod, and was called *Essen,* [the breastplate,] which in the Greek language signifies the *Oracle.* This piece exactly filled up the void space in the ephod. It was united to it by golden rings at every corner, the like rings being annexed to the ephod, and a blue riband was made use of to tie them together by those rings; and that the space between the rings might not appear empty, they contrived to fill it up with stitches of blue ribands. There were also two sardonyxes upon the ephod, at the shoulders, to fasten it in the nature of buttons, having each

---

9. The use of these golden bells at the bottom of the high priest's long garment, seems to me to have been this: That by shaking his garment at the time of his offering incense in the temple, on the great day of expiation, or at other proper periods of his sacred ministrations there, on the great festivals, the people might have notice of it, and might fall to their own prayers at the time of incense, or other proper periods; and so the whole congregation might at once offer those common prayers jointly with the high priest himself to the Almighty (see Luke 1:10; Revelation 8:3, 4). Nor probably is the son of Sirach to be otherwise understood, when he says of Aaron, the first high priest (Ecclus. 45:9), "And God encompassed Aaron with pomegranates, and with many golden bells round about, that as he went there might be a sound, and a noise made that might be heard in the temple, for a memorial to the children of his people."

end running to the sardonyxes of gold, that they might be buttoned by them. On these were engraven the names of the sons of Jacob, in our own country letters, and in our own tongue, six on each of the stones, on either side; and the elder sons' names were on the right shoulder. Twelve stones also there were upon the breast-plate, extraordinary in largeness and beauty; and they were an ornament not to be purchased by men, because of their immense value. These stones, however, stood in three rows, by four in a row, and were inserted into the breastplate itself, and they were set in ouches of gold, that were themselves inserted in the breastplate, and were so made that they might not fall out low the first three stones were a sardonyx, a topaz, and an emerald. The second row contained a carbuncle, a jasper, and a sapphire. The first of the third row was a ligure, then an amethyst, and the third an agate, being the ninth of the whole number. The first of the fourth row was a chrysolite, the next was an onyx, and then a beryl, which was the last of all. Now the names of all those sons of Jacob were engraven in these stones, whom we esteem the heads of our tribes, each stone having the honor of a name, in the order according to which they were born. And whereas the rings were too weak of themselves to bear the weight of the stones, they made two other rings of a larger size, at the edge of that part of the breastplate which reached to the neck, and inserted into the very texture of the breastplate, to receive chains finely wrought, which connected them with golden bands to the tops of the shoulders, whose extremity turned backwards, and went into the ring, on the prominent back part of the ephod; and this was for the security of the breastplate, that it might not fall out of its place. There was also a girdle sewed to the breastplate, which was of the forementioned colors, with gold intermixed, which, when it had gone once round, was tied again upon the seam, and hung down. There were also golden loops that admitted its fringes at each extremity of the girdle, and included them entirely.

6. The high priest's mitre was the same that we described before, and was wrought like that of all the other priests; above which there was another, with swathes of blue embroidered, and round it was a golden crown polished, of three rows, one above another; out of which arose a cup of gold, which resembled the herb which we call *Saccharus;* but those Greeks that are skillful in botany call it *Hyoscyamus.* Now, lest anyone that has seen this herb, but has not been taught its name, and is unacquainted with its nature, or, having known its name, knows not the herb when he sees it, I shall give such, as these are a description of it. This herb is oftentimes in tallness above three spans, but its root is like that of a turnip (for he that should compare it thereto would not be mistaken); but its leaves are like the leaves of mint. Out of its branches it sends

out a calyx, cleaving to the branch; and a coat encompasses it, which it naturally puts off when it is changing, in order to produce its fruit. This calyx is of the bigness of the bone of the little finger, but in the compass of its aperture is like a cup. This I will further describe, for the use of those that are unacquainted with it. Suppose a sphere be divided into two parts, round at the bottom, but having another segment that grows up to a circumference from that bottom; suppose it become narrower by degrees, and that the cavity of that part grow decently smaller, and then gradually grow wider again at the brim, such as we see in the navel of a pomegranate, with its notches. And indeed such a coat grows over this plant as renders it a hemisphere, and that, as one may say, turned accurately in a lathe, and having its notches extant above it, which, as I said, grow like a pomegranate, only that they are sharp, and end in nothing but prickles. Now the fruit is preserved by this coat of the calyx, which fruit is like the seed of the herb Sideritis: it sends out a flower that may seem to resemble that of poppy. Of this was a crown made, as far from the hinder part of the head to each of the temples; but this *Ephielis,* for so this calyx may be called, did not cover the forehead, but it was covered with a golden plate,[10] which had inscribed upon it the name of God in sacred characters. And such were the ornaments of the high priest.

7. Now here one may wonder at the ill-will which men bear to us, and which they profess to bear on account of our despising that Deity which they pretend to honor; for if anyone do but consider the fabric of the tabernacle, and take a view of the garments of the high priest, and of those vessels which we make use of in our sacred ministration, he will find that our legislator was a divine man, and that we are unjustly reproached by others; for if anyone do without prejudice, and with judgment, look upon these things, he will find they were every one made in way of imitation and representation of the universe. When Moses distinguished the tabernacle into three parts, and allowed two of them to the priests, as a place accessible and common, he denoted the land and the sea, these being of general access to all; but he set apart the third division for God, because heaven is inaccessible to men. And when he ordered twelve loaves to be set on the table, he denoted the year, as distinguished into so many months. By branching out the candlestick into seventy parts, he secretly intimated the *Decani,* or seventy divisions of the planets; and as to the seven lamps upon the candlesticks, they referred to the course of the planets, of which

---

10. The reader ought to take notice here, that the very Mosaic Petalon, or golden plate, for the forehead of the Jewish high priest, was itself preserved, not only till the days of Josephus, but of Origen; and that its inscription, Holiness to the Lord, was in the Samaritan characters.

that is the number. The veils, too, which were composed of four things, they declared the four elements; for the fine linen was proper to signify the earth, because the flax grows out of the earth; the purple signified the sea, because that color is dyed by the blood of a sea shell-fish; the blue is fit to signify the air; and the scarlet will naturally be an indication of fire. Now the vestment of the high priest being made of linen, signified the earth; the blue denoted the sky, being like lightning in its pomegranates, and in the noise of the bells resembling thunder. And for the ephod, it showed that God had made the universe of four elements; and as for the gold interwoven, I suppose it related to the splendor by which all things are enlightened. He also appointed the breastplate to be placed in the middle of the ephod, to resemble the earth, for that has the very middle place of the world. And the girdle which encompassed the high priest round, signified the ocean, for that goes round about and includes the universe. Each of the sardonyxes declares to us the sun and the moon; those, I mean, that were in the nature of buttons on the high priest's shoulders. And for the twelve stones, whether we understand by them the months, or whether we understand the like number of the signs of that circle which the Greeks call the *Zodiac,* we shall not be mistaken in their meaning. And for the mitre, which was of a blue color, it seems to me to mean heaven; for how otherwise could the name of God be inscribed upon it? That it was also illustrated with a crown, and that of gold also, is because of that splendor with which God is pleased. Let this explication suffice at present,[11] since the course of my narration will often, and on many occasions, afford me the opportunity of enlarging upon the virtue of our legislator.

8: THE PRIESTHOOD OF AARON

1. When what has been described was brought to a conclusion, gifts not being yet presented, God appeared to Moses, and enjoined him to

---

11. This explication of the mystical meaning of the Jewish tabernacle and its vessels, with the garments of the high priest, is taken out of Philo, and fitted to Gentile philosophical notions. This may possibly be forgiven in Jews, greatly versed in heathen learning and philosophy, as Philo had ever been, and as Josephus had long been when he wrote these *Antiquities.* In the meantime, it is not to be doubted, but in their education they must have both learned more Jewish interpretations, such as we meet with in the Epistle of Barnabas, in that to the Hebrews, and elsewhere among the old Jews. Accordingly when Josephus wrote his books of the Jewish War, for the use of the Jews, at which time he was comparatively young, and less used to Gentile books, we find one specimen of such a Jewish interpretation; for there (book 7, chapter 5, section 5) he makes the seven branches of the temple-candlestick, with their seven lamps, an emblem of the seven days of creation and rest, which are here emblems of the seven planets. Nor certainly ought ancient Jewish emblems to be explained any other way than according to ancient Jewish, and not Gentile, notions.

bestow the high priesthood upon Aaron his brother, as upon him that best of them all deserved to obtain that honor, on account of his virtue. And when he had gathered the multitude together, he gave them an account of Aaron's virtue, and of his good-will to them, and of the dangers he had undergone for their sakes. Upon which, when they had given testimony to him in all respects, and showed their readiness to receive him, Moses said to them, "O you Israelites, this work is already brought to a conclusion, in a manner most acceptable to God, and according to our abilities. And now since you see that he is received into this tabernacle, we shall first of all stand in need of one that may officiate for us, and may minister to the sacrifices, and to the prayers that are to be put up for us. And indeed had the inquiry after such a person been left to me, I should have thought myself worthy of this honor, both because all men are naturally fond of themselves, and because I am conscious to myself that I have taken a great deal of pains for your deliverance; but now God himself has determined that Aaron is worthy of this honor, and has chosen him for his priest, as knowing him to be the most righteous person among you. So that he is to put on the vestments which are consecrated to God; he is to have the care of the altars, and to make provision for the sacrifices; and he it is that must put up prayers for you to God, who will readily hear them, not only because he is himself solicitous for your nation, but also because he will receive them as offered by one that he hath himself chosen to this office. The Hebrews were pleased with what was said, and they gave their approbation to him whom God had ordained; for Aaron was of them all the most deserving of this honor, on account of his own stock and gift of prophecy, and his brother's virtue. He had at that time four sons, Nadab, Abihu, Eleazar, and Ithamar.

2. Now Moses commanded them to make use of all the utensils which were more than were necessary to the structure of the tabernacle, for covering the tabernacle itself, the candlestick, and altar of incense, and the other vessels, that they might not be at all hurt when they journeyed, either by the rain, or by the rising of the dust. And when he had gathered the multitude together again, he ordained that they should offer half a shekel for every man, as an oblation to God; which shekel is a piece among the Hebrews, and is equal to four Athenian drachmae. Whereupon they readily obeyed what Moses had commanded; and the number of the offerers was six hundred and five thousand five hundred and fifty. Now this money that was brought by the men that were free, was given by such as were about twenty years old, but under fifty; and what was collected was spent in the uses of the tabernacle.

3. Moses now purified the tabernacle and the priests; which purification was performed after the following manner:—He commanded them to take five hundred shekels of choice myrrh, an equal quantity of cassia, and half the foregoing weight of cinnamon and calamus (this last is a sort of sweet spice); to beat them small, and wet them with an bin of oil of olives (an *hin* is our own country measure, and contains two Athenian *choas,* or *congiuses);* then mix them together, and boil them, and prepare them after the art of the apothecary, and make them into a very sweet ointment; and afterward to take it to anoint and to purify the priests themselves, and all the tabernacle, as also the sacrifices. There were also many, and those of various kinds, of sweet spices, that belonged to the tabernacle, and such as were of very great price, and were brought to the golden altar of incense; the nature of which I do not now describe, lest it should be troublesome to my readers; but incense was to be offered twice a-day, both before sunrising and at sun-setting. They were also to keep oil already purified for the lamps; three of which were to give light all day long, upon the sacred candlestick, before God, and the rest were to be lighted at the evening.

4. Now all was finished. Besaleel and Aholiab appeared to be the most skillful of the workmen; for they invented finer works than what others had done before them, and were of great abilities to gain notions of what they were formerly ignorant of; and of these, Besaleel was judged to be the best. Now the whole time they were about this work was the interval of seven months; and after this it was that was ended the first year since their departure out of Egypt. But at the beginning of the second year, on the month *Xanthicus,* as the Macedonians call it, but on the month *Nisan,* as the Hebrews call it, on the new moon, they consecrated the tabernacle, and all its vessels, which I have already described.

5. Now God showed himself pleased with the work of the Hebrews, and did not permit their labors to be in vain; nor did he disdain to make use of what they had made, but he came and sojourned with them, and pitched his tabernacle in the holy house. And in the following manner did he come to it:—The sky was clear, but there was a mist over the tabernacle only, encompassing it, but not with such a very deep and thick cloud as is seen in the winter season, nor yet in so thin a one as men might be able to discern anything through it, but from it there dropped a sweet dew, and such a one as showed the presence of God to those that desired and believed it.

6. Now when Moses had bestowed such honorary presents on the workmen, as it was fit they should receive, who had wrought so well, he offered sacrifices in the open court of the tabernacle, as God commanded him; a bull, a ram, and a kid of the goats, for a sin-offering. Now I shall speak of what we do in our sacred offices in my discourse about sacrifices; and

therein shall inform men in what cases Moses bid us offer a whole burnt-offering, and in what cases the law permits us to partake of them as of food. And when Moses had sprinkled Aaron's vestments, himself, and his sons, with the blood of the beasts that were slain, and had purified them with spring waters and ointment, they became God's priests. After this manner did he consecrate them and their garments for seven days together. The same he did to the tabernacle, and the vessels thereto belonging, both with oil first incensed, as I said, and with the blood of bulls and of rams, slain day by day one, according to its kind. But on the eighth day he appointed a feast for the people, and commanded them to offer sacrifice according to their ability. Accordingly they contended one with another, and were ambitious to exceed each other in the sacrifices which they brought, and so fulfilled Moses's injunctions. But as the sacrifices lay upon the altar, a sudden fire was kindled from among them of its own accord, and appeared to the sight like fire from a flash of lightning, and consumed whatsoever was upon the altar.

7. Hereupon an affliction befell Aaron, considered as a man and a father, but was undergone by him with true fortitude; for he had indeed a firmness of soul in such accidents, and he thought this calamity came upon him according to God's will: for whereas he had four sons, as I said before, the two elder of them, Nadab and Abihu, did not bring those sacrifices which Moses bade them bring, but which they used to offer formerly, and were burnt to death. Now when the fire rushed upon them, and began to burn them, nobody could quench it. Accordingly they died in this manner. And Moses bid their father and their brethren to take up their bodies, to carry them out of the camp, and to bury them magnificently. Now the multitude lamented them, and were deeply affected at this their death, which so unexpectedly befell them. But Moses entreated their brethren and their father not to be troubled for them, and to prefer the honor of God before their grief about them; for Aaron had already put on his sacred garments.

8. But Moses refused all that honor which he saw the multitude ready to bestow upon him, and attended to nothing else but the service of God. He went no more up to Mount Sinai; but he went into the tabernacle, and brought back answers from God for what he prayed for. His habit was also that of a private man, and in all other circumstances he behaved himself like one of the common people, and was desirous to appear without distinguishing himself from the multitude, but would have it known that he did nothing else but take care of them. He also set down in writing the form of their government, and those laws by obedience whereto they would lead their lives so as to please God, and so as to have no quarrels one among another. However, the laws he ordained were such

as God suggested to him; so I shall now discourse concerning that form of government, and those laws.

9. I will now treat of what I before omitted, the garment of the high priest: for he [Moses] left no room for the evil practices of [false] prophets; but if some of that sort should attempt to abuse the Divine authority, he left it to God to be present at his sacrifices when he pleased, and when he pleased to be absent. And he was willing this should be known, not to the Hebrews only, but to those foreigners also who were there. For as to those stones,[12] which we told you before, the high priest bare on his shoulders, which were sardonyxes, (and I think it needless to describe

---

12. These answers by the oracle of Urim and Thummim, which words signify, light and perfection, or, as the Septuagint render them, revelation and truth, and denote nothing further, that I see, but the shining stones themselves, which were used, in this method of illumination, in revealing the will of God, after a perfect and true manner, to his people Israel: I say, these answers were not made by the shining of the precious stones, after an awkward manner, in the high priest's breastplate, as the modern Rabbins vainly suppose; for certainly the shining of the stones might precede or accompany the oracle, without itself delivering that oracle (see book 6, section 4); but rather by an audible voice from the mercy-seat between the cherubims. . . . This oracle had been silent, as Josephus here informs us, two hundred years before he wrote his *Antiquities*, or ever since the days of the last good high priest of the family of the Maccabees, John Hyrcanus. Now it is here very well worth our observation, that the oracle before us was that by which God appeared to be present with, and gave directions to, his people Israel as their King, all the while they submitted to him in that capacity; and did not set over them such independent kings as governed according to their own wills and political maxims, instead of Divine directions. Accordingly we meet with this oracle (besides angelic and prophetic admonitions) all along from the days of Moses and Joshua to the anointing of Saul, the first of the succession of the kings (Numbers 27:21; Joshua 6:6, etc.; 19:50; Judges 1:1; 18:4-6, 30, 31; 20:18, 23, 26-28; 21:1, etc.; 1 Samuel 1:17, 18; 3; 4), nay, till Saul's rejection of the Divine commands in the war with Amalek, when he took upon him to act as he thought fit (1 Samuel 14:3, 18, 19, 36, 37), then this oracle left Saul entirely, which indeed he had seldom consulted before (1 Samuel 14:35; 1 Chronicles 10:14; 13:3); and accompanied David, who was anointed to succeed him, and who consulted God by it frequently, and complied with its directions constantly (1 Samuel 14:37, 41; 15:26; 22:13, 15; 23:9, 10; 30:7, 8, 18; 2 Samuel 2:1; 5:19, 23; 21:1; 23:14; 1 Chronicles 14:10, 14). Saul, indeed, long after his rejection by God, and when God had given him up to destruction for his disobedience, did once afterwards endeavor to consult God when it was too late; but God would not then answer him, neither by dreams, nor by Urim, nor by prophets (1 Samuel 28:6). Nor did any of David's successors, the kings of Judah, that we know of, consult God by this oracle, till the very Babylonish captivity itself, when those kings were at an end; they taking upon them, I suppose, too much of despotic power and royalty, and too little owning the God of Israel for the supreme King of Israel, though a few of them consulted the prophets sometimes, and were answered by them. At the return of the two tribes, without the return of the kingly government, the restoration of this oracle was expected (Nehemiah 7:63; 1 Esd. 5:40; 1 Macc. 4:46; 14:41). And indeed it may seem to have been restored for some time after the Babylonish captivity, at least in the days of that excellent high priest, John Hyrcanus, whom Josephus esteemed as a king, a priest, and a prophet; and who, he says, foretold several things that came to pass accordingly; but about the time of his death, he here implies, that this oracle quite ceased, and not before. The following high priests now putting diadems on their heads, and ruling according to their own will, and by their own authority, like the other kings of the pagan countries about them; so that while the God of Israel was allowed to be the supreme King of Israel, and his

their nature, they being known to everybody,) the one of them shined out when God was present at their sacrifices; I mean that which was in the nature of a button on his right shoulder, bright rays darting out thence, and being seen even by those that were most remote; which splendor yet was not before natural to the stone. This has appeared a wonderful thing to such as have not so far indulged themselves in philosophy, as to despise Divine revelation. Yet will I mention what is still more wonderful than this: for God declared beforehand, by those twelve stones which the high priest bare on his breast, and which were inserted into his breastplate, when they should be victorious in battle; for so great a splendor shone forth from them before the army began to march, that all the people were sensible of God's being present for their assistance. Whence it came to pass that those Greeks, who had a veneration for our laws, because they could not possibly contradict this, called that breastplate *the Oracle*. Now this breastplate, and this sardonyx, left off shining two hundred years before I composed this book, God having been displeased at the transgressions of his laws. Of which things we shall further discourse on a fitter opportunity; but I will now go on with my proposed narration.

10. The tabernacle being now consecrated, and a regular order being settled for the priests, the multitude judged that God now dwelt among them, and betook themselves to sacrifices and praises to God as being now delivered from all expectation of evils and as entertaining a hopeful prospect of better times hereafter. They offered also gifts to God some as

---

directions to be their authentic guides, God gave them such directions as their supreme King and Governor, and they were properly under a theocracy, by this oracle of Urim, but no longer . . . ; though I confess I cannot but esteem the high priest Jaddus's divine dream (*Antiquities*, book 11, chapter 8, section 4), and the high priest Caiaphas's most remarkable prophecy (John 11:47-52), as two small remains or specimens of this ancient oracle, which properly belonged to the Jewish high priests: nor perhaps ought we entirely to forget that eminent prophetic dream of our Josephus himself, (one next to a high priest, as of the family of the Asamoneans or Maccabees,) as to the succession of Vespasian and Titus to the Roman empire, and that in the days of Nero, and before either Galba, Otho, or Vitellius were thought of to succeed him. . . . This, I think, may well be looked on as the very last instance of anything like the prophetic Urim among the Jewish nation, and just preceded their fatal desolation: but how it could possibly come to pass that such great men as Sir John Marsham and Dr. Spenser, should imagine that this oracle of Urim and Thummim with other practices as old or older than the law of Moses, should have been ordained in imitation of somewhat like them among the Egyptians, which we never hear of till the days of Diodorus Siculus, Aelian, and Maimonides, or little earlier than the Christian era at the highest, is almost unaccountable; while the main business of the law of Moses was evidently to preserve the Israelites from the idolatrous and superstitious practices of the neighboring pagan nations; and while it is so undeniable, that the evidence for the great antiquity of Moses's law is incomparably beyond that for the like or greater antiquity of such customs in Egypt or other nations, which indeed is generally none at all, it is most absurd to derive any of Moses's laws from the imitation of those heathen practices, Such hypotheses demonstrate to us how far inclination can prevail over evidence, in even some of the most learned part of mankind.

common to the whole nation, and others as peculiar to themselves, and these tribe by tribe; for the heads of the tribes combined together, two by two, and brought a wagon and a yoke of oxen. These amounted to six, and they carried the tabernacle when they journeyed. Besides which, each head of a tribe brought a bowl, and a charger, and a spoon, of ten darics, full of incense. Now the charger and the bowl were of silver, and together they weighed two hundred shekels, but the bowl cost no more than seventy shekels; and these were full of fine flour mingled with oil, such as they used on the altar about the sacrifices. They brought also a young bullock, and a ram, with a lamb of a year old, for a whole burnt-offering, as also a goat for the forgiveness of sins. Every one of the heads of the tribes brought also other sacrifices, called *peace-offerings,* for every day two bulls, and five rams, with lambs of a year old, and kids of the goats. These heads of tribes were twelve days in sacrificing, one sacrificing every day. Now Moses went no longer up to Mount Sinai, but went into the tabernacle, and learned of God what they were to do, and what laws should be made; which laws were preferable to what have been devised by human understanding, and proved to be firmly observed for all time to come, as being believed to be the gift of God, insomuch that the Hebrews did not transgress any of those laws, either as tempted in times of peace by luxury, or in times of war by distress of affairs. But I say no more here concerning them, because I have resolved to compose another work concerning our laws.

9: THE MANNER OF OUR OFFERING SACRIFICES

1. I will now, however, make mention of a few of our laws which belong to purifications, and the like sacred offices, since I am accidentally come to this matter of sacrifices. These sacrifices were of two sorts; of those sorts one was offered for private persons, and the other for the people in general; and they are done in two different ways. In the one case, what is slain is burnt, as a whole burnt-offering, whence that name is given to it; but the other is a thank-offering, and is designed for feasting those that sacrifice. I will speak of the former. Suppose a private man offer a burnt-offering, he must slay either a bull, a lamb, or a kid of the goats, and the two latter of the first year, though of bulls he is permitted to sacrifice those of a greater age; but all burnt-offerings are to be of males. When they are slain, the priests sprinkle the blood round about the altar; they then cleanse the bodies, and divide them into parts, and salt them with salt, and lay them upon the altar, while the pieces of wood are piled one upon another, and the fire is burning; they next cleanse the feet of the sacrifices, and the inwards, in an accurate manner and so lay them to the

rest to be purged by the fire, while the priests receive the hides. This is the way of offering a burnt-offering.

2. But those that offer thank-offerings do indeed sacrifice the same creatures, but such as are unblemished, and above a year old; however, they may take either males or females. They also sprinkle the altar with their blood; but they lay upon the altar the kidneys and the caul, and all the fat, and the lobe of the liver, together with the rump of the lamb; then, giving the breast and the right shoulder to the priests, the offerers feast upon the remainder of the flesh for two days; and what remains they burn.

3. The sacrifices for sins are offered in the same manner as is the thank-offering. But those who are unable to purchase complete sacrifices, offer two pigeons, or turtle doves; the one of which is made a burnt-offering to God, the other they give as food to the priests. But we shall treat more accurately about the oblation of these creatures in our discourse concerning sacrifices. But if a person fall into sin by ignorance, he offers an ewe lamb, or a female kid of the goats, of the same age; and the priests sprinkle the blood at the altar, not after the former manner, but at the corners of it. They also bring the kidneys and the rest of the fat, together with the lobe of the liver, to the altar, while the priests bear away the hides and the flesh, and spend it in the holy place, on the same day; for the law does not permit them to leave of it until the morning. But if anyone sin, and is conscious of it himself, but hath nobody that can prove it upon him, he offers a ram, the law enjoining him so to do; the flesh of which the priests eat, as before, in the holy place, on the same day. And if the rulers offer sacrifices for their sins, they bring the same oblations that private men do; only they so far differ, that they are to bring for sacrifices a bull or a kid of the goats, both males.

4. Now the law requires, both in private and public sacrifices, that the finest flour be also brought; for a lamb the measure of one tenth deal,—for a ram two,—and for a bull three. This they consecrate upon the altar, when it is mingled with oil; for oil is also brought by those that sacrifice; for a bull the half of an hin, and for a ram the third part of the same measure, and one quarter of it for a lamb. This hin is an ancient Hebrew measure, and is equivalent to two Athenian choas (or congiuses). They bring the same quantity of oil which they do of wine, and they pour the wine about the altar; but if anyone does not offer a complete sacrifice of animals, but brings fine flour only for a vow, he throws a handful upon the altar as its first-fruits, while the priests take the rest for their food, either boiled or mingled with oil, but made into cakes of bread. But whatsoever it be that a priest himself offers, it must of necessity be all burnt. Now the law forbids us to sacrifice any animal at the same time with its dam;

and, in other cases, not till the eighth day after its birth. Other sacrifices there are also appointed for escaping distempers, or for other occasions, in which meat-offerings are consumed, together with the animals that are sacrificed; of which it is not lawful to leave any part till the next day, only the priests are to take their own share.

10: THE FESTIVALS

1. The law requires, that out of the public expenses a lamb of the first year be killed every day, at the beginning and at the ending of the day; but on the seventh day, which is called the *Sabbath,* they kill two, and sacrifice them in the same manner. At the new moon, they both perform the daily sacrifices, and slay two bulls, with seven lambs of the first year, and a kid of the goats also, for the expiation of sins; that is, if they have sinned through ignorance.

2. But on the seventh month, which the Macedonians call *Hyperbere-taeus,* they make an addition to those already mentioned, and sacrifice a bull, a ram, and seven lambs, and a kid of the goats, for sins.

3. On the tenth day of the same lunar month, they fast till the evening; and this day they sacrifice a bull, and two rams, and seven lambs, and a kid of the goats, for sins. And, besides these, they bring two kids of the goats; the one of which is sent alive out of the limits of the camp into the wilderness for the scapegoat, and to be an expiation for the sins of the whole multitude; but the other is brought into a place of great cleanness, within the limits of the camp, and is there burnt, with its skin, without any sort of cleansing. With this goat was burnt a bull, not brought by the people, but by the high priest, at his own charges; which, when it was slain, he brought of the blood into the holy place, together with the blood of the kid of the goats, and sprinkled the ceiling with his finger seven times, as also its pavement, and again as often toward the most holy place, and about the golden altar: he also at last brings it into the open court, and sprinkles it about the great altar. Besides this, they set the extremities, and the kidneys, and the fat, with the lobe of the liver, upon the altar. The high priest likewise presents a ram to God as a burnt-offering.

4. Upon the fifteenth day of the same month, when the season of the year is changing for winter, the law enjoins us to pitch tabernacles in every one of our houses, so that we preserve ourselves from the cold of that time of the year; as also that when we should arrive at our own country, and come to that city which we should have then for our metropolis, because of the temple therein to be built, and keep a festival for eight days, and offer burnt-offerings, and sacrifice thank-offerings, that we should then carry in

our hands a branch of myrtle, and willow, and a bough of the palm-tree, with the addition of the pome citron: That the burnt-offering on the first of those days was to be a sacrifice of thirteen bulls, and fourteen lambs, and fifteen rams, with the addition of a kid of the goats, as an expiation for sins; and on the following days the same number of lambs, and of rams, with the kids of the goats; but abating one of the bulls every day till they amounted to seven only. On the eighth day all work was laid aside, and then, as we said before, they sacrificed to God a bullock, a ram, and seven lambs, with a kid of the goats, for an expiation of sins. And this is the accustomed solemnity of the Hebrews, when they pitch their tabernacles.

5. In the month of Xanthicus, which is by us called *Nisan,* and is the beginning of our year, on the fourteenth day of the lunar month, when the sun is in Aries, (for in this month it was that we were delivered from bondage under the Egyptians,) the law ordained that we should every year slay that sacrifice which I before told you we slew when we came out of Egypt, and which was called the *Passover;* and so we do celebrate this passover in companies, leaving nothing of what we sacrifice till the day following. The feast of unleavened bread succeeds that of the passover, and falls on the fifteenth day of the month, and continues seven days, wherein they feed on unleavened bread; on every one of which days two bulls are killed, and one ram, and seven lambs. Now these lambs are entirely burnt, besides the kid of the goats which is added to all the rest, for sins; for it is intended as a feast for the priest on every one of those days. But on the second day of unleavened bread, which is the sixteenth day of the month, they first partake of the fruits of the earth, for before that day they do not touch them. And while they suppose it proper to honor God, from whom they obtain this plentiful provision, in the first place, they offer the first-fruits of their barley, and that in the manner following: They take a handful of the ears, and dry them, then beat them small, and purge the barley from the bran; they then bring one tenth deal to the altar, to God; and, casting one handful of it upon the fire, they leave the rest for the use of the priest. And after this it is that they may publicly or privately reap their harvest. They also at this participation of the first-fruits of the earth, sacrifice a lamb, as a burnt-offering to God.

6. When a week of weeks has passed over after this sacrifice, (which weeks contain forty and nine days,) on the fiftieth day, which is Pentecost, but is called by the Hebrews *Asartha,* which signifies *Pentecost,* they bring to God a loaf, made of wheat flour, of two tenth deals, with leaven; and for sacrifices they bring two lambs; and when they have only presented them to God, they are made ready for supper for the priests; nor is it permitted to leave anything of them till the day following. They also slay

three bullocks for a burnt-offering, and two rams; and fourteen lambs, with two kids of the goats, for sins; nor is there anyone of the festivals but in it they offer burnt-offerings; they also allow themselves to rest on every one of them. Accordingly, the law prescribes in them all what kinds they are to sacrifice, and how they are to rest entirely, and must slay sacrifices, in order to feast upon them.

7. However, out of the common charges, baked bread [was set on the table of shew-bread], without leaven, of twenty-four tenth deals of flour, for so much is spent upon this bread; two heaps of these were baked, they were baked the day before the sabbath, but were brought into the holy place on the morning of the sabbath, and set upon the holy table, six on a heap, one loaf still standing over against another; where two golden cups full of frankincense were also set upon them, and there they remained till another sabbath, and then other loaves were brought in their stead, while the loaves were given to the priests for their food, and the frankincense was burnt in that sacred fire wherein all their offerings were burnt also; and so other frankincense was set upon the loaves instead of what was there before. The [high priest] also, of his own charges, offered a sacrifice, and that twice every day. It was made of flour mingled with oil, and gently baked by the fire; the quantity was one tenth deal of flour; he brought the half of it to the fire in the morning, and the other half at night. The account of these sacrifices I shall give more accurately hereafter; but I think I have premised what for the present may be sufficient concerning them.

11: THE PURIFICATIONS

1. Moses took out the tribe of Levi from communicating with the rest of the people, and set them apart to be a holy tribe; and purified them by water taken from perpetual springs, and with such sacrifices as were usually offered to God on the like occasions. He delivered to them also the tabernacle, and the sacred vessels, and the other curtains, which were made for covering the tabernacle, that they might minister under the conduct of the priests, who had been already consecrated to God.

2. He also determined concerning animals; which of them might be used for food, and which they were obliged to abstain from; which matters, when this work shall give me occasion, shall be further explained; and the causes shall be added by which he was moved to allot some of them to be our food, and enjoined us to abstain from others. However, he entirely forbade us the use of blood for food, and esteemed it to contain the soul and spirit. He also forbade us to eat the flesh of an animal that died of itself, as also the caul, and the fat of goats, and sheep, and bulls.

3. He also ordered that those whose bodies were afflicted with leprosy, and that had a gonorrhea, should not come into the city;[13] nay, he removed the women, when they had their natural purgations, till the seventh day; after which he looked on them as pure, and permitted them to come in again. The law permits those also who have taken care of funerals to come in after the same manner, when this number of days is over; but if any continued longer than that number of days in a state of pollution, the law appointed the offering two lambs for a sacrifice; the one of which they are to purge by fire, and for the other, the priests take it for themselves. In the same manner do those sacrifice who have had the gonorrhea. But he that sheds his seed in his sleep, if he go down into cold water, has the same privilege with those that have lawfully accompanied with their wives. And for the lepers, he suffered them not to come into the city at all, nor to live with any others, as if they were in effect dead persons; but if anyone had obtained by prayer to God, the recovery from that distemper, and had gained a healthful complexion again, such a one returned thanks to God, with several sorts of sacrifices; concerning which we will speak hereafter.

4. Whence one cannot but smile at those who say that Moses was himself afflicted with the leprosy when he fled out of Egypt, and that he became the conductor of those who on that account left that country, and led them into the land of Canaan; for had this been true, Moses would not have made these laws to his own dishonor, which indeed it was more likely he would have opposed, if others had endeavored to introduce them; and this the rather, because there are lepers in many nations, who yet are in honor, and not only free from reproach and avoidance, but who have been great captains of armies, and been intrusted with high offices in the commonwealth, and have had the privilege of entering into holy places and temples; so that nothing hindered, but if either Moses himself, or the multitude that was with him, had been liable to such a misfortune in the color of his skin, he might have made laws about them for their credit and advantage, and have laid no manner of difficulty upon them. Accordingly, it is a plain case, that it is out of violent prejudice only that they report these things about us. But Moses was pure from any such distemper, and lived with countrymen who were pure of it also, and thence made the laws which concerned others that had the distemper. He did this for the honor of God. But as to these matters, let everyone consider them after what manner he pleases.

---

13. We may here note, that Josephus frequently calls the camp the city, and the court of the Mosaic tabernacle a temple, and the tabernacle itself a holy house, with allusion to the latter city, temple, and holy house, which he knew so well long afterwards.

5. As to the women, when they have born a child, Moses forbade them to come into the temple, or touch the sacrifices, before forty days were over, supposing it to be a boy; but if she hath born a girl, the law is that she cannot be admitted before twice that number of days be over. And when after the before-mentioned time appointed for them, they perform their sacrifices, the priests distribute them before God.

6. But if anyone suspect that his wife has been guilty of adultery, he was to bring a tenth deal of barley flour; they then cast one handful to God and gave the rest of it to the priests for food. One of the priests set the woman at the gates that are turned towards the temple, and took the veil from her head, and wrote the name of God on parchment, and enjoined her to swear that she had not at all injured her husband; and to wish that, if she had violated her chastity, her right thigh might be put out of joint; that her belly might swell; and that she might die thus: but that if her husband, by the violence of his affection, and of the jealousy which arose from it, had been rashly moved to this suspicion, that she might bear a male child in the tenth month. Now when these oaths were over, the priest wiped the name of God out of the parchment, and wrung the water into a vial. He also took some dust out of the temple, if any happened to be there, and put a little of it into the vial, and gave it her to drink; whereupon the woman, if she were unjustly accused, conceived with child, and brought it to perfection in her womb: but if she had broken her faith of wedlock to her husband, and had sworn falsely before God, she died in a reproachful manner; her thigh fell off from her, and her belly swelled with a dropsy. And these are the ceremonies about sacrifices, and about the purifications thereto belonging, which Moses provided for his countrymen. He also prescribed the following laws to them:—

12: SEVERAL LAWS

1. As for adultery, Moses forbade it entirely, as esteeming it a happy thing that men should be wise in the affairs of wedlock; and that it was profitable both to cities and families that children should be known to be genuine. He also abhorred men's lying with their mothers, as one of the greatest crimes; and the like for lying with the father's wife, and with aunts, and sisters, and sons' wives, as all instances of abominable wickedness. He also forbade a man to lie with his wife when she was defiled by her natural purgation: and not to come near brute beasts; nor to approve of the lying with a male, which was to hunt after unlawful pleasures on account of beauty. To those who were guilty of such insolent behavior, he ordained death for their punishment.

2. As for the priests, he prescribed to them a double degree of purity for he restrained them in the instances above, and moreover forbade them to marry harlots. He also forbade them to marry a slave, or a captive, and such as got their living by cheating trades, and by keeping inns; as also a woman parted from her husband, on any account whatsoever. Nay, he did not think it proper for the high priest to marry even the widow of one that was dead, though he allowed that to the priests; but he permitted him only to marry a virgin, and to retain her. Whence it is that the high priest is not to come near to one that is dead, although the rest are not prohibited from coming near to their brethren, or parents, or children, when they are dead; but they are to be unblemished in all respects. He ordered that the priest who had any blemish, should have his portion indeed among the priests, but he forbade him to ascend the altar, or to enter into the holy house. He also enjoined them, not only to observe purity in their sacred ministrations, but in their daily conversation, that it might be unblamable also. And on this account it is that those who wear the sacerdotal garments are without spot, and eminent for their purity and sobriety: nor are they permitted to drink wine so long as they wear those garments.[14] Moreover, they offer sacrifices that are entire, and have no defect whatsoever.

3. And truly Moses gave them all these precepts, being such as were observed during his own lifetime; but though he lived now in the wilderness, yet did he make provision how they might observe the same laws when they should have taken the land of Canaan. He gave them rest to the land from ploughing and planting every seventh year, as he had prescribed to them to rest from working every seventh day; and ordered, that then what grew of its own accord out of the earth should in common belong to all that pleased to use it, making no distinction in that respect between their own countrymen and foreigners: and he ordained, that they should do the same after seven times seven years, which in all are fifty years; and that fiftieth year is called by the Hebrews *The Jubilee,* wherein debtors are freed from their debts, and slaves are set at liberty; which slaves became such, though they were of the same stock, by transgressing some of those laws the punishment of which was not capital, but they were punished by this method of slavery. This year also restores the land to its former possessors in the manner following:—When the Jubilee is come, which name denotes *liberty,* he that sold the land, and he that bought it, meet together, and make an estimate, on one hand, of the fruits gathered; and,

---

14. The precept given to the priests of not drinking wine while they wore the sacred garments, is equivalent; to their abstinence from it all the while they ministered in the temple; because they then always, and then only, wore those sacred garments, which were laid up there from one time of ministration to another.

on the other hand, of the expenses laid out upon it. If the fruits gathered come to more than the expenses laid out, he that sold it takes the land again; but if the expenses prove more than the fruits, the present possessor receives of the former owner the difference that was wanting, and leaves the land to him; and if the fruits received, and the expenses laid out, prove equal to one another, the present possessor relinquishes it to the former owners. Moses would have the same law obtain as to those houses also which were sold in villages; but he made a different law for such as were sold in a city; for if he that sold it tendered the purchaser his money again within a year, he was forced to restore it; but in case a whole year had intervened, the purchaser was to enjoy what he had bought. This was the constitution of the laws which Moses learned of God when the camp lay under Mount Sinai, and this he delivered in writing to the Hebrews.

4. Now when this settlement of laws seemed to be well over, Moses thought fit at length to take a review of the host, as thinking it proper to settle the affairs of war. So he charged the heads of the tribes, excepting the tribe of Levi, to take an exact account of the number of those that were able to go to war; for as to the Levites, they were holy, and free from all such burdens. Now when the people had been numbered, there were found six hundred thousand that were able to go to war, from twenty to fifty years of age, besides three thousand six hundred and fifty. Instead of Levi, Moses took Manasseh, the son of Joseph, among the heads of tribes; and Ephraim instead of Joseph. It was indeed the desire of Jacob himself to Joseph, that he would give him his sons to be his own by adoption, as I have before related.

5. When they set up the tabernacle, they received it into the midst of their camp, three of the tribes pitching their tents on each side of it; and roads were cut through the midst of these tents. It was like a well-appointed market; and everything was there ready for sale in due order; and all sorts of artificers were in the shops; and it resembled nothing so much as a city that sometimes was movable, and sometimes fixed. The priests had the first places about the tabernacle; then the Levites, who, because their whole multitude was reckoned from thirty days old, were twenty-three thousand eight hundred and eighty males; and during the time that the cloud stood over the tabernacle, they thought proper to stay in the same place, as supposing that God there inhabited among them; but when that removed, they journeyed also.

6. Moreover, Moses was the inventor of the form of their trumpet, which was made of silver. Its description is this:—In length it was little less than a cubit. It was composed of a narrow tube, somewhat thicker than a flute, but with so much breadth as was sufficient for admission of the breath

of a man's mouth: it ended in the form of a bell, like common trumpets. Its sound was called in the Hebrew tongue *Asosra.* Two of these being made, one of them was sounded when they required the multitude to come together to congregations. When the first of them gave a signal, the heads of the tribes were to assemble, and consult about the affairs to them properly belonging; but when they gave the signal by both of them, they called the multitude together. Whenever the tabernacle was removed, it was done in this solemn order:—At the first alarm of the trumpet, those whose tents were on the east quarter prepared to remove; when the second signal was given, those that were on the south quarter did the like; in the next place, the tabernacle was taken to pieces, and was carried in the midst of six tribes that went before, and of six that followed, all the Levites assisting about the tabernacle; when the third signal was given, that part which had their tents towards the west put themselves in motion; and at the fourth signal those on the north did so likewise. They also made use of these trumpets in their sacred ministrations, when they were bringing their sacrifices to the altar as well on the Sabbaths as on the rest of the [festival] days; and now it was that Moses offered that sacrifice which was called the *Passover in the Wilderness,* as the first he had offered after the departure out of Egypt.

13: HOW MOSES CONDUCTED THE PEOPLE TO THE BORDERS OF THE CANAANITES

A little while afterwards he rose up, and went from Mount Sinai; and, having passed through several mansions, of which we will speak he came to a place called *Hazeroth,* where the multitude began again to be mutinous, and to Moses for the misfortunes they had suffered their travels; and that when he had persuaded to leave a good land, they at once had lost land, and instead of that happy state he had them, they were still wandering in their miserable condition, being already in want water; and if the manna should happen to fail, must then utterly perish. Yet while they spake many and sore things against the there was one of them who exhorted them to be unmindful of Moses, and of what great pains he had been at about their common safety; not to despair of assistance from God. The multitude thereupon became still more unruly, and mutinous against Moses than before. Hereupon Moses, although he was so basely abused by them encouraged them in their despairing conditioned and promised that he would procure them a quantity of flesh-meat, and that not for a few days only, but for many days. This they were not to believe; and when one of them asked, whence he could obtain such vast plenty of what he promised, he replied, "Neither God nor I, we hear such opprobrious language from will leave off our labors for you; and this soon appear also." As soon as ever he had this, the whole camp was filled with quails, they stood round about them, and gathered great numbers. However, it was not long ere God punished the Hebrews for their insolence, those reproaches they had used towards him, no small number of them died; and still to this day the place retains the memory of this destruction and is named *Kibrothhattaavah,* which is, *Graves of Lust.*

14: HOW MOSES SENT SOME PERSONS TO SEARCH OUT THE LAND OF THE CANAANITES; AND HOW THE DISCOURAGED PEOPLE WERE RESOLVED TO RETURN TO EGYPT

1. When Moses had led the Hebrews away from thence to a place called *Paran,* which was near to the borders of the Canaanites, and a place difficult to be continued in, he gathered the multitude together to a congregation; and standing in the midst of them, he said, "Of the two things that God determined to bestow upon us, liberty, and the possession of a Happy Country, the one of them ye already are partakers of, by the gift of God, and the other you will quickly obtain; for we now have our abode near the borders of the Canaanites, and nothing can hinder the acquisition of it, when we now at last are fallen upon it: I say, not only no king nor city, but neither the whole race of mankind, if they were all gathered together, could do it. Let us therefore prepare ourselves for the work, for the Canaanites will not resign up their land to us without fighting, but it must be wrested from them by great struggles in war. Let us then send spies, who may take a view of the goodness of the land, and what strength it is of; but, above all things, let us be of one mind, and let us honor God, who above all is our helper and assister."

2. When Moses had said thus, the multitude requited him with marks of respect; and chose twelve spies, of the most eminent men, one out of each tribe, who, passing over all the land of Canaan, from the borders of Egypt, came to the city Hamath, and to Mount Lebanon; and having learned the nature of the land, and of its inhabitants, they came home, having spent forty days in the whole work. They also brought with them of the fruits which the land bare; they also showed them the excellency of those fruits, and gave an account of the great quantity of the good things that land afforded, which were motives to the multitude to go to war. But then they terrified them again with the great difficulty there was in obtaining it; that the rivers were so large and deep that they could not be passed over; and that the hills were so high that they could not travel along for them;

that the cities were strong with walls, and their firm fortifications round about them. They told them also, that they found at Hebron the posterity of the giants. Accordingly these spies, who had seen the land of Canaan, when they perceived that all these difficulties were greater there than they had met with since they came out of Egypt, they were affrighted at them themselves, and endeavored to affright the multitude also.

3. So they supposed, from what they had heard, that it was impossible to get the possession of the country. And when the congregation was dissolved, they, their wives and children, continued their lamentation, as if God would not indeed assist them, but only promised them fair. They also again blamed Moses, and made a clamor against him and his brother Aaron, the high priest. Accordingly they passed that night very ill, and with contumelious language against them; but in the morning they ran to a congregation, intending to stone Moses and Aaron, and so to return back into Egypt.

4. But of the spies, there were Joshua the son of Nun, of the tribe of Ephraim, and Caleb of the tribe of Judah, that were afraid of the consequence, and came into the midst of them, and stilled the multitude, and desired them to be of good courage; and neither to condemn God, as having told them lies, nor to hearken to those who had affrighted them, by telling them what was not true concerning the Canaanites, but to those that encouraged them to hope for good success; and that they should gain possession of the happiness promised them, because neither the height of mountains, nor the depth of rivers, could hinder men of true courage from attempting them, especially while God would take care of them beforehand, and be assistant to them. "Let us then go," said they, "against our enemies, and have no suspicion of ill success, trusting in God to conduct us, and following those that are to be our leaders." Thus did these two exhort them, and endeavor to pacify the rage they were in. But Moses and Aaron fell on the ground, and besought God, not for their own deliverance, but that he would put a stop to what the people were unwarily doing, and would bring their minds to a quiet temper, which were now disordered by their present passion. The cloud also did now appear, and stood over the tabernacle, and declared to them the presence of God to be there.

15: HOW MOSES FORETOLD THAT GOD WAS ANGRY AND THAT THEY SHOULD CONTINUE IN THE WILDERNESS FOR FORTY YEARS

1. Moses came now boldly to the multitude, and informed them that God was moved at their abuse of him, and would inflict punishment upon

them, not indeed such as they deserved for their sins, but such as parents inflict on their children, in order to their correction. For, he said, that when he was in the tabernacle, and was bewailing with ears that destruction which was coming upon them God put him in mind what things he had done for them, and what benefits they had received from him, and yet how ungrateful they had been to him that just now they had been induced, through the timorousness of the spies, to think that their words were truer than his own promise to them; and that on this account, though he would not indeed destroy them all, nor utterly exterminate their nation, which he had honored more than any other part of mankind, yet he would not permit them to take possession of the land of Canaan, nor enjoy its happiness; but would make them wander in the wilderness, and live without a fixed habitation, and without a city, for forty years together, as a punishment for this their transgression; but that he had promised to give that land to our children, and that he would make them the possessors of those good things which, by your ungoverned passions, you have deprived yourselves of.

2. When Moses had discoursed thus to them according to the direction of God, the multitude, grieved, and were in affliction; and entreated Most to procure their reconciliation to God, and to permit them no longer to wander in the wilderness, but bestow cities upon them. But he replied, that God would not admit of any such trial, for that God was not moved to this determination from any human levity or anger, but that he had judicially condemned them to that punishment. Now we are not to disbelieve that Moses, who was but a single person, pacified so many ten thousands when they were in anger, and converted them to a mildness temper; for God was with him, and prepared way to his persuasions of the multitude; and as they had often been disobedient, they were now sensible that such disobedience was disadvantageous to them and that they had still thereby fallen into calamities.

3. But this man was admirable for his virtue, and powerful in making men give credit to what he delivered, not only during the time of his natural life, but even there is still no one of the Hebrews who does not act even now as if Moses were present, and ready to punish him if he should do anything that is indecent; nay, there is no one but is obedient to what laws he ordained, although they might be concealed in their transgressions. There are also many other demonstrations that his power was more than human, for still some there have been, who have come from the parts beyond Euphrates, a journey of four months, through many dangers, and at great expenses, in honor of our temple; and yet, when they had offered their oblations, could not partake of their own sacrifices, because Moses had forbidden it, by somewhat in the law that did not

permit them, or somewhat that had befallen them, which our ancient customs made inconsistent therewith; some of these did not sacrifice at all, and others left their sacrifices in an imperfect condition; many were not able, even at first, so much as to enter the temple, but went their ways in this as preferring a submission to the laws of Moses before the fulfilling of their own inclinations, they had no fear upon them that anybody could convict them, but only out of a reverence to their own conscience. Thus this legislation, which appeared to be divine, made this man to be esteemed as one superior to his own nature. Nay, further, a little before the beginning of this war, when Claudius was emperor of the Romans, and Ismael was our high priest, and when so great a famine was come upon us, that one tenth deal [of wheat] was sold for four drachmae, and when no less than seventy cori of flour were brought into the temple, at the feast of unleavened bread, (these cori are thirty-one Sicilian, but forty-one Athenian medimni,) not one of the priests was so hardy as to eat one crumb of it, even while so great a distress was upon the land; and this out of a dread of the law, and of that wrath which God retains against acts of wickedness, even when no one can accuse the actors. Whence we are not to wonder at what was then done, while to this very day the writings left by Moses have so great a force, that even those that hate us do confess, that he who established this settlement was God, and that it was by the means of Moses, and of his virtue; but as to these matters, let everyone take them as he thinks fit.

Chapter 3

THE REJECTION OF THAT GENERATION TO THE
DEATH OF MOSES

1: FIGHT OF THE HEBREWS WITH THE CANAANITES WITHOUT THE CONSENT OF MOSES; AND THEIR DEFEAT

1. Now this life of the Hebrews in the wilderness was so disagreeable and troublesome to them, and they were so uneasy at it, that although God had forbidden them to meddle with the Canaanites, yet could they not be persuaded to be obedient to the words of Moses, and to be quiet; but supposing they should be able to beat their enemies, without his approbation, they accused him, and suspected that he made it his business to keep in a distressed condition, that they might always stand in need of his assistance. Accordingly they resolved to fight with the Canaanites, and said that God gave them his assistance, not out of regard to Moses's intercessions, but because he took care of their entire nation, on account of their forefathers, whose affairs he took under his own conduct; as also, that it was on account of their own virtue that he had formerly procured them their liberty, and would be assisting to them, now they were willing to take pains for it. They also said that they were possessed of abilities sufficient for the conquest of their enemies, although Moses should have a mind to alienate God from them; that, however, it was for their advantage to be their own masters, and not so far to rejoice in their deliverance from the indignities they endured under the Egyptians, as to bear the tyranny of Moses over them, and to suffer themselves to be deluded, and live according to his pleasure, as though God did only foretell what concerns us out of his kindness to him, as if they were not all the posterity of Abraham; that God made him alone the author of all the knowledge we have, and we must still learn it from him; that it would be a piece of prudence to oppose his arrogant pretenses, and to put their confidence in

God, and to resolve to take possession of that land which he had promised them, and not to give ear to him, who on this account, and under the pretense of Divine authority, forbade them so to do. Considering, therefore, the distressed state they were in at present, and that in those desert places they were still to expect things would be worse with them, they resolved to fight with the Canaanites, as submitting only to God, their supreme Commander, and not waiting for any assistance from their legislator.

2. When, therefore, they had come to this resolution, as being best for them, they went against their enemies; but those enemies were not dismayed either at the attack itself, or at the great multitude that made it, and received them with great courage. Many of the Hebrews were slain; and the remainder of the army, upon the disorder of their troops, were pursued, and fled, after a shameful manner, to their camp. Whereupon this unexpected misfortune made them quite despond; and they hoped for nothing that was good; as gathering from it, that this affliction came from the wrath of God, because they rashly went out to war without his approbation.

3. But when Moses saw how deeply they were affected with this defeat, and being afraid lest the enemies should grow insolent upon this victory, and should be desirous of gaining still greater glory, and should attack them, he resolved that it was proper to withdraw the army into the wilderness to a further distance from the Canaanites: so the multitude gave themselves up again to his conduct, for they were sensible that, without his care for them, their affairs could not be in a good condition; and he caused the host to remove, and he went further into the wilderness, as intending there to let them rest, and not to permit them to fight the Canaanites before God should afford them a more favorable opportunity.

2: THE SEDITION OF CORAH AND OF THE MULTITUDE AGAINST MOSES AND HIS BROTHER

1. That which is usually the case of great armies, and especially upon ill success, to be hard to be pleased, and governed with difficulty, did now befall the Jews; for they being in number six hundred thousand, and by reason of their great multitude not readily subject to their governors, even in prosperity, they at this time were more than usually angry, both against one another and against their leader, because of the distress they were in, and the calamities they then endured. Such a sedition overtook them, as we have not the like example either among the Greeks or the Barbarians, by which they were in danger of being all destroyed, but were notwithstanding saved by Moses, who would not remember that he had

been almost stoned to death by them. Nor did God neglect to prevent their ruin; but, notwithstanding the indignities they had offered their legislator and the laws, and disobedience to the commandments which he had sent them by Moses, he delivered them from those terrible calamities which, without his providential care, had been brought upon them by this sedition. So I will first explain the cause whence this sedition arose, and then will give an account of the sedition itself; as also of what settlements made for their government after it was over.

2. Corah, a Hebrew of principal account, both by his family and by his wealth, one that was also able to speak well, and one that could easily persuade the people by his speeches, saw that Moses was in an exceeding great dignity, and was at it, and envied him on that account, (he of the same tribe with Moses, and of kin to him,) was particularly grieved, because he thought he better deserved that honorable post on account of great riches, and not inferior to him in his birth. So he raised a clamor against him among the Levites, who were of the same tribe, and among his kindred, saying, "That it was a very sad thing that they should overlook Moses, while hunted after and paved the way to glory for himself, and by ill arts should obtain it, under the pretense of God's command, while, contrary to laws, he had given the priesthood to Aaron, the common suffrage of the multitude, but by his own vote, as bestowing dignities in a way on whom he pleased." He added, "That this concealed way of imposing on them was harder to be borne than if it had been done by an open force upon them, because he did now not only their power without their consent, but even they were unapprised of his contrivances against them; for whosoever is conscious to himself that he deserves any dignity, aims to get it by persuasion, and not by an arrogant method of violence; those that believe it impossible to obtain honors justly, make a show of goodness, and do not introduce force, but by cunning tricks grow wickedly powerful. That it was proper for the multitude to punish such men, even while they think themselves concealed in their designs, and not suffer them to gain strength till they have them for their open enemies. For what account," added he, "is Moses able to give, why he has bestowed the priesthood on Aaron and his sons? for if God had determined to bestow that honor on one of the tribe of Levi, I am more worthy of it than he is; I myself being equal to Moses by my family, and superior to him both in riches and in age: but if God had determined to bestow it on the eldest be, that of Reuben might have it most justly; and then Dathan, and Abiram, and [On, the son of] Peleth, would have it; for these are the oldest men of that tribe, and potent on account of their great wealth also."

3. Now Corah, when he said this, had a mind to appear to take care of the public welfare, but in reality he was endeavoring to procure to have that dignity transferred by the multitude to himself. Thus did he, out of a malignant design, but with discourse to those of his own tribe; when these words did gradually spread to more people, and when the hearers still added to what tended to the scandals that were cast upon the whole army was full of them. Now of those that conspired with Corah, there were two hundred and fifty, and those of the principal men also, who were eager to have the priesthood taken away from Moses's brother, and to bring him into disgrace: nay, the multitude themselves were provoked to be seditious, and attempted to stone Moses, wad gathered themselves together after an indecent manner, with confusion and disorder. And now all were, in a tumultuous manner, raising a before the tabernacle of God, to prosecute the tyrant, and to relieve the multitude from their slavery under him who, under color of the Divine laid violent injunctions upon them; for had it been God who chose one that was to the office of a priest, he would have raised person to that dignity, and would not [have] produced such a one as was inferior to many others nor have given him that office; and that in he had judged it fit to bestow it on Aaron, he would have permitted it to the multitude to bestow it, and not have left it to be bestowed by his own brother.

4. Now although Moses had a great while ago foreseen this calumny of Corah, and had seen the people were irritated, yet was he not affrighted at it; but being of good courage, because given them right advice about their affairs, and knowing that his brother had been made partaker of the priesthood at the command of God, and not by his own favor to him, he came to the assembly; and as for the multitude, he said not a word to them, but spake as loud to Corah as he could; and being very skillful in making speeches, and having this natural talent, among others, that he could greatly move the multitude with his discourses, he said, "O Corah, both thou and all these with thee (pointing to the two hundred and fifty men) seem to be worthy of this honor; nor do I pretend but that this whole company may be worthy of the like dignity, although they may not be so rich or so great as you are: nor have I taken and given this office to my brother because he excelled others in riches, for thou exceedest us both in the greatness of thy wealth;[1] nor indeed because he was of an eminent family, for God, by giving us the same common ancestor, has made our families equal: nay, nor was it out of brotherly affection, which

---

1. Although our Bibles say little or nothing of these riches of Corah, both the Jews and Mahommedans, as well as Josephus, are full of it.

another might yet have justly done; for certainly, unless I had bestowed this honor out of regard to God, and to his laws, I had not passed by myself, and given it to another, as being nearer of kin to myself than to my brother, and having a closer intimacy with myself than I have with him; for surely it would not be a wise thing for me to expose myself to the dangers of offending, and to bestow the happy employment on this account upon another. But I am above such base practices: nor would God have overlooked this matter, and seen himself thus despised; nor would he have suffered you to be ignorant of what you were to do, in order to please him; but he hath himself chosen one that is to perform that sacred office to him, and thereby freed us from that care. So that it was not a thing that I pretend to give, but only according to the determination of God; I therefore propose it still to be contended for by such as please to put in for it, only desiring that he who has been already preferred, and has already obtained it, may be allowed now also to offer himself for a candidate. He prefers your peace, and your living without sedition, to this honorable employment, although in truth it was with your approbation that he obtained it; for though God were the donor, yet do we not offend when we think fit to accept it with your good-will; yet would it have been an instance of impiety not to have taken that honorable employment when he offered it; nay, it had been exceedingly unreasonable, when God had thought fit anyone should have it for all time to come, and had made it secure and firm to him, to have refused it. However, he himself will judge again who it shall be whom he would have to offer sacrifices to him, and to have the direction of matters of religion; for it is absurd that Corah, who is ambitious of this honor, should deprive God of the power of giving it to whom he pleases. Put an end, therefore, to your sedition and disturbance on this account; and tomorrow morning do every one of you that desire the priesthood bring a censer from home, and come hither with incense and fire: and do thou, O Corah, leave the judgment to God, and await to see on which side he will give his determination upon this occasion, but do not thou make thyself greater than God. Do thou also come, that this contest about this honorable employment may receive determination. And I suppose we may admit Aaron without offense, to offer himself to this scrutiny, since he is of the same lineage with thyself, and has done nothing in his priesthood that can be liable to exception. Come ye therefore together, and offer your incense in public before all the people; and when you offer it, he whose sacrifice God shall accept shall be ordained to the priesthood, and shall be clear of the present calumny on Aaron, as if I had granted him that favor because he was my brother."

3: HOW THOSE THAT STIRRED UP THIS SEDITION WERE DESTROYED

1. When Moses had said this, the multitude left off the turbulent behavior they had indulged, and the suspicion they had of Moses, and commended what he had said; for those proposals were good, and were so esteemed of the people. At that time therefore they dissolved the assembly. But on the next day they came to the congregation, in order to be present at the sacrifice, and at the determination that was to be made between the candidates for the priesthood. Now this congregation proved a turbulent one, and the multitude were in great suspense in expectation of what was to be done; for some of them would have been pleased if Moses had been convicted of evil practices, but the wiser sort desired that they might be delivered from the present disorder and disturbance; for they were afraid, that if this sedition went on, the good order of their settlement would rather be destroyed; but the whole body of the people do naturally delight in clamors against their governors, and, by changing their opinions upon the harangues of every speaker, disturb the public tranquility. And now Moses sent messengers for Abiram and Dathan, and ordered them to come to the assembly, and wait there for the holy offices that were to be performed. But they answered the messenger, that they would not obey his summons; nay, would not overlook Moses's behavior, who was growing too great for them by evil practices. Now when Moses heard of this their answer, he desired the heads of the people to follow him, and he went to the faction of Dathan, not thinking it any frightful thing at all to go to these insolent people; so they made no opposition, but went along with him. But Dathan, and his associates, when they understood that Moses and the principal of the people were coming to them, came out, with their wives and children, and stood before their tents, and looked to see what Moses would do. They had also their servants about them to defend themselves, in case Moses should use force against them.

2. But he came near, and lifted up his hands to heaven, and cried out with a loud voice, in order to be heard by the whole multitude, and said, "O Lord of the creatures that are in the heaven, in the earth, and in the sea; for thou art the most authentic witness to what I have done, that it has all been done by thy appointment, and that it was thou that affordedst us assistance when we attempted anything, and showedst mercy on the Hebrews in all their distresses; do thou come now, and hear all that I say, for no action or thought escapes thy knowledge; so that thou wilt not disdain to speak what is true, for my vindication, without any regard to the ungrateful imputations of these men. As for what was done before I was

born, thou knowest best, as not learning them by report, but seeing them, and being present with them when they were done; but for what has been done of late, and which these men, although they know them well enough, unjustly pretend to suspect, be thou my witness. When I lived a private quiet life, I left those good things which, by my own diligence, and by thy counsel, I enjoyed with Raguel my father-in-law; and I gave myself up to this people, and underwent many miseries on their account. I also bore great labors at first, in order to obtain liberty for them, and now in order to their preservation; and have always showed myself ready to assist them in every distress of theirs. Now, therefore, since I am suspected by those very men whose being is owing to my labors, come thou, as it is reasonable to hope thou wilt; thou, I say, who showedst me that fire at mount Sinai, and madest me to hear its voice, and to see the several wonders which that place afforded thou who commandedst me to go to Egypt, and declare thy will to this people; thou who disturbest the happy estate of the Egyptians, and gavest us the opportunity of flying away from our under them, and madest the dominion of Pharaoh inferior to my dominion; thou who didst make the sea dry land for us, when we knew not whither to go, and didst overwhelm the Egyptians with those destructive waves which had been divided for us; thou who didst bestow upon us the security of weapons when we were naked; thou who didst make the fountains that were corrupted to flow, so as to be fit for drinking, and didst furnish us with water that came out of the rocks, when we were in want of it; thou who didst preserve our lives with [quails, which was] food from the sea, when the fruits of the ground failed us; thou didst send us such food from heaven as had never been seen before; thou who didst suggest to us the knowledge of thy laws, and appoint to us a of government,—come thou, I say, O Lord of the whole world, and that as such a Judge and a Witness to me as cannot be bribed, and show how I never admitted of any gift against justice from any of the Hebrews; and have never condemned a man that ought to have been acquitted, on account of one that was rich; and have never attempted to hurt this commonwealth. I am now and am suspected of a thing the remotest from my intentions, as if I had given the priesthood to Aaron, not at thy command, but out of my own favor to him; do thou at this time demonstrate that all things are administered by thy providence and that nothing happens by chance, but is governed by thy will, and thereby attains its end: as also demonstrate that thou takest care that have done good to the Hebrews; demonstrate this, I say, by the punishment of Abiram and Dathan, who condemn thee as an insensible Being, and one overcome by my contrivances. This thou do by inflicting such an open punishment on these men who so madly fly in the face of thy glory, as will take them out of the world, not in an manner, but so that it may appear they do die after the manner of other men: let that ground which they tread upon open about them and consume them, with their families and goods. This will be a demonstration of thy power to all and this method of their sufferings will be an instruction of wisdom for those that entertain profane sentiments of thee. By this means I shall be a good servant, in the precepts thou hast given by me. But if the calumnies they have raised against me be true, mayst thou preserve these men from every evil accident, and bring all that destruction on me which I have imprecated upon them. And when thou hast inflicted punishment on those that have endeavored to deal unjustly with this people, bestow upon them concord and peace. Save this multitude that follow thy commandments, and preserve them free from harm, and let them not partake of the punishment of those that have sinned; for thou knowest thyself it is not just, that for the wickedness of those men the whole body of the Israelites should suffer punishment."

3. When Moses had said this, with tears in his eyes, the ground was moved on a sudden; and the agitation that set it in motion was like that which the wind produces in waves of the sea. The people were all affrighted; and the ground that was about their tents sunk down at the great noise, with a terrible sound, and carried whatsoever was dear to the seditious into itself, who so entirely perished, that there was not the least appearance that any man had ever been seen there, the earth that had opened itself about them, closing again, and becoming entire as it was before, insomuch that such as saw it afterward did not perceive that any such accident had happened to it. Thus did these men perish, and become a demonstration of the power of God. And truly, anyone would lament them, not only on account of this calamity that befell them, which yet deserves our commiseration, but also because their kindred were pleased with their sufferings; for they forgot the relation they bare to them, and at the sight of this sad accident approved of the judgment given against them; and because they looked upon the people about Dathan as pestilent men, they thought they perished as such, and did not grieve for them.

4. And now Moses called for those that contended about the priesthood, that trial might be made who should be priest, and that he whose sacrifice God was best pleased with might be ordained to that function. There attended two hundred and fifty men, who indeed were honored by the people, not only on account of the power of their ancestors, but also on account of their own, in which they excelled the others: Aaron also and Corah came forth, and they all offered incense, in those censers of theirs which they brought with them, before the tabernacle. Hereupon so great a fire shone out as no one ever saw in any that is made by the hand

of man, neither in those eruptions out of the earth that are caused by subterraneous burn-rags, nor in such fires as arise of their own accord in the woods, when the agitation is caused by the trees rubbing one against another: but this fire was very bright, and had a terrible flame, such as is kindled at the command of God; by whose irruption on them, all the company, and Corah himself, were destroyed, and this so entirely, that their very bodies left no remains behind them. Aaron alone was preserved, and not at all hurt by the fire, because it was God that sent the fire to burn those only who ought to be burned. Hereupon Moses, after these men were destroyed, was desirous that the memory of this judgment might be delivered down to posterity, and that future ages might be acquainted with it; and so he commanded Eleazar, the son of Aaron, to put their censers near the brazen altar, that they might be a memorial to posterity of what these men suffered, for supposing that the power of God might be eluded. And thus Aaron was now no longer esteemed to have the priesthood by the favor of Moses, but by the public judgment of God; and thus he and his children peaceably enjoyed that honor afterward.

4: WHAT HAPPENED TO THE HEBREWS DURING THIRTY-EIGHT YEARS IN THE WILDERNESS

1. However, this sedition was so far from ceasing upon this destruction, that it grew much stronger, and became more intolerable. And the occasion of its growing worse was of that nature, as made it likely the calamity would never cease, but last for a long time; for the men, believing already that nothing is done without the providence of God, would have it that these things came thus to pass not without God's favor to Moses; they therefore laid the blame upon him that God was so angry, and that this happened not so much because of the wickedness of those that were punished, as because Moses procured the punishment; and that these men had been destroyed without any sin of theirs, only because they were zealous about the Divine worship; as also, that he who had been the cause of this diminution of the people, by destroying so many men, and those the most excellent of them all, besides his escaping any punishment himself, had now given the priesthood to his brother so firmly, that nobody could any longer dispute it with him; for no one else, to be sure, could now put in for it, since he must have seen those that first did so to have miserably perished. Nay, besides this, the kindred of those that were destroyed made great entreaties to the multitude to abate the arrogance of Moses, because it would be safest for them so to do.

2. Now Moses, upon his hearing for a good while that the people were tumultuous, was afraid that they would attempt some other innovation,

and that some great and sad calamity would be the consequence. He called the multitude to a congregation, and patiently heard what apology they had to make for themselves, without opposing them, and this lest he should embitter the multitude: he only desired the heads of the tribes to bring their rods, with the names of their tribes inscribed upon them, and that he should receive the priesthood in whose rod God should give a sign. This was agreed to. So the rest brought their rods, as did Aaron also, who had written the tribe of Levi on his rod. These rods Moses laid up in the tabernacle of God. On the next day he brought out the rods, which were known from one another by those who brought them, they having distinctly noted them, as had the multitude also; and as to the rest, in the same form Moses had received them, in that they saw them still; but they also saw buds and branches grown out of Aaron's rod, with ripe fruits upon them; they were almonds, the rod having been cut out of that tree. The people were so amazed at this strange sight, that though Moses and Aaron were before under some degree of hatred, they now laid that hatred aside, and began to admire the judgment of God concerning them; so that hereafter they applauded what God had decreed, and permitted Aaron to enjoy the priesthood peaceably. And thus God ordained him priest three several times, and he retained that honor without further disturbance. And hereby this sedition of the Hebrews, which had been a great one, and had lasted a great while, was at last composed.

3. And now Moses, because the tribe of Levi was made free from war and warlike expeditions, and was set apart for the Divine worship, lest they should want and seek after the necessaries of life, and so neglect the temple, commanded the Hebrews, according to the will of God, that when they should gain the possession of the land of Canaan, they should assign forty-eight good and fair cities to the Levites; and permit them to enjoy their suburbs, as far as the limit of two thousand cubits would extend from the walls of the city. And besides this, he appointed that the people should pay the tithe of their annual fruits of the earth, both to the Levites and to the priests. And this is what that tribe receives of the multitude; but I think it necessary to set down what is paid by all, peculiarly to the priests.

4. Accordingly he commanded the Levites to yield up to the priests thirteen of their forty-eight cities, and to set apart for them the tenth part of the tithes which they every year receive of the people; as also, that it was but just to offer to God the first-fruits of the entire product of the ground; and that they should offer the first-born of those four-footed beasts that are appointed for sacrifices, if it be a male, to the priests, to be slain, that they and their entire families may eat them in the holy city; but that the owners of those first-born which are not appointed for sacrifices in the

laws of our country, should bring a shekel and a half in their stead: but
for the first-born of a man, five shekels: that they should also have the
first-fruits out of the shearing of the sheep; and that when any baked bread
corn, and made loaves of it, they should give somewhat of what they had
baked to them. Moreover, when any have made a sacred vow, I mean those
that are called *Nazarites,* that suffer their hair to grow long, and use no
wine, when they consecrate their hair, and offer it for a sacrifice, they are
to allot that hair for the priests [to be thrown into the fire]. Such also as
dedicate themselves to God, as a corban, which denotes what the Greeks
call a *gift,* when they are desirous of being freed from that ministration,
are to lay down money for the priests; thirty shekels if it be a woman,
and fifty if it be a man; but if any be too poor to pay the appointed sum,
it shall be lawful for the priests to determine that sum as they think fit.
And if any slay beasts at home for a private festival, but not for a religious
one, they are obliged to bring the maw and the cheek, [or breast,] and the
right shoulder of the sacrifice, to the priests. With these Moses contrived
that the priests should be plentifully maintained, besides what they had
out of those offerings for sins which the people gave them, as I have set
it down in the foregoing book. He also ordered, that out of everything
allotted for the priests, their servants, [their sons,] their daughters, and
their wives, should partake, as well as themselves, excepting what came
to them out of the sacrifices that were offered for sins; for of those none
but the males of the family of the priests might eat, and this in the temple
also, and that the same day they were offered.

5. When Moses had made these constitutions, after the sedition was
over, he removed, together with the whole army, and came to the borders
of Idumea. He then sent ambassadors to the king of the Idumeans, and
desired him to give him a passage through his country; and agreed to
send him what hostages he should desire, to secure him from an injury. He
desired him also, that he would allow his army liberty to buy provisions;
and, if he insisted upon it, he would pay down a price for the very water
they should drink. But the king was not pleased with this embassage from
Moses: nor did he allow a passage for the army, but brought his people
armed to meet Moses, and to hinder them, in case they should endeavor to
force their passage. Upon which Moses consulted God by the oracle, who
would not have him begin the war first; and so he withdrew his forces,
and traveled round about through the wilderness.

6. Then it was that Miriam, the sister of Moses, came to her end, having
completed her fortieth year since she left Egypt, on the first day of the
lunar month Xanthicus. They then made a public funeral for her, at a great
expense. She was buried upon a certain mountain, which they call *Sin:* and

when they had mourned for her thirty days, Moses purified the people after this manner: He brought a heifer that had never been used to the plough or to husbandry, that was complete in all its parts, and entirely of a red color, at a little distance from the camp, into a place perfectly clean. This heifer was slain by the high priest, and her blood sprinkled with his finger seven times before the tabernacle of God; after this, the entire heifer was burnt in that state, together with its skin and entrails; and they threw cedar-wood, and hyssop, and scarlet wool, into the midst of the fire; then a clean man gathered all her ashes together, and laid them in a place perfectly clean. When therefore any persons were defiled by a dead body, they put a little of these ashes into spring water, with hyssop, and, dipping part of these ashes in it, they sprinkled them with it, both on the third day, and on the seventh, and after that they were clean. This he enjoined them to do also when the tribes should come into their own land.

7. Now when this purification, which their leader made upon the mourning for his sister, as it has been now described, was over, he caused the army to remove and to march through the wilderness and through Arabia; and when he came to a place which the Arabians esteem their metropolis, which was formerly called *Arce,* but has now the name of *Petra,* at this place, which was encompassed with high mountains, Aaron went up one of them in the sight of the whole army, Moses having before told him that he was to die, for this place was over against them. He put off his pontifical garments, and delivered them to Eleazar his son, to whom the high priesthood belonged, because he was the elder brother; and died while the multitude looked upon him. He died in the same year wherein he lost his sister, having lived in all a hundred twenty and three years. He died on the first day of that lunar month which is called by the Athenians *Hecatombaeon,* by the Macedonians *Lous,* but by the Hebrews *Abba.*

5: HOW MOSES CONQUERED SIHON AND OG AND THEN DIVIDED THEIR LAND

1. The people mourned for Aaron thirty days, and when this mourning was over, Moses removed the army from that place, and came to the river Arnon, which, issuing out of the mountains of Arabia, and running through all that wilderness, falls into the lake Asphaltitis, and becomes the limit between the land of the Moabites and the land of the Amorites. This land is fruitful, and sufficient to maintain a great number of men, with the good things it produces. Moses therefore sent messengers to Sihon, the king of this country, desiring that he would grant his army a passage, upon what security he should please to require; he promised that he should be no

way injured, neither as to that country which Sihon governed, nor as to its inhabitants; and that he would buy his provisions at such a price as should be to their advantage, even though he should desire to sell them their very water. But Sihon refused his offer, and put his army into battle array, and was preparing everything in order to hinder their passing over Arnon.

2. When Moses saw that the Amorite king was disposed to enter upon hostilities with them, he thought he ought not to bear that insult; and, determining to wean the Hebrews from their indolent temper, and prevent the disorders which arose thence, which had been the occasion of their former sedition, (nor indeed were they now thoroughly easy in their minds,) he inquired of God, whether he would give him leave to fight? which when he had done, and God also promised him the victory, he was himself very courageous, and ready to proceed to fighting. Accordingly he encouraged the soldiers; and he desired of them that they would take the pleasure of fighting, now God gave them leave so to do. They then, upon the receipt of this permission, which they so much longed for, put on their whole armor, and set about the work without delay. But the Amorite king was not now like to himself when the Hebrews were ready to attack him; but both he himself was affrighted at the Hebrews, and his army, which before had showed themselves to be of good courage, were then found to be timorous: so they could not sustain the first onset, nor bear up against the Hebrews, but fled away, as thinking this would afford them a more likely way for their escape than fighting, for they depended upon their cities, which were strong, from which yet they reaped no advantage when they were forced to fly to them; for as soon as the Hebrews saw them giving ground, they immediately pursued them close; and when they had broken their ranks, they greatly terrified them, and some of them broke off from the rest, and ran away to the cities. Now the Hebrews pursued them briskly, and obstinately persevered in the labors they had already undergone; and being very skillful in slinging, and very dexterous in throwing of darts, or anything else of that kind, and also having nothing but light armor, which made them quick in the pursuit, they overtook their enemies; and for those that were most remote, and could not be overtaken, they reached them by their slings and their bows, so that many were slain; and those that escaped the slaughter were sorely wounded, and these were more distressed with thirst than with any of those that fought against them, for it was the summer season; and when the greatest number of them were brought down to the river out of a desire to drink, as also when others fled away by troops, the Hebrews came round them, and shot at them; so that, what with darts and what with arrows, they made a slaughter of them all. Sihon their king was also slain. So the Hebrews

spoiled the dead bodies, and took their prey. The land also which they took was full of abundance of fruits, and the army went all over it without fear, and fed their cattle upon it; and they took the enemies prisoners, for they could no way put a stop to them, since all the fighting men were destroyed. Such was the destruction which overtook the Amorites, who were neither sagacious in counsel, nor courageous in action. Hereupon the Hebrews took possession of their land, which is a country situate between three rivers, and naturally resembled an island: the river Arnon being its southern; the river Jabbok determining its northern side, which running into Jordan loses its own name, and takes the other; while Jordan itself runs along by it, on its western coast.

3. When matters were come to this state, Og, the king of Gilead and Gaulanitis, fell upon the Israelites. He brought an army with him, and in haste to the assistance of his friend Sihon: but though he found him already slain, yet did he resolve still to come and fight the Hebrews, supposing he should be too hard for them, and being desirous to try their valor; but failing of his hope, he was both himself slain in the battle, and all his army was destroyed. So Moses passed over the river Jabbok, and overran the kingdom of Og. He overthrew their cities, and slew all their inhabitants, who yet exceeded in riches all the men in that part of the continent, on account of the goodness of the soil, and the great quantity of their wealth. Now Og had very few equals, either in the largeness of his body, or handsomeness of his appearance. He was also a man of great activity in the use of his hands, so that his actions were not unequal to the vast largeness and handsome appearance of his body. And men could easily guess at his strength and magnitude when they took his bed at Rabbath, the royal city of the Ammonites; its structure was of iron, its breadth four cubits, and its length a cubit more than double thereto. However, his fall did not only improve the circumstances of the Hebrews for the present, but by his death he was the occasion of further good success to them; for they presently took those sixty cities, which were encompassed with excellent walls, and had been subject to him, and all got both in general and in particular a great prey.

6: BALAAM THE PROPHET AND WHAT KIND OF MAN HE WAS

1. Now Moses, when he had brought his army to Jordan; pitched his camp in the great plain over against Jericho. This city is a very happy situation, and very fit for producing palm-trees and balsam. And now the Israelites began to be very proud of themselves, and were very eager for fighting. Moses then, after he had offered for a few days sacrifices of

thanksgiving to God, and feasted the people, sent a party of armed men to lay waste the country of the Midianites, and to take their cities. Now the occasion which he took for making war upon them was this that follows:–

2. When Balak, the king of the Moabites, who had from his ancestors a friendship and league with the Midianites, saw how great the Israelites were grown, he was much affrighted on account of his own and his kingdom's danger; for he was not acquainted with this, that the Hebrews would not meddle with any other country, but were to be contented with the possession of the land of Canaan, God having forbidden them to go any farther. So he, with more haste than wisdom, resolved to make an attempt upon them by words; but he did not judge it prudent to fight against them, after they had such prosperous successes, and even became out of ill successes more happy than before, but he thought to hinder them, if he could, from growing greater, and so he resolved to send ambassadors to the Midianites about them. Now these Midianites knowing there was one Balaam, who lived by Euphrates, and was the greatest of the prophets at that time, and one that was in friendship with them, sent some of their honorable princes along with the ambassadors of Balak, to entreat the prophet to come to them, that he might imprecate curses to the destruction of the Israelites. So Balsam received the ambassadors, and treated them very kindly; and when he had supped, he inquired what was God's will, and what this matter was for which the Midianites entreated him to come to them. But when God opposed his going, he came to the ambassadors, and told them that he was himself very willing and desirous to comply with their request, but informed them that God was opposite to his intentions, even that God who had raised him to great reputation on account of the truth of his predictions; for that this army, which they entreated him to come and curse, was in the favor of God; on which account he advised them to go home again, and not to persist in their enmity against the Israelites; and when he had given them that answer, he dismissed the ambassadors.

3. Now the Midianites, at the earnest request and fervent entreaties of Balak, sent other ambassadors to Balaam, who, desiring to gratify the men, inquired again of God; but he was displeased at [second] trial and bid him by no means to contradict the ambassadors.[2] Now Balsam did not

---

2. Note that Josephus never supposes Balaam to be an idolater, nor to seek idolatrous enchantments, or to prophesy falsely, but to be no other than an ill-disposed prophet of the true God; and intimates that God's answer the second time, permitting him to go, was ironical, and on design that he deceived (which sort of deception, by way of punishment for former crimes, Josephus never scruples to admit, as ever esteeming such wicked men justly and providentially deceived). But perhaps we had better keep here close to the text which

imagine that God gave this injunction in order to deceive him, so he went along with the ambassadors; but when the divine angel met him in the way, when he was in a narrow passage, and hedged in with a wall on both sides, the ass on which Balaam rode understood that it was a divine spirit that met him, and thrust Balaam to one of the walls, without regard to the stripes which Balaam, when he was hurt by the wall, gave her; but when the ass, upon the angel's continuing to distress her, and upon the stripes which were given her, fell down, by the will of God, she made use of the voice of a man, and complained of Balaam as acting unjustly to her; that whereas he had no fault find with her in her former service to him, he now inflicted stripes upon her, as not understanding that she was hindered from serving him in what he was now going about, by the providence of God. And when he was disturbed by reason of the voice of the ass, which was that of a man, the angel plainly appeared to him, and blamed him for the stripes he had given his ass; and informed him that the brute creature was not in fault, but that he was himself come to obstruct his journey, as being contrary to the will of God. Upon which Balaam was afraid, and was preparing to return back again: yet did God excite him to go on his intended journey, but added this injunction, that he should declare nothing but what he himself should suggest to his mind.

4. When God had given him this charge, he came to Balak; and when the king had entertained him in a magnificent manner, he desired him to go to one of the mountains to take a view of the state of the camp of the Hebrews. Balak himself also came to the mountain, and brought the prophet along with him, with a royal attendance. This mountain lay over their heads, and was distant sixty furlongs from the camp. Now when he saw them, he desired the king to build him seven altars, and to bring him as many bulls and rams; to which desire the king did presently conform. He then slew the sacrifices, and offered them as burnt-offerings, that he might observe some signal of the flight of the Hebrews. Then said he, "Happy is this people, on whom God bestows the possession of innumerable good things, and grants them his own providence to be their assistant and their guide; so that there is not any nation among mankind but you will be

---

says (Numbers 23:20, 21), that God only permitted Balaam to go along with the ambassadors, in case they came and called him, or positively insisted on his going along with them, on any terms; whereas Balaam seems out of impatience to have risen up in the morning, and saddled his ass, and rather to have called them, than staid for their calling him, so zealous does he seem to have been for his reward of divination, his wages of unrighteousness (Numbers 23:7, 17, 18, 37; 2 Peter 2:15; Jude 5, 11); which reward or wages the truly religious prophets of God never required nor accepted, as our Josephus justly takes notice in the cases of Samuel (*Antiquities*, book 5, chapter 4, section 1), and Daniel (*Antiquities*, book 10, chapter 11, section 3). (See also Genesis 14:22, 23; 2 Kings 5:15, 16, 26, 27; and Acts 8:17-24.)

esteemed superior to them in virtue, and in the earnest prosecution of the best rules of life, and of such as are pure from wickedness, and will leave those rules to your excellent children; and this out of the regard that God bears to you, and the provision of such things for you as may render you happier than any other people under the sun. You shall retain that land to which he hath sent you, and it shall ever be under the command of your children; and both all the earth, as well as the seas, shall be filled with your glory: and you shall be sufficiently numerous to supply the world in general, and every region of it in particular, with inhabitants out of your stock. However, O blessed army! wonder that you are become so many from one father: and truly, the land of Canaan can now hold you, as being yet comparatively few; but know ye that the whole world is proposed to be your place of habitation forever. The multitude of your posterity also shall live as well in the islands as on the continent, and that more in number than are the stars of heaven. And when you are become so many, God will not relinquish the care of you, but will afford you an abundance of all good things in times of peace, with victory and dominion in times of war. May the children of your enemies have an inclination to fight against you; and may they be so hardy as to come to arms, and to assault you in battle, for they will not return with victory, nor will their return be agreeable to their children and wives. To so great a degree of valor will you be raised by the providence of God, who is able to diminish the affluence of some, and to supply the wants of others."

5. Thus did Balaam speak by inspiration, as not being in his own power, but moved to say what he did by the Divine Spirit. But then Balak was displeased, and said he had broken the contract he had made, whereby he was to come, as he and his confederates had invited him, by the promise of great presents: for whereas he came to curse their enemies, he had made an encomium upon them, and had declared that they were the happiest of men. To which Balaam replied, "O Balak, if thou rightly considerest this whole matter, canst thou suppose that it is in our power to be silent, or to say anything, when the Spirit of God seizes upon us?—for he puts such words as he pleases in our mouths, and such discourses as we are not ourselves conscious of. I well remember by what entreaties both you and the Midianites so joyfully brought me hither, and on that account I took this journey. It was my prayer, that I might not put any affront upon you, as to what you desired of me; but God is more powerful than the purposes I had made to serve you; for those that take upon them to foretell the affairs of mankind, as from their own abilities, are entirely unable to do it, or to forbear to utter what God suggests to them, or to offer violence to his will; for when he prevents us and enters into us, nothing that we say is our

own. I then did not intend to praise this army, nor to go over the several good things which God intended to do to their race; but since he was so favorable to them, and so ready to bestow upon them a happy life and eternal glory, he suggested the declaration of those things to me: but now, because it is my desire to oblige thee thyself, as well as the Midianites, whose entreaties it is not decent for me to reject, go to, let us again rear other altars, and offer the like sacrifices that we did before, that I may see whether I can persuade God to permit me to bind these men with curses." Which, when Balak had agreed to, God would not, even upon second sacrifices, consent to his cursing the Israelites. Then fell Balaam upon his face, and foretold what calamities would befall the several kings of the nations, and the most eminent cities, some of which of old were not so much as inhabited; which events have come to pass among the several people concerned, both in the foregoing ages, and in this, till my own memory, both by sea and by land. From which completion of all these predictions that he made, one may easily guess that the rest will have their completion in time to come.

6. But Balak being very angry that the Israelites were not cursed, sent away Balaam without thinking him worthy of any honor. Whereupon, when he was just upon his journey, in order to pass the Euphrates, he sent for Balak, and for the princes of the Midianites, and spake thus to them:— "O Balak, and you Midianites that are here present, (for I am obliged even without the will of God to gratify you,) it is true no entire destruction can seize upon the nation of the Hebrews, neither by war, nor by plague, nor by scarcity of the fruits of the earth, nor can any other unexpected accident be their entire ruin; for the providence of God is concerned to preserve them from such a misfortune; nor will it permit any such calamity to come upon them whereby they may all perish; but some small misfortunes, and those for a short time, whereby they may appear to be brought low, may still befall them; but after that they will flourish again, to the terror of those that brought those mischiefs upon them. So that if you have a mind to gain a victory over them for a short space of time, you will obtain it by following my directions:—Do you therefore set out the handsomest of such of your daughters as are most eminent for beauty,[3] and proper to force and conquer the modesty of those that behold them, and these decked and trimmed to the highest degree able. Then do you send them to be near camp, and give them in charge, that the young men of the Hebrews desire

---

3. Such a large and distinct account of this perversion of the Israelites by the Midianite women, of which our other copies give us but short intimations (Numbers 31:16; 2 Peter 2:15; Jude 11; Revelation 2:14), is preserved, . . . in the Samaritan Chronicle, in Philo, and in other writings of the Jews, as well as here by Josephus.

their allow it them; and when they see they are enamored of them, let them take leaves; and if they entreat them to stay, let give their consent till they have persuaded leave off their obedience to their own laws, the worship of that God who established them to worship the gods of the Midianites and for by this means God will be angry at them.[4] Accordingly, when Balaam had suggested counsel to them, he went his way.

7. So when the Midianites had sent their daughters, as Balaam had exhorted them, the Hebrew men were allured by their beauty, and came with them, and besought them not to grudge them the enjoyment of their beauty, nor to deny them their conversation. These daughters of Midianites received their words gladly, and consented to it, and staid with them; but when they brought them to be enamored of them, and their inclinations to them were grown to ripeness, they began to think of departing from them: then it was that these men became greatly disconsolate at the women's departure, and they were urgent with them not to leave them, but begged they would continue there, and become their wives; and they promised them they should be owned as mistresses all they had. This they said with an oath, and called God for the arbitrator of what they promised; and this with tears in their eyes, and all such marks of concern, as might shew how miserable they thought themselves without them, and so might move their compassion for them. So the women, as soon as they perceived they had made their slaves, and had caught them with their conservation began to speak thus to them:—

8. "O you illustrious young men! we have of our own at home, and great plenty of good things there, together with the natural, affectionate parents and friends; nor is it out of our want of any such things that we came to discourse with you; nor did we admit of your invitation with design to prostitute the beauty of our bodies for gain; but taking you for brave and worthy men, we agreed to your request, that we might treat you with such honors as hospitality required: and now seeing you say that you have a great affection for us, and are troubled when you think we are departing, we are not averse to your entreaties; and if we may receive such assurance of your good-will as we think can be alone sufficient, we will be glad to lead our lives with you as your wives; but we are afraid that you will in time be weary of our company, and will then abuse us, and send us back to our parents, after an ignominious manner." And they desired that they would excuse them in their guarding

---

4. This grand maxim, That God's people of Israel could never be hurt nor destroyed, but by drawing them to sin against God, appears to be true, by the entire history of that people, both in the Bible and in Josephus; and is often taken notice of in them both. See in particular a most remarkable Ammonite testimony to this purpose in Judith 5:5-21.

against that danger. But the young men professed they would give them any assurance they should desire; nor did they at all contradict what they requested, so great was the passion they had for them. "If then," said they, "this be your resolution, since you make use of such customs and conduct of life as are entirely different from all other men,[5] insomuch that your kinds of food are peculiar to yourselves, and your kinds of drink not common to others, it will be absolutely necessary, if you would have us for your wives, that you do withal worship our gods. Nor can there be any other demonstration of the kindness which you say you already have, and promise to have hereafter to us, than this, that you worship the same gods that we do. For has anyone reason to complain, that now you are come into this country, you should worship the proper gods of the same country? especially while our gods are common to all men, and yours such as belong to nobody else but yourselves." So they said they must either come into such methods of divine worship as all others came into, or else they must look out for another world, wherein they may live by themselves, according to their own laws.

9. Now the young men were induced by the fondness they had for these women to think they spake very well; so they gave themselves up to what they persuaded them, and transgressed their own laws, and supposing there were many gods, and resolving that they would sacrifice to them according to the laws of that country which ordained them, they both were delighted with their strange food, and went on to do everything that the women would have them do, though in contradiction to their own laws; so far indeed that this transgression was already gone through the whole army of the young men, and they fell into a sedition that was much worse than the former, and into danger of the entire abolition of their own institutions; for when once the youth had tasted of these strange customs, they went with insatiable inclinations into them; and even where some of the principal men were illustrious on account of the virtues of their fathers, they also were corrupted together with the rest.

10. Even Zimri, the head of the tribe of Simeon accompanied with Cozbi, a Midianitish women, who was the daughter of Sur, a man of authority

---

5. What Josephus here puts into the mouths of these Midianite women, who came to entice the Israelites to lewdness and idolatry, viz., that their worship of the God of Israel, in opposition to their idol gods, implied their living according to the holy laws which the true God had given them by Moses, in opposition to those impure laws which were observed under their false gods, well deserves our consideration; and gives us a substantial reason for the great concern that was ever shown under the law of Moses to preserve the Israelites from idolatry, and in the worship of the true God; it being of no less consequence than whether God's people should be governed by the holy laws of the true God, or by the impure laws derived from demons, under the pagan idolatry.

in that country; and being desired by his wife to disregard the laws of Moses, and to follow those she was used to, he complied with her, and this both by sacrificing after a manner different from his own, and by taking a stranger to wife. When things were thus, Moses was afraid that matters should grow worse, and called the people to a congregation, but then accused nobody by name, as unwilling to drive those into despair who, by lying concealed, might come to repentance; but he said that they did not do what was either worthy of themselves, or of their fathers, by preferring pleasure to God, and to the living according to his will; that it was fit they should change their courses while their affairs were still in a good state, and think that to be true fortitude which offers not violence to their laws, but that which resists their lusts. And besides that, he said it was not a reasonable thing, when they had lived soberly in the wilderness, to act madly now when they were in prosperity; and that they ought not to lose, now they have abundance, what they had gained when they had little:—and so did he endeavor, by saying this, to correct the young inert, and to bring them to repentance for what they had done.

11. But Zimri arose up after him, and said, "Yes, indeed, Moses, thou art at liberty to make use of such laws as thou art so fond of, and hast, by accustoming thyself to them, made them firm; otherwise, if things had not been thus, thou hadst often been punished before now, and hadst known that the Hebrews are not easily put upon; but thou shalt not have me one of thy followers in thy tyrannical commands, for thou dost nothing else hitherto, but, under pretense of laws, and of God, wickedly impose on us slavery, and gain dominion to thyself, while thou deprivest us of the sweetness of life, which consists in acting according to our own wills, and is the right of free-men, and of those that have no lord over them. Nay, indeed, this man is harder upon the Hebrews then were the Egyptians themselves, as pretending to punish, according to his laws, every one's acting what is most agreeable to himself; but thou thyself better deservest to suffer punishment, who presumest to abolish what everyone acknowledges to be what is good for him, and aimest to make thy single opinion to have more force than that of all the rest; and what I now do, and think to be right, I shall not hereafter deny to be according to my own sentiments. I have married, as thou sayest rightly, a strange woman, and thou hearest what I do from myself as from one that is free, for truly I did not intend to conceal myself. I also own that I sacrificed to those gods to whom you do not think it fit to sacrifice; and I think it right to come at truth by inquiring of many people, and not like one that lives under tyranny, to suffer the whole hope of my life to depend upon one

man; nor shall anyone find cause to rejoice who declares himself to have more authority over my actions than myself."

12. Now when Zimri had said these things, about what he and some others had wickedly done, the people held their peace, both out of fear of what might come upon them, and because they saw that their legislator was not willing to bring his insolence before the public any further, or openly to contend with him; for he avoided that, lest many should imitate the impudence of his language, and thereby disturb the multitude. Upon this the assembly was dissolved. However, the mischievous attempt had proceeded further, if Zimri had not been first slain, which came to pass on the following occasion:—Phineas, a man in other respects better than the rest of the young men, and also one that surpassed his contemporaries in the dignity of his father, (for he was the son of Eleazar the high priest, and the grandson of [Aaron] Moses's brother,) who was greatly troubled at what was done by Zimri, he resolved in earnest to inflict punishment on him, before his unworthy behavior should grow stronger by impunity, and in order to prevent this transgression from proceeding further, which would happen if the ringleaders were not punished. He was of so great magnanimity, both in strength of mind and body, that when he undertook any very dangerous attempt, he did not leave it off till he overcame it, and got an entire victory. So he came into Zimri's tent, and slew him with his javelin, and with it he slew Cozbi also, Upon which all those young men that had a regard to virtue, and aimed to do a glorious action, imitated Phineas's boldness, and slew those that were found to be guilty of the same crime with Zimri. Accordingly many of those that had transgressed perished by the magnanimous valor of these young men; and the rest all perished by a plague, which distemper God himself inflicted upon them; so that all those their kindred, who, instead of hindering them from such wicked actions, as they ought to have done, had persuaded them to go on, were esteemed by God as partners in their wickedness, and died. Accordingly there perished out of the army no fewer than fourteen [twenty-four] thousand at this time.

13. This was the cause why Moses was provoked to send an army to destroy the Midianites, concerning which expedition we shall speak presently, when we have first related what we have omitted; for it is but just not to pass over our legislator's due encomium, on account of his conduct here, because, although this Balaam, who was sent for by the Midianites to curse the Hebrews, and when he was hindered from doing it by Divine Providence, did still suggest that advice to them, by making use of which our enemies had well nigh corrupted the whole multitude of the Hebrews with their wiles, till some of them were deeply infected with their

opinions; yet did he do him great honor, by setting down his prophecies in writing. And while it was in his power to claim this glory to himself, and make men believe they were his own predictions, there being no one that could be a witness against him, and accuse him for so doing, he still gave his attestation to him, and did him the honor to make mention of him on this account. But let everyone think of these matters as he pleases.

7: HOW THE HEBREWS FOUGHT WITH THE MIDIANITES, AND OVERCAME THEM

1. Now Moses sent an army against the land of Midian, for the causes forementioned, in all twelve thousand, taking an equal number out of every tribe, and appointed Phineas for their commander; of which Phineas we made mention a little before, as he that had guarded the laws of the Hebrews, and had inflicted punishment on Zimri when he had transgressed them. Now the Midianites perceived beforehand how the Hebrews were coming, and would suddenly be upon them: so they assembled their army together, and fortified the entrances into their country, and there awaited the enemy's coming. When they were come, and they had joined battle with them, an immense multitude of the Midianites fell; nor could they be numbered, they were so very many: and among them fell all their kings, five in number, viz. Evi, Zur, Reba, Hur, and Rekem, who was of the same name with a city, the chief and capital of all Arabia, which is still now so called by the whole Arabian nation, *Arecem,* from the name of the king that built it; but is by the Greeks called *Petra.* Now when the enemies were discomfited, the Hebrews spoiled their country, and took a great prey, and destroyed the men that were its inhabitants, together with the women; only they let the virgins alone, as Moses had commanded Phineas to do, who indeed came back, bringing with him an army that had received no harm, and a great deal of prey; fifty-two thousand beeves, seventy-five thousand six hundred sheep, sixty thousand asses, with an immense quantity of gold and silver furniture, which the Midianites made use of in their houses; for they were so wealthy, that they were very luxurious. There were also led captive about thirty-two thousand virgins.[6] So Moses parted the prey into parts, and gave one fiftieth part to Eleazar and the two priests, and

---

6. The slaughter of all the Midianite women that had prostituted themselves to the lewd Israelites, and the preservation of those that had not been guilty therein; the last of which were no fewer than thirty-two thousand, both here and Numbers 31:15-17, 35, 40, 46, and both by the particular command of God; are highly remarkable, and show that, even in nations otherwise for their wickedness doomed to destruction, the innocent were sometimes particularly and providentially taken care of, and delivered from that destruction; which directly implies, that it was the wickedness of the nations of Canaan, and nothing else, that

another fiftieth part to the Levites; and distributed the rest of the prey among the people. After which they lived happily, as having obtained an abundance of good things by their valor, and there being no misfortune that attended them, or hindered their enjoyment of that happiness.

2. But Moses was now grown old, and appointed Joshua for his successor, both to receive directions from God as a prophet, and for a commander of the army, if they should at any time stand in need of such a one; and this was done by the command of God, that to him the care of the public should be committed. Now Joshua had been instructed in all those kinds of learning which concerned the laws and God himself, and Moses had been his instructor.

3. At this time it was that the two tribes of Gad and Reuben, and the half tribe of Manasseh, abounded in a multitude of cattle, as well as in all other kinds of prosperity; whence they had a meeting, and in a body came and besought Moses to give them, as their peculiar portion, that land of the Amorites which they had taken by right of war, because it was fruitful, and good for feeding of cattle; but Moses, supposing that they were afraid of fighting with the Canaanites, and invented this provision for their cattle as a handsome excuse for avoiding that war, he called them *arrant cowards,* and said they had only contrived a decent excuse for that cowardice; and that they had a mind to live in luxury and ease, while all the rest were laboring with great pains to obtain the land they were desirous to have; and that they were not willing to march along, and undergo the remaining hard service, whereby they were, under the Divine promise, to pass over Jordan, and overcome those our enemies which God had shown them, and so obtain their land. But these tribes, when they saw that Moses was angry with them, and when they could not deny but he had a just cause to be displeased at their petition, made an apology for themselves; and said, that it was not on account of their fear of dangers, nor on account of their laziness, that they made this request to him, but that they might leave the prey they had gotten in places of safety,

---

occasioned their excision. (See Genesis 15; 16; 1 Samuel 15:18, 33.) In the first of which places, the reason of the delay of the punishment of the Amorites is given, because "their iniquity was not yet full." In the secured, Saul is ordered to go and "destroy the sinners, the Amalekites;" plainly implying that they were therefore to be destroyed, because they were sinners, and not otherwise. In the third, the reason is given why king Agag was not to be spared, viz. because of his former cruelty: "As thy sword hath made the (Hebrew) women childless, so shall thy mother be made childless among women by the Hebrews." In the last place, the apostles, or their amanuensis Clement, gave this reason for the necessity of the coming of Christ, that "men had formerly perverted both the positive law, and that of nature; and had cast out of their mind the memory of the Flood, the burning of Sodom, the plagues of the Egyptians, and the slaughter of the inhabitants of Palestine," as signs of the most amazing impenitence and insensibility, under the punishments of horrid wickedness.

and thereby might be more expedite, and ready to undergo difficulties, and to fight battles. They added this also, that when they had built cities, wherein they might preserve their children, and wives, and possessions, if he would bestow them upon them, they would go along with the rest of the army. Hereupon Moses was pleased with what they said; so he called for Eleazar the high priest, and Joshua, and the chief of the tribes, and permitted these tribes to possess the land of the Amorites; but upon this condition, that they should join with their kinsmen in the war until all things were settled. Upon which condition they took possession of the country, and built them strong cities, and put into them their children and their wives, and whatsoever else they had that might be an impediment to the labors of their future marches.

4. Moses also now built those ten cities which were to be of the number of the forty-eight [for the Levites;]; three of which he allotted to those that slew any person involuntarily, and fled to them; and he assigned the same time for their banishment with that of the life of that high priest under whom the slaughter and flight happened; after which death of the high priest he permitted the slayer to return home. During the time of his exile, the relations of him that was slain may, by this law, kill the manslayer, if they caught him without the bounds of the city to which he fled, though this permission was not granted to any other person. Now the cities which were set apart for this flight were these: Bezer, at the borders of Arabia; Ramoth, of the land of Gilead; and Golan, in the land of Bashan. There were to be also, by Moses's command, three other cities allotted for the habitation of these fugitives out of the cities of the Levites, but not till after they should be in possession of the land of Canaan.

5. At this time the chief men of the tribe of Manasseh came to Moses, and informed him that there was an eminent man of their tribe dead, whose name was Zelophehad, who left no male children, but left daughters; and asked him whether these daughters might inherit his land or not. He made this answer, That if they shall marry into their own tribe, they shall carry their estate along with them; but if they dispose of themselves in marriage to men of another tribe, they shall leave their inheritance in their father's tribe. And then it was that Moses ordained, that every one's inheritance should continue in his own tribe.

8: THE POLITY SETTLED BY MOSES; AND HOW HE DISAPPEARED FROM AMONG MANKIND

1. When forty years were completed, within thirty days, Moses gathered the congregation together near Jordan, where the city Abila now stands,

a place full of palm-trees; and all the people being come together, he spake thus to them:—

2. "O you Israelites and fellow soldiers, who have been partners with me in this long and uneasy journey; since it is now the will of God, and the course of old age, at a hundred and twenty, requires it that I should depart out of this life; and since God has forbidden me to be a patron or an assistant to you in what remains to be done beyond Jordan; I thought it reasonable not to leave off my endeavors even now for your happiness, but to do my utmost to procure for you the eternal enjoyment of good things, and a memorial for myself, when you shall be in the fruition of great plenty and prosperity. Come, therefore, let me suggest to you by what means you may be happy, and may leave an eternal prosperous possession thereof to your children after you, and then let me thus go out of the world; and I cannot but deserve to be believed by you, both on account of the great things I have already done for you, and because, when souls are about to leave the body, they speak with the sincerest freedom. O children of Israel! there is but one source of happiness for all mankind, the favor of God for he alone is able to give good things to those that deserve them, and to deprive those of them that sin against him; towards whom, if you behave yourselves according to his will, and according to what I, who well understand his mind, do exhort you to, you will both be esteemed blessed, and will be admired by all men; and will never come into misfortunes, nor cease to be happy: you will then preserve the possession of the good things you already have, and will quickly obtain those that you are at present in want of,—only do you be obedient to those whom God would have you to follow. Nor do you prefer any other constitution of government before the laws now given you; neither do you disregard that way of Divine worship which you now have, nor change it for any other form: and if you do this, you will be the most courageous of all men, in undergoing the fatigues of war, and will not be easily conquered by any of your enemies; for while God is present with you to assist you, it is to be expected that you will be able to despise the opposition of all mankind; and great rewards of virtue are proposed for you, if you preserve that virtue through your whole lives. Virtue itself is indeed the principal and the first reward, and after that it bestows abundance of others; so that your exercise of virtue towards other men will make your own lives happy, and render you more glorious than foreigners can be, and procure you an undisputed reputation with posterity. These blessings you will be able to obtain, in case you hearken to and observe those laws which, by Divine revelation, I have ordained for you; that is, in case you withal meditate upon the wisdom that is in them. I am going from you myself, rejoicing in the good things you enjoy;

and I recommend you to the wise conduct of your law, to the becoming order of your polity, and to the virtues of your commanders, who will take care of what is for your advantage. And that God, who has been till now your Leader, and by whose goodwill I have myself been useful to you, will not put a period now to his providence over you, but as long as you desire to have him your Protector in your pursuits after virtue, so long will you enjoy his care over you. Your high priest also Eleazar, as well as Joshua, with the senate, and chief of your tribes, will go before you, and suggest the best advices to you; by following which advices you will continue to be happy: to whom do you give ear without reluctance, as sensible that all such as know well how to be governed, will also know how to govern, if they be promoted to that authority themselves. And do not you esteem liberty to consist in opposing such directions as your governors think fit to give you for your practice,—as at present indeed you place your liberty in nothing else but abusing your benefactors; which error if you can avoid for the time to come, your affairs will be in a better condition than they have hitherto been. Nor do you ever indulge such a degree of passion in these matters, as you have oftentimes done when you have been very angry at me; for you know that I have been oftener in danger of death from you than from our enemies. What I now put you in mind of, is not done in order to reproach you; for I do not think it proper, now I am going out of the world, to bring this to your remembrance, in order to leave you offended at me, since, at the time when I underwent those hardships from you, I was not angry at you; but I do it in order to make you wiser hereafter, and to teach you that this will be for your security; I mean, that you never be injurious to those that preside over you, even when you are become rich, as you will he to a great degree when you have passed over Jordan, and are in possession of the land of Canaan. Since, when you shall have once proceeded so far by your wealth, as to a contempt and disregard of virtue, you will also forfeit the favor of God; and when you have made him your enemy, you will be beaten in war, and will have the land which you possess taken away again from you by your enemies, and this with great reproaches upon your conduct. You will be scattered over the whole world, and will, as slaves, entirely fill both sea and land; and when once you have had the experience of what I now say, you will repent, and remember the laws you have broken, when it is too late. Whence I would advise you, if you intend to preserve these laws, to leave none of your enemies alive when you have conquered them, but to look upon it as for your advantage to destroy them all, lest, if you permit them to live, you taste of their manners, and thereby corrupt your own proper institutions. I also do further exhort you, to overthrow their altars, and their groves, and whatsoever temples they have among them, and to burn all such, their nation, and their very memory with fire; for by this means alone the safety of your own happy constitution can be firmly secured to you. And in order to prevent your ignorance of virtue, and the degeneracy of your nature into vice, I have also ordained you laws, by Divine suggestion, and a form of government, which are so good, that if you regularly observe them, you will be esteemed of all men the most happy."

3. When he had spoken thus, he gave them the laws and the constitution of government written in a book. Upon which the people fell into tears, and appeared already touched with the sense that they should have a great want of their conductor, because they remembered what a number of dangers he had passed through, and what care he had taken of their preservation: they desponded about what would come upon them after he was dead, and thought they should never have another governor like him; and feared that God would then take less care of them when Moses was gone, who used to intercede for them. They also repented of what they had said to him in the wilderness when they were angry, and were in grief on those accounts, insomuch that the whole body of the people fell into tears with such bitterness, that it was past the power of words to comfort them in their affliction. However, Moses gave them some consolation; and by calling them off the thought how worthy he was of their weeping for him, he exhorted them to keep to that form of government he had given them; and then the congregation was dissolved at that time.

4. Accordingly, I shall now first describe this form of government which was agreeable to the dignity and virtue of Moses; and shall thereby inform those that read these Antiquities, what our original settlements were, and shall then proceed to the remaining histories. Now those settlements are all still in writing, as he left them; and we shall add nothing by way of ornament, nor anything besides what Moses left us; only we shall so far innovate, as to digest the several kinds of laws into a regular system; for they were by him left in writing as they were accidentally scattered in their delivery, and as he upon inquiry had learned them of God. On which account I have thought it necessary to premise this observation beforehand, lest any of my own countrymen should blame me, as having been guilty of an offense herein. Now part of our constitution will include the laws that belong to our political state. As for those laws which Moses left concerning our common conversation and intercourse one with another, I have reserved that for a discourse concerning our manner of life, and the occasions of those laws; which I propose to myself, with God's assistance, to write, after I have finished the work I am now upon.

5. When you have possessed yourselves of the land of Canaan, and have leisure to enjoy the good things of it, and when you have afterward determined to build cities, if you will do what is pleasing to God, you will have a secure state of happiness. Let there be then one city of the land of Canaan, and this situate in the most agreeable place for its goodness, and very eminent in itself, and let it be that which God shall choose for himself by prophetic revelation. Let there also be one temple therein, and one altar, not reared of hewn stones, but of such as you gather together at random; which stones, when they are whited over with mortar, will have a handsome appearance, and be beautiful to the sight. Let the ascent to it be not by steps but by an acclivity of raised earth.[7] And let there be neither an altar nor a temple in any other city; for God is but one, and the nation of the Hebrews is but one.

6. He that blasphemeth God, let him be stoned; and let him hang upon a tree all that day, and then let him be buried in an ignominious and obscure manner.

7. Let those that live as remote as the bounds of the land which the Hebrews shall possess, come to that city where the temple shall be, and this three times in a year, that they may give thanks to God for his former benefits, and may entreat him for those they shall want hereafter; and let them, by this means, maintain a friendly correspondence with one another by such meetings and feastings together, for it is a good thing for those that are of the same stock, and under the same institution of laws, not to be unacquainted with each other; which acquaintance will be maintained by thus conversing together, and by seeing and talking with one another, and so renewing the memorials of this union; for if they do not thus converse together continually, they will appear like mere strangers to one another.

8. Let there be taken out of your fruits a tenth, besides that which you have allotted to give to the priests and Levites. This you may indeed sell in the country, but it is to be used in those feasts and sacrifices that are to be celebrated in the holy city; for it is fit that you should enjoy those fruits of the earth which God gives you to possess, so as may be to the honor of the donor.

---

7. This law, both here and Exodus 20:25, 26, of not going up to God's altar by ladder-steps, but on an acclivity, seems not to have belonged to the altar of the tabernacle, which was in all but three cubits high (Exodus 27:4); nor to that of Ezekiel, which was expressly to be gone up to by steps (Ezekiel 43:17); but rather to occasional altars of any considerable altitude and largeness; as also probably to Solomon's altar, to which it is here applied by Josephus, as well as to that in Zorobabel's and Herod's temple, which were, I think, all ten cubits high. (See 2 Chronicles 4:1.) The reason why these temples, and these only, were to have this ascent on an acclivity, and not by steps, is obvious, that before the invention of stairs, such as we now use, decency could not be otherwise provided for in the loose garments which the priests wore, as the law required.

9. You are not to offer sacrifices out of the hire of a woman who is a harlot for the Deity is not pleased with anything that arises from such abuses of nature; of which sort none can be worse than this prostitution of the body. In like manner no one may take the price of the covering of a bitch, either of one that is used in hunting, or in keeping of sheep, and thence sacrifice to God.

10. Let no one blaspheme those gods which other cities esteem such; nor may anyone steal what belongs to strange temples, nor take away the gifts that are dedicated to any god.

11. Let not any one of you wear a garment made of woolen and linen, for that is appointed to be for the priests alone.

12. When the multitude are assembled together unto the holy city for sacrificing every seventh year, at the feast of tabernacles, let the high priest stand upon a high desk, whence he may be heard, and let him read the laws to all the people; and let neither the women nor the children be hindered from hearing, no, nor the servants neither; for it is a good thing that those laws should be engraven in their souls, and preserved in their memories, that so it may not be possible to blot them out; for by this means they will not be guilty of sin, when they cannot plead ignorance of what the laws have enjoined them. The laws also will have a greater authority among them, as foretelling what they will suffer if they break them; and imprinting in their souls by this hearing what they command them to do, that so there may always be within their minds that intention of the laws which they have despised and broken, and have thereby been the causes of their own mischief. Let the children also learn the laws, as the first thing they are taught, which will be the best thing they can be taught, and will be the cause of their future felicity.

13. Let everyone commemorate before God the benefits which he bestowed upon them at their deliverance out of the land of Egypt, and this twice every day, both when the day begins and when the hour of sleep comes on, gratitude being in its own nature a just thing, and serving not only by way of return for past, but also by way of invitation of future favors. They are also to inscribe the principal blessings they have received from God upon their doors, and show the same remembrance of them upon their arms; as also they are to bear on their forehead and their arm those wonders which declare the power of God, and his good-will towards them, that God's readiness to bless them may appear everywhere conspicuous about them.[8]

---

8. Whether these phylacteries, and other Jewish memorials of the law here mentioned by Josephus, and by Moses (besides the fringes on the borders of their garments, Numbers

14. Let there be seven men to judge in every city, and these such as have been before most zealous in the exercise of virtue and righteousness. Let every judge have two officers allotted him out of the tribe of Levi. Let those that are chosen to judge in the several cities be had in great honor; and let none be permitted to revile any others when these are present, nor to carry themselves in an insolent manner to them; it being natural that reverence towards those in high offices among men should procure men's fear and reverence towards God. Let those that judge be permitted to determine according as they think to be right, unless anyone can show that they have taken bribes, to the perversion of justice, or can allege any other accusation against them, whereby it may appear that they have passed an unjust sentence; for it is not fit that causes should be openly determined out of regard to gain, or to the dignity of the suitors, but that the judges should esteem what is right before all other things, otherwise God will by that means be despised, and esteemed inferior to those, the dread of whose power has occasioned the unjust sentence; for justice is the power of God. He therefore that gratifies those in great dignity, supposes them more potent than God himself. But if these judges be unable to give a just sentence about the causes that come before them, (which case is not infrequent in human affairs,) let them send the cause undetermined to the holy city, and there let the high priest, the prophet, and the sanhedrim, determine as it shall seem good to them.

15. But let not a single witness be credited, but three, or two at the least, and those such whose testimony is confirmed by their good lives. But let not the testimony of women be admitted, on account of the levity and boldness of their sex.[9] Nor let servants be admitted to give testimony, on account of the ignobility of their soul; since it is probable that they may not speak truth, either out of hope of gain, or fear of punishment. But if anyone be believed to have borne false witness, let him, when he is convicted, suffer all the very same punishments which he against whom he bore witness was to have suffered.

15:37), were literally meant by God, I much question. That they have been long observed by the Pharisees and Rabbinical Jews is certain; however, the Karaites, who receive not the unwritten traditions of the elders, but keep close to the written law, with Jerome and Grotius, think they were not literally to be understood. . . . Nor indeed do I remember that, either in the ancienter books of the Old Testament, or in the books we call Apocrypha, there are any signs of such literal observations appearing among the Jews, though their real or mystical signification, i.e., the constant remembrance and observation of the laws of God by Moses, be frequently inculcated in all the sacred writings.

9. I have never observed elsewhere, that in the Jewish government women were not admitted as legal witnesses in courts of justice. None of our copies of the Pentateuch say a word of it. It is very probable, however, that this was the exposition of the scribes and Pharisees, and the practice of the Jews in the days of Josephus.

16. If a murder be committed in any place, and he that did it be not found, nor is there any suspicion upon one as if he had hated the man, and so had killed him, let there be a very diligent inquiry made after the man, and rewards proposed to anyone who will discover him; but if still no information can be procured, let the magistrates and senate of those cities that lie near the place in which the murder was committed, assemble together, and measure the distance from the place where the dead body lies; then let the magistrates of the nearest city thereto purchase a heifer, and bring it to a valley, and to a place therein where there is no land ploughed or trees planted, and let them cut the sinews of the heifer; then the priests and Levites, and the senate of that city, shall take water and wash their hands over the head of the heifer; and they shall openly declare that their hands are innocent of this murder, and that they have neither done it themselves, nor been assisting to any that did it. They shall also beseech God to be merciful to them, that no such horrid act may any more be done in that land.

17. Aristocracy, and the way of living under it, is the best constitution: and may you never have any inclination to any other form of government; and may you always love that form, and have the laws for your governors, and govern all your actions according to them; for you need no supreme governor but God. But if you shall desire a king, let him be one of your own nation; let him be always careful of justice and other virtues perpetually; let him submit to the laws, and esteem God's commands to be his highest wisdom; but let him do nothing without the high priest and the votes of the senators: let him not have a great number of wives, nor pursue after abundance of riches, nor a multitude of horses, whereby he may grow too proud to submit to the laws. And if he affect any such things, let him be restrained, lest he become so potent that his state be inconsistent with your welfare.

18. Let it not be esteemed lawful to remove boundaries, neither our own, nor of those with whom we are at peace. Have a care you do not take those landmarks away which are, as it were, a divine and unshaken limitation of rights made by God himself, to last forever; since this going beyond limits, and gaining ground upon others, is the occasion of wars and seditions; for those that remove boundaries are not far off an attempt to subvert the laws.

19. He that plants a piece of land, the trees of which produce fruits before the fourth year, is not to bring thence any first-fruits to God, nor is he to make use of that fruit himself, for it is not produced in its proper season; for when nature has a force put upon her at an unseasonable time, the fruit is not proper for God, nor for the master's use; but let the owner

gather all that is grown on the fourth car, for then it is in its proper season. And let him that has gathered it carry it to the holy city, and spend that, together with the tithe of his other fruits, in feasting with his friends, with the orphans, and the widows. But on the fifth year the fruit is his own, and he may use it as he pleases.

20. You are not to sow with seed a piece of land which is planted with vines, for it is enough that it supply nourishment to that plant, and be not harassed by ploughing also. You are to plough your land with oxen, and not to oblige other animals to come under the same yoke with them; but to till your land with those beasts that are of the same kind with each other. The seeds are also to be pure, and without mixture, and not to be compounded of two or three sorts, since nature does not rejoice in the union of things that are not in their own nature alike; nor are you to permit beasts of different kinds to gender together, for there is reason to fear that this unnatural abuse may extend from beasts of different kinds to men, though it takes its first rise from evil practices about such smaller things. Nor is anything to be allowed, by imitation whereof any degree of subversion may creep into the constitution. Nor do the laws neglect small matters, but provide that even those may be managed after an unblamable manner.

21. Let not those that reap, and gather in the corn that is reaped, gather in the gleanings also; but let them rather leave some handfuls for those that are in want of the necessaries of life, that it may be a support and a supply to them, in order to their subsistence. In like manner when they gather their grapes, let them leave some smaller bunches for the poor, and let them pass over some of the fruits of the olive-trees, when they gather them, and leave them to be partaken of by those that have none of their own; for the advantage arising from the exact collection of all, will not be so considerable to the owners as will arise from the gratitude of the poor. And God will provide that the land shall more willingly produce what shall be for the nourishment of its fruits, in case you do not merely take care of your own advantage, but have regard to the support of others also. Nor are you to muzzle the mouths of the oxen when they tread the ears of corn in the thrashing-floor; for it is not just to restrain our fellow-laboring animals, and those that work in order to its production, of this fruit of their labors. Nor are you to prohibit those that pass by at the time when your fruits are ripe to touch them, but to give them leave to fill themselves full of what you have; and this whether they be of your own country or strangers,—as being glad of the opportunity of giving them some part of your fruits when they are ripe; but let it not be esteemed lawful for them to carry any away. Nor let those that gather the grapes, and carry them to the wine-presses, restrain those whom they meet from eating of them;

for it is unjust, out of envy, to hinder those that desire it, to partake of the good things that come into the world according to God's will, and this while the season is at the height, and is hastening away as it pleases God. Nay, if some, out of bashfulness, are unwilling to touch these fruits, let them be encouraged to take of them (I mean, those that are Israelites) as if they were themselves the owners and lords, on account of the kindred there is between them. Nay, let them desire men that come from other countries, to partake of these tokens of friendship which God has given in their proper season; for that is not to be deemed as idly spent, which anyone out of kindness communicates to another, since God bestows plenty of good things on men, not only for themselves to reap the advantage, but also to give to others in a way of generosity; and he is desirous, by this means, to make known to others his peculiar kindness to the people of Israel, and how freely he communicates happiness to them, while they abundantly communicate out of their great superfluities to even these foreigners also. But for him that acts contrary to this law, let him be beaten with forty stripes save one by the public executioner; let him undergo this punishment, which is a most ignominious one for a free-man, and this because he was such a slave to gain as to lay a blot upon his dignity; for it is proper for you who have had the experience of the afflictions in Egypt, and of those in the wilderness, to make provision for those that are in the like circumstances; and while you have now obtained plenty yourselves, through the mercy and providence of God, to distribute of the same plenty, by the like sympathy, to such as stand in need of it.

22. Besides those two tithes, which I have already said you are to pay every year, the one for the Levites, the other for the festivals, you are to bring every third year a third tithe to be distributed to those that want; to women also that are widows, and to children that are orphans. But as to the ripe fruits, let them carry that which is ripe first of all into the temple; and when they have blessed God for that land which bare them, and which he had given them for a possession, when they have also offered those sacrifices which the law has commanded them to bring, let them give the first-fruits to the priests. But when anyone hath done this, and hath brought the tithe of all that he hath, together with those first-fruits that are for the Levites, and for the festivals, and when he is about to go home, let him stand before the holy house, and return thanks to God, that he hath delivered them from the injurious treatment they had in Egypt, and hath given them a good land, and a large, and lets them enjoy the fruits thereof; and when he hath openly testified that he hath fully paid the tithes [and other dues] according to the laws of Moses, let him entreat God that he will be ever merciful and gracious to him, and continue so to be to all the

Hebrews, both by preserving the good things which he hath already given them, and by adding what it is still in his power to bestow upon them.

23. Let the Hebrews marry, at the age fit for it, virgins that are free, and born of good parents. And he that does not marry a virgin, let him not corrupt another man's wife, and marry her, nor grieve her former husband. Nor let free men marry slaves, although their affections should strongly bias any of them so to do; for it is decent, and for the dignity of the persons themselves, to govern those their affections. And further, no one ought to marry a harlot, whose matrimonial oblations, arising from the prostitution of her body, God will not receive; for by these means the dispositions of the children will be liberal and virtuous; I mean, when they are not born of base parents, and of the lustful conjunction of such as marry women that are not free. If anyone has been espoused to a woman as to a virgin, and does not afterward find her so to be, let him bring his action, and accuse her, and let him make use of such indications[10] to prove his accusation as he is furnished withal; and let the father or the brother of the damsel, or someone that is after them nearest of kin to her, defend her If the damsel obtain a sentence in her favor, that she had not been guilty, let her live with her husband that accused her; and let him not have any further power at all to put her away, unless she give him very great occasions of suspicion, and such as can be no way contradicted. But for him that brings an accusation and calumny against his wife in an impudent and rash manner, let him be punished by receiving forty stripes save one, and let him pay fifty shekels to her father: but if the damsel be convicted, as having been corrupted, and is one of the common people, let her be stoned, because she did not preserve her virginity till she were lawfully married; but if she were the daughter of a priest, let her be burnt alive. If anyone has two wives, and if he greatly respect and be kind to one of them, either out of his affection to her, or for her beauty, or for some other reason, while the other is of less esteem with him; and if the son of her that is beloved be the younger by birth than another born of the other wife, but endeavors to obtain the right of primogeniture from his father's kindness to his mother, and would thereby obtain a double portion

---

10. These tokens of virginity, as the Hebrew and Septuagint style them (Deuteronomy 22:15, 17, 20), seem to me very different from what our later interpreters suppose. They appear rather to have been such close linen garments as were never put off virgins, after, a certain age, till they were married, but before witnesses, and which, while they were entire, were certain evidences of such virginity. (See 2 Samuel 13:18; Isaiah 6:1.) Josephus here determines nothing what were these particular tokens of virginity or of corruption: perhaps he thought he could not easily describe them to the heathens, without saying what they might have thought a breach of modesty; which seeming breach of modesty laws cannot always wholly avoid.

of his father's substance, for that double portion is what I have allotted him in the laws,—let not this be permitted; for it is unjust that he who is the elder by birth should be deprived of what is due to him, on the father's disposition of his estate, because his mother was not equally regarded by him. He that hath corrupted a damsel espoused to another man, in case he had her consent, let both him and her be put to death, for they are both equally guilty; the man, because he persuaded the woman willingly to submit to a most impure action, and to prefer it to lawful wedlock; the woman, because she was persuaded to yield herself to be corrupted, either for pleasure or for gain. However, if a man light on a woman when she is alone, and forces her, where nobody was present to come to her assistance, let him only be put to death. Let him that hath corrupted a virgin not yet espoused marry her; but if the father of the damsel be not willing that she should be his wife, let him pay fifty shekels as the price of her prostitution. He that desires to be divorced from his wife for any cause whatsoever, (and many such causes happen among men,) let him in writing give assurance that he will never use her as his wife anymore; for by this means she may be at liberty to marry another husband, although before this bill of divorce be given, she is not to be permitted so to do: but if she be misused by him also, or if, when he is dead, her first husband would marry her again, it shall not be lawful for her to return to him. If a woman's husband die, and leave her without children, let his brother marry her, and let him call the son that is born to him by his brother's name, and educate him as the heir of his inheritance, for this procedure will be for the benefit of the public, because thereby families will not fail, and the estate will continue among the kindred; and this will be for the solace of wives under their affliction, that they are to be married to the next relation of their former husbands. But if the brother will not marry her, let the woman come before the senate, and protest openly that this brother will not admit her for his wife, but will injure the memory of his deceased brother, while she is willing to continue in the family, and to hear him children. And when the senate have inquired of him for what reason it is that he is averse to this marriage, whether he gives a bad or a good reason, the matter must come to this issue, That the woman shall loose the sandals of the brother, and shall spit in his face, and say, He deserves this reproachful treatment from her, as having injured the memory of the deceased. And then let him go away out of the senate, and bear this reproach upon him all his life long; and let her marry to whom she pleases, of such as seek her in marriage. But now, if any man take captive, either a virgin, or one that hath been married,[11] and has a mind to marry her, let him not be allowed to bring her to bed to him, or to live with her as his wife, before she hath her head shaven, and hath put on her mourning habit, and lamented her relations and friends that were slain in the battle, that by this means she may give vent to her sorrow for them, and after that may betake herself to feasting and matrimony; for it is good for him that takes a woman, in order to have children by her, to be complaisant to her inclinations, and not merely to pursue his own pleasure, while he hath no regard to what is agreeable to her. But when thirty days are past, as the time of mourning, for so many are sufficient to prudent persons for lamenting the dearest friends, then let them proceed to the marriage; but in case when he hath satisfied his lust, he be too proud to retain her for his wife, let him not have it in his power to make her a slave, but let her go away whither she pleases, and have that privilege of a free woman.

24. As to those young men that despise their parents, and do not pay them honor, but offer them affronts, either because they are ashamed of them or think themselves wiser than they,—in the first place, let their parents admonish them in words, (for they are by nature of authority sufficient for becoming their judges,) and let them say thus to them:— That they cohabited together, not for the sake of pleasure, nor for the augmentation of their riches, by joining both their stocks together, but that they might have children to take care of them in their old age, and might by them have what they then should want. And say further to him, "That when thou wast born, we took thee up with gladness, and gave God the greatest thanks for thee, and brought time up with great care, and spared for nothing that appeared useful for thy preservation, and for thy instruction in what was most excellent. And now, since it is reasonable to forgive the sins of those that are young, let it suffice thee to have given so many indications Of thy contempt of us; reform thyself, and act more wisely for the time to come; considering that God is displeased with those that are insolent towards their parents, because he is himself the Father of the whole race of mankind, and seems to bear part of that dishonor which falls upon those that have the same name, when they do not meet with dire returns from their children. And on such the law inflicts inexorable punishment; of which punishment mayst thou never have the experience." Now if the insolence of young men be thus cured, let them escape the reproach which their former errors deserved; for by

---

11. Here it is supposed that this captive's husband, if she were before a married woman, was dead before, or rather was slain in this very battle, otherwise it would have been adultery in him that married her.

this means the lawgiver will appear to be good, and parents happy, while they never behold either a son or a daughter brought to punishment. But if it happen that these words and instructions, conveyed by them in order to reclaim the man, appear to be useless, then the offender renders the laws implacable enemies to the insolence he has offered his parents; let him therefore be brought forth by these very parents out of the city, with a multitude following him, and there let him be stoned; and when he has continued there for one whole day, that all the people may see him, let him be buried in the night. And thus it is that we bury all whom the laws condemn to die, upon any account whatsoever. Let our enemies that fall in battle be also buried; nor let anyone's dead body lie above the ground, or suffer a punishment beyond what justice requires.

25. Let no one lend to any one of the Hebrews upon usury, neither usury of what is eaten or what is drunken, for it is not just to make advantage of the misfortunes of one of thy own countrymen; but when thou hast been assistant to his necessities, think it thy gain if thou obtainest their gratitude to thee; and withal that reward which will come to thee from God, for thy humanity towards him.

26. Those who have borrowed either silver or any sort of fruits, whether dry or wet, (I mean this, when the Jewish affairs shall, by the blessing of God, be to their own mind,) let the borrowers bring them again, and restore them with pleasure to those who lent them, laying them up, as it were, in their own treasuries, and justly expecting to receive them thence, if they shall want them again. But if they be without shame, and do not restore it, let not the lender go to the borrower's house, and take a pledge himself, before judgment be given concerning it; but let him require the pledge, and let the debtor bring it of himself, without the least opposition to him that comes upon him under the protection of the law. And if he that gave the pledge be rich, let the creditor retain it till what he lent be paid him again; but if he be poor, let him that takes it return it before the going down of the sun, especially if the pledge be a garment, that the debtor may have it for a covering in his sleep, God himself naturally showing mercy to the poor. It is also not lawful to take a millstone, nor any utensil thereto belonging, for a pledge, that the debtor, may not be deprived of instruments to get their food withal, and lest they be undone by their necessity.

27. Let death be the punishment for stealing a man; but he that hath purloined gold or silver, let him pay double. If anyone kill a man that is stealing something out of his house, let him be esteemed guiltless, although the man were only breaking in at the wall. Let him that hath stolen cattle pay fourfold what is lost, excepting the case of an ox, for which let the

thief pay fivefold. Let him that is so poor that he cannot pay what mulct is laid upon him, be his servant to whom he was adjudged to pay it.

28. If anyone be sold to one of his own nation, let him serve him six years, and on the seventh let him go free. But if he have a son by a woman servant in his purchaser's house, and if, on account of his good-will to his master, and his natural affection to his wife and children, he will be his servant still, let him be set free only at the coming of the year of jubilee, which is the fiftieth year, and let him then take away with him his children and wife, and let them be free also.

29. If anyone find gold or silver on the road, let him inquire after him that lost it, and make proclamation of the place where he found it, and then restore it to him again, as not thinking it right to make his own profit by the loss of another. And the same rule is to be observed in cattle found to have wandered away into a lonely place. If the owner be not presently discovered, let him that is the finder keep it with himself, and appeal to God that he has not purloined what belongs to another.

30. It is not lawful to pass by any beast that is in distress, when in a storm it is fallen down in the mire, but to endeavor to preserve it, as having a sympathy with it in its pain.

31. It is also a duty to show the roads to those who do not know them, and not to esteem it a matter for sport, when we hinder others' advantages, by setting them in a wrong way.

32. In like manner, let no one revile a person blind or dumb.

33. If men strive together, and there be no instrument of iron, let him that is smitten be avenged immediately, by inflicting the same punishment on him that smote him: but if when he is carried home he lie sick many days, and then die, let him that smote him not escape punishment; but if he that is smitten escape death, and yet be at great expense for his cure, the smiter shall pay for all that has been expended during the time of his sickness, and for all that he has paid the physician. He that kicks a woman with child, so that the woman miscarry,[12] let him pay a fine in money, as the judges shall determine, as having diminished the multitude by the destruction of what was in her womb; and let money also be given the woman's husband by him that kicked her; but if she die of the stroke,

---

12. Philo and others appear to have understood this law (Exodus 21:22, 23) better than Josephus, who seems to allow, that though the infant in the mother's womb, even after the mother were quick, and so the infant had a rational soul, were killed by the stroke upon the mother, yet if the mother escaped, the offender should only be fined, and not put to death; while the law seems rather to mean, that if the infant in that case be killed, though the mother escape, the offender must be put to death, and not only when the mother is killed, as Josephus understood it. It seems this was the exposition of the Pharisees in the days of Josephus.

let him also be put to death, the law judging it equitable that life should go for life.

34. Let no one of the Israelites keep any poison that may cause death, or any other harm; but if he be caught with it, let him be put to death, and suffer the very same mischief that he would have brought upon them for whom the poison was prepared.[13]

35. He that maimeth anyone, let him undergo the like himself, and be deprived of the same member of which he hath deprived the other, unless he that is maimed will accept of money instead of it for the law makes the sufferer the judge of the value of what he hath suffered, and permits him to estimate it, unless he will be more severe.[14]

36. Let him that is the owner of an ox which pusheth with his horn, kill him: but if he pushes and gores anyone in the thrashing-floor, let him be put to death by stoning, and let him not be thought fit for food: but if his owner be convicted as having known what his nature was, and hath not kept him up, let him also be put to death, as being the occasion of the ox's having killed a man. But if the ox have killed a man-servant, or a maid-servant, let him be stoned; and let the owner of the ox pay thirty shekels to the master of him that was slain; but if it be an ox that is thus smitten and killed, let both the oxen, that which smote the other and that which was killed, be sold, and let the owners of them divide their price between them.

37. Let those that dig a well or a pit be careful to lay planks over them, and so keep them shut up, not in order to hinder any persons from drawing water, but that there may be no danger of falling into them. But if anyone's beast fall into such a well or pit thus digged, and not shut up, and perish, let the owner pay its price to the owner of the beast. Let there be a battlement round the tops of your houses instead of a wall, that may prevent any persons from rolling down and perishing.

38. Let him that has received anything in trust for another, take care to keep it as a sacred and divine thing; and let no one invent any contrivance whereby to deprive him that hath intrusted it with him of the same, and this whether he be a man or a woman; no, not although he or she were to gain an immense sum of gold, and this where he cannot be convicted of it by anybody; for it is fit that a man's own conscience, which knows what he hath, should in all cases oblige him to do well. Let this conscience be his witness, and make him always act so as may procure him commendation

---

13. What we render a witch, according to our modern notions of witchcraft (Exodus 22:15), Philo and Josephus understood of a poisoner, or one who attempted by secret and unlawful drugs or philtra, to take away the senses or the lives of men.

14. This permission of redeeming this penalty with money is not in our copies (Exodus 21:24, 25; Leviticus 24:20; Deuteronomy 19:21).

from others; but let him chiefly have regard to God, from whom no wicked man can lie concealed: but if he in whom the trust was reposed, without any deceit of his own, lose what he was intrusted withal, let him come before the seven judges, and swear by God that nothing hath been lost willingly, or with a wicked intention, and that he hath not made use of any part thereof, and so let him depart without blame; but if he hath made use of the least part of what was committed to him, and it be lost, let him be condemned to repay all that he had received. After the same manner as in these trusts it is to be, if anyone defraud those that undergo bodily labor for him. And let it be always remembered, that we are not to defraud a poor man of his wages, as being sensible that God has allotted these wages to him instead of land and other possessions; nay, this payment is not at all to be delayed, but to be made that very day, since God is not willing to deprive the laborer of the immediate use of what he hath labored for.

39. You are not to punish children for the faults of their parents, but on account of their own virtue rather to vouchsafe them commiseration, because they were born of wicked parents, than hatred, because they were born of bad ones. Nor indeed ought we to impute the sin of children to their fathers, while young persons indulge themselves in many practices different from what they have been instructed in, and this by their proud refusal of such instruction.

40. Let those that have made themselves eunuchs be had in detestation; and do you avoid any conversation with them who have deprived themselves of their manhood, and of that fruit of generation which God has given to men for the increase of their kind: let such be driven away, as if they had killed their children, since they beforehand have lost what should procure them; for evident it is, that while their soul is become effeminate, they have withal transfused that effeminacy to their body also. In like manner do you treat all that is of a monstrous nature when it is looked on; nor is it lawful to geld men or any other animals.

41. Let this be the constitution of your political laws in time of peace, and God will be so merciful as to preserve this excellent settlement free from disturbance: and may that time never come which may innovate anything, and change it for the contrary. But since it must needs happen that mankind fall into troubles and dangers, either undesignedly or intentionally, come let us make a few constitutions concerning them, that so being apprised beforehand what ought to be done, you may have salutary counsels ready when you want them, and may not then be obliged to go to seek what is to be done, and so be unprovided, and fall into dangerous circumstances. May you be a laborious people, and exercise your souls in virtuous actions, and thereby possess and inherit the land without wars; while neither any

foreigners make war upon it, and so afflict you, nor any internal sedition seize upon it, whereby you may do things that are contrary to your fathers, and so lose the laws which they have established. And may you continue in the observation of those laws which God hath approved of, and hath delivered to you. Let all sort of warlike operations, whether they befall you now in your own time, or hereafter in the times of your posterity, be done out of your own borders: but when you are about to go to war, send embassages and heralds to those who are your voluntary enemies, for it is a right thing to make use of words to them before you come to your weapons of war; and assure them thereby, that although you have a numerous army, with horses and weapons, and, above these, a God merciful to you, and ready to assist you, you do however desire them not to compel you to fight against them, nor to take from them what they have, which will indeed be our gain, but what they will have no reason to wish we should take to ourselves. And if they hearken to you, it will be proper for you to keep peace with them; but if they trust in their own strength, as superior to yours, and will not do you justice, lead your army against them, making use of God as your supreme Commander, but ordaining for a lieutenant under him one that is of the greatest courage among you; for these different commanders, besides their being an obstacle to actions that are to be done on the sudden, are a disadvantage to those that make use of them. Lead an army pure, and of chosen men, composed of all such as have extraordinary strength of body and hardiness of soul; but do you send away the timorous part, lest they run away in the time of action, and so afford an advantage to your enemies. Do you also give leave to those that have lately built them houses, and have not yet lived in them a year's time; and to those that have planted them vineyards, and have not yet been partakers of their fruits,—to continue in their own country; as well as those also who have betrothed, or lately married them wives, lest they have such an affection for these things that they he too sparing of their lives, and, by reserving themselves for these enjoyments, they become voluntary cowards, on account of their wives.

42. When you have pitched your camp, take care that you do nothing that is cruel. And when you are engaged in a siege; and want timber for the making of warlike engines, do not you render the land naked by cutting down trees that bear fruit, but spare them, as considering that they were made for the benefit of men; and that if they could speak, they would have a just plea against you, because, though they are not occasions of the war, they are unjustly treated, and suffer in it, and would, if they were able, remove themselves into another land. When you have beaten your enemies in battle, slay those that have fought against you; but preserve

the others alive, that they may pay you tribute, excepting the nation of the Canaanites; for as to that people, you must entirely destroy them.

43. Take care, especially in your battles, that no woman use the habit of a man, nor man the garment of a woman.

44. This was the form of political government which was left us by Moses. Moreover, he had already delivered laws in writing in the fortieth year [after they came out of Egypt], concerning which we will discourse in another book. But now on the following days (for he called them to assemble continually) he delivered blessings to them, and curses upon those that should not live according to the laws, but should transgress the duties that were determined for them to observe. After this, he read to them a poetic song, which was composed in hexameter verse, and left it to them in the holy book: it contained a prediction of what was to come to pass afterward; agreeably whereto all things have happened all along, and do still happen to us; and wherein he has not at all deviated from the truth. Accordingly, he delivered these books to the priest, with the ark; into which he also put the ten commandments, written on two tables. He delivered to them the tabernacle also, and exhorted the people, that when they had conquered the land, and were settled in it, they should not forget the injuries of the Amalekites, but make war against them, and inflict punishment upon them for what mischief they did them when they were in the wilderness; and that when they had got possession of the land of the Canaanites, and when they had destroyed the whole multitude of its inhabitants, as they ought to do, they should erect an altar that should face the rising sun, not far from the city of Shechem, between the two mountains, that of Gerizzim, situate on the right hand, and that called Ebal, on the left; and that the army should be so divided, that six tribes should stand upon each of the two mountains, and with them the Levites and the priests. And that first, those that were upon Mount Gerizzim should pray for the best blessings upon those who were diligent about the worship of God, and the observation of his laws, and who did not reject what Moses had said to them; while the other wished them all manner of happiness also; and when these last put up the like prayers, the former praised them. After this, curses were denounced upon those that should transgress those laws, they answering one another alternately, by way of confirmation of what had been said. Moses also wrote their blessings and their curses, that they might learn them so thoroughly, that they might never be forgotten by length of time. And when he was ready to die, he wrote these blessings and curses upon the altar, on each side of it; where he says also the people stood, and then sacrificed and offered burnt-offerings, though after that day they never offered upon it any other sacrifice, for it was not lawful

so to do. These are the constitutions of Moses; and the Hebrew nation still live according to them.

45. On the next day, Moses called the people together, with the women and children, to a congregation, so as the very slaves were present also, that they might engage themselves to the observation of these laws by oath; and that, duly considering the meaning of God in them, they might not, either for favor of their kindred, or out of fear of anyone, or indeed for any motive whatsoever, think anything ought to be preferred to these laws, and so might transgress them. That in case any one of their own blood, or any city, should attempt to confound or dissolve their constitution of government, they should take vengeance upon them, both all in general, and each person in particular; and when they had conquered them, should overturn their city to the very foundations, and, if possible, should not leave the least footsteps of such madness: but that if they were not able to take such vengeance, they should still demonstrate that what was done was contrary to their wills. So the multitude bound themselves by oath so to do.

46. Moses taught them also by what means their sacrifices might be the most acceptable to God; and how they should go forth to war, making use of the stones (in the high priest's breastplate) for their direction, as I have before signified. Joshua also prophesied while Moses was present. And when Moses had recapitulated whatsoever he had done for the preservation of the people, both in their wars and in peace, and had composed them a body of laws, and procured them an excellent form of government, he foretold, as God had declared to him "That if they transgressed that institution for the worship of God, they should experience the following miseries:—Their land should be full of weapons of war from their enemies, and their cities should be overthrown, and their temple should be burnt that they should be sold for slaves, to such men as would have no pity on them in their afflictions; that they would then repent, when that repentance would no way profit them under their sufferings. "Yet," said he, "will that God who founded your nation, restore your cities to your citizens, with their temple also; and you shall lose these advantages not once only, but often."

47. Now when Moses had encouraged Joshua to lead out the army against the Canaanites, by telling him that God would assist him in all his undertakings, and had blessed the whole multitude, he said, "Since I am going to my forefathers, and God has determined that this should be the day of my departure to them, I return him thanks while I am still alive and present with you, for that providence he hath exercised over you, which hath not only delivered us from the miseries we lay under, but hath bestowed a state of prosperity upon us; as also, that he hath assisted me in

the pains I took, and in all the contrivances I had in my care about you, in order to better your condition, and hath on all occasions showed himself favorable to us; or rather he it was who first conducted our affairs, and brought them to a happy conclusion, by making use of me as a vicarious general under him, and as a minister in those matters wherein he was willing to do you good: on which account I think it proper to bless that Divine Power which will take care of you for the time to come, and this in order to repay that debt which I owe him, and to leave behind me a memorial that we are obliged to worship and honor him, and to keep those laws which are the most excellent gift of all those he hath already bestowed upon us, or which, if he continue favorable to us, he will bestow upon us hereafter. Certainly a human legislator is a terrible enemy when his laws are affronted, and are made to no purpose. And may you never experience that displeasure of God which will be the consequence of the neglect of these his laws, which he, who is your Creator, hath given you."

48. When Moses had spoken thus at the end of his life, and had foretold what would befall to every one of their tribes afterward,[15] with the addition of a blessing to them, the multitude fell into tears, insomuch that even the women, by beating their breasts, made manifest the deep concern they had when he was about to die. The children also lamented still more, as not able to contain their grief; and thereby declared, that even at their age they were sensible of his virtue and mighty deeds; and truly there seemed to be a strife betwixt the young and the old who should most grieve for him. The old grieved because they knew what a careful protector they were to be deprived of, and so lamented their future state; but the young grieved, not only for that, but also because it so happened that they were to be left by him before they had well tasted of his virtue. Now one may make a guess at the excess of this sorrow and lamentation of the multitude, from what happened to the legislator himself; for although he was always persuaded that he ought not to be cast down at the approach of death, since the undergoing it was agreeable to the will of God and the law of nature, yet what the people did so overbore him, that he wept himself. Now as he went thence to the place where he was to vanish out of their sight, they all followed after him weeping; but Moses beckoned with his hand to those that were remote from him, and bade them stay behind in quiet, while he exhorted those that were near to him that they would not render his departure so lamentable. Whereupon they thought they ought

---

15. Since Josephus assures us here, as is most naturally to be supposed, and as the Septuagint gives the text (Deuteronomy 33:6), that Moses blessed every one of the tribes of Israel, it is evident that Simeon was not omitted in his copy, as it unhappily now is, both in our Hebrew and Samaritan copies.

to grant him that favor, to let him depart according as he himself desired; so they restrained themselves, though weeping still towards one another. All those who accompanied him were the senate, and Eleazar the high priest, and Joshua their commander. Now as soon as they were come to the mountain called *Abarim,* (which is a very high mountain, situate over against Jericho, and one that affords, to such as are upon it, a prospect of the greatest part of the excellent land of Canaan,) he dismissed the senate; and as he was going to embrace Eleazar and Joshua, and was still discoursing with them, a cloud stood over him on the sudden, and he disappeared in a certain valley, although he wrote in the holy books that he died, which was done out of fear, lest they should venture to say that, because of his extraordinary virtue, he went to God.

49. Now Moses lived in all one hundred and twenty years; a third part of which time, abating one month, he was the people's ruler; and he died on the last month of the year, which is called by the Macedonians *Dystrus,* but by us *Adar,* on the first day of the month. He was one that exceeded all men that ever were in understanding, and made the best use of what that understanding suggested to him. He had a very graceful way of speaking and addressing himself to the multitude; and as to his other qualifications, he had such a full command of his passions, as if he hardly had any such in his soul, and only knew them by their names, as rather perceiving them in other men than in himself. He was also such a general of an army as is seldom seen, as well as such a prophet as was never known, and this to such a degree, that whatsoever he pronounced, you would think you heard the voice of God himself. So the people mourned for him thirty days: nor did ever any grief so deeply affect the Hebrews as did this upon the death of Moses: nor were those that had experienced his conduct the only persons that desired him, but those also that perused the laws he left behind him had a strong desire after him, and by them gathered the extraordinary virtue he was master of. And this shall suffice for the declaration of the manner of the death of Moses.

APPENDIX

"MOSES," FROM *Jewish Encyclopedia*

BIBLICAL DATA

The birth of Moses occurred at a time when Pharaoh had commanded that all male children born to Hebrew captives should be thrown into the Nile (Ex. ii.; comp. i.). Jochebed, the wife of the Levite Amram, bore a son, and kept the child concealed for three months. When she could keep him hidden no longer, rather than deliver him to death she set him adrift on the Nile in an ark of bulrushes. The daughter of Pharaoh, coming opportunely to the river to bathe, discovered the babe, was attracted to him, adopted him as her son, and named him "Moses." Thus it came about that the future deliverer of Israel was reared as the son of an Egyptian princess (Ex. ii. 1-10).

When Moses was grown to manhood, he went one day to see how it fared with his brethren, bondmen to the Egyptians. Seeing an Egyptian maltreating a Hebrew, he killed the Egyptian and hid his body in the sand, supposing that no one who would be disposed to reveal the matter knew of it. The next day, seeing two Hebrews quarreling, he endeavored to separate them, whereupon the Hebrew who was wronging his brother taunted Moses with slaying the Egyptian. Moses soon discovered from a higher source that the affair was known, and that Pharaoh was likely to put him to death for it; he therefore made his escape to the Sinaitic Peninsula and settled with Hobab, or Jethro, priest of Midian, whose daughter Zipporah he in due time married. There he sojourned forty years, following the occupation of a shepherd, during which time his son Gershom was born (Ex. ii., 11-22).

One day, as Moses led his flock to Mount Horeb, he saw a bush burning but without being consumed. When he turned aside to look more closely at the marvel, Yhwh spoke to him from the bush and commissioned him to return to Egypt and deliver his brethren from their bondage (Ex. iii. 1-10). According to Ex. iii. 13 *et seq.*, it was at this time that the name of Yhwh was revealed, though it is frequently used throughout the patriarchal narratives, from the second chapter of Genesis on. Armed with this new name and with certain signs which he could give in attestation of his mission, he returned to Egypt (Ex. iv. 1-9, 20). On the way he was met by Yhwh, who would have killed him; but Zipporah, Moses' wife, circumcised her son and Yhwh's anger abated (Ex. iv. 24-26). Moses was met and assisted on his arrival in Egypt by his elder brother, Aaron, and readily gained a hearing with his oppressed brethren (Ex. iv. 27-31). It was a more difficult matter, however, to persuade Pharaoh to let the Hebrews depart. Indeed, this was not accomplished until, through the agency of Moses, ten plagues had come upon the Egyptians (Ex. vii.-xii.). These plagues culminated in the slaying of the Egyptian firstborn (Ex. xii. 29), whereupon such terror seized the Egyptians that they urged the Hebrews to leave.

In the Wilderness

The children of Israel, with their flocks and herds, started toward the eastern border at the southern part of the Isthmus of Suez. The long procession moved slowly, and found it necessary to encamp three times before passing the Egyptian frontier at the Bitter Lakes. Meanwhile Pharaoh had repented and was in pursuit of them with a large army (Ex. xiv. 5-9). Shut in between this army and the Red Sea, or the Bitter Lakes, which were then connected with it, the Israelites despaired, but Yhwh divided the waters of the sea so that they passed safely across; when the Egyptians attempted to follow, He permitted the waters to return upon them and drown them (Ex. xiv. 10-31). Moses led the Hebrews to Sinai, or Horeb, where Jethro celebrated their coming by a great sacrifice in the presence of Moses, Aaron, and the elders of Israel (Ex. xviii.). At Horeb, or Sinai, Yhwh welcomed Moses upon the sacred mountain and talked with him face to face (Ex. xix.). He gave him the Ten Commandments and the Law and entered into a covenant with Israel through him. This covenant bound Yhwh to be Israel's God, if Israel would keep His commandments (Ex. xix. *et seq.*).

Moses and the Israelites sojourned at Sinai about a year (comp. Num. x. 11), and Moses had frequent communications from Yhwh. As a result of these the Tabernacle, according to the last chapters of Exodus, was constructed, the priestly law ordained, the plan of encampment arranged both for the Levites and the non-priestly tribes (comp. Num. i. 50-ii. 34), and the Tabernacle consecrated. While at Sinai Joshua had become general of the armies of Israel and the special minister, or assistant, of Moses (Ex. xvii. 9). From Sinai Moses led the people to Kadesh, whence the spies were sent to Canaan. Upon the return of the spies the people were so discouraged by their report that they refused to go forward, and were condemned to remain in the wilderness until that generation had passed away (Num. xiii.-xiv.).

After the lapse of thirty-eight years Moses led the people eastward. Having gained friendly permission to do so, they passed through the territory of Esau (where Aaron died, on Mount Hor; Num. xx. 22-29), and then, by a similar arrangement, through the land of Moab. But Sihon, king of the Amorites, whose capital was at Heshbon, refused permission, and was conquered by Moses, who allotted his territory to the tribes of Reuben and Gad. Og, King of Bashan, was similarly overthrown (comp. Num. xxi.), and his territory assigned to the half-tribe of Manasseh.

Death of Moses

After all this was accomplished Moses was warned that he would not be permitted to lead Israel across the Jordan, but would die on the eastern side (Num. xx. 12). He therefore assembled the tribes and delivered to them a parting address, which forms the Book of Deuteronomy. In this address it is commonly supposed that he recapitulated the Law, reminding them of its most important features. When this was finished, and he had pronounced a blessing upon the people, he went up Mount Nebo to the top of Pisgah, looked over the country spread out before him, and died, at the age of one hundred and twenty. Yhwh Himself buried him in an unknown grave (Deut. xxxiv.). Moses was thus the human instrument in the creation of the Israelitish nation; he communicated to it all its laws. More meek than any other man (Num. xii. 3), he enjoyed unique privileges, for "there hath not arisen a prophet since in Israel like unto Moses, whom the Lord knew face to face" (Deut. xxxiv. 10).

IN RABBINICAL LITERATURE

Of all Biblical personages Moses has been chosen most frequently as the subject of later legends; and his life has been recounted in full detail in the poetic haggadah. As liberator, lawgiver, and leader of a people which was transformed by him from an unorganized horde into a nation, he occupies a more important place in popular legend than the Patriarchs and all the other national heroes. His many-sided activity also offered more abundant scope for imaginative embellishment. A cycle of legends has been woven around nearly every trait of his character and every event of his life; and groups of the most different and often contradictory stories have been connected with his career. It would be interesting to investigate the origin of the different cycles, and the relation of the several cycles to one another and to the original source, if there was one. The present article attempts to give, without claiming completeness, a picture of the character of Moses according to Jewish legend and a narrative of the most important incidents of his life. (The following special abbreviations of book-titles are used: "D. Y." = "Dibre ha-Yamim le-Mosheh Rabbenu," in Jellinek, "B. H." ii.; "S. Y." = "Sefer ha-Yashar"; "M. W." = "Midrash Wayosha'," in Jellinek, *l.c.*)

The Beginnings

Moses' influence and activity reach back to the days of the Creation. Heaven and earth were created only for his sake (Lev. R. xxxvi. 4). The account of the creation of the water on the second day (Gen. i. 6-8), therefore, does not close with the usual formula, "And God saw that it was good," because God foresaw that Moses would suffer through water (Gen. R. iv. 8). Although Noah was not worthy to be saved from the Flood, yet he was saved because Moses was destined to descend from him (*ib.* xxvi. 15). The angels which Jacob in his nocturnal vision saw ascending to and descending from heaven (Gen. vii. 12) were really Moses and Aaron (Gen. R. lxviii. 16). The birth of Moses as the liberator of the people of Israel was foretold to Pharaoh by his soothsayers, in consequence of which he issued the cruel command to cast all the male children into the river (Ex. i. 22). Later on Miriam also foretold to her father, Amram, that a son would be born to him who would liberate Israel from the yoke of Egypt (Sotah 11b, 12a; Meg. 14a; Ex. R. i. 24; "S. Y.," Shemot, pp. 111a, 112b; comp. Josephus, "Ant." ii. 9, § 3). Moses was born on Adar 7 (Meg. 13b) in the year 2377 after the creation of the world (Book of Jubilees, xlvii. 1). He was born circumcised (Sotah 12a), and was able to walk immediately after his birth (Yalk., Wayelek, 940); but according to another story he was circumcised on the eighth day after birth (Pirke R. El. xlviii.). A peculiar and glorious light filled the entire house at his birth (*ib.*; "S. Y." p. 112b), indicating that he was worthy of the gift of prophecy (Sotah*l.c.*). He spoke with his father and mother on the day of his birth, and prophesied at the age of three (Midr. Petirat Mosheh, in Jellinek, "B. H." i. 128). His mother kept his birth secret for three months, when Pharaoh was informed that she had borne a son. The mother put the child into a casket, which she hid among the reeds of the sea before the king's officers came to her (Jubilees, *l.c.* 47; "D. Y." in Jellinek, "B. H." ii. 3; "S. Y." p. 112b). For seven days his mother went to him at night to nurse him, his sister Miriam protecting him from the birds by day (Jubilees, *l.c.* 4).

Pharaoh's Daughter

Then God sent a fierce heat upon Egypt ("D. Y." *l.c.*), and Pharaoh's daughter Bithiah (comp. I. Chron. iv. 18; Tarmut [Thermutis], according to Josephus, *l.c.* and Jubilees, *l.c.*), who was afflicted with leprosy, went to bathe in the river. Hearing a child cry, she beheld a casket in the reeds. She caused it to be brought to her, and on touching it was cured of her leprosy (Ex. R. i. 27). For this reason she was kindly disposed toward the child. When she opened the casket she was astonished at his beauty (Philo, "Vita Mosis," ii.), and saw the Shekinah with him (Ex. R. i. 28). Noticing that the child was circumcised, she knew that the parents must have been Hebrews (Sotah 12b). Gabriel struck Moses, so as to make him cry and arouse the pity of the princess (Ex. R. i. 28). She wished to save the child; but as her maids told her she must not transgress her father's commands, she set him down again (Midr. Abkir, in Yalk., Ex. 166). Then Gabriel threw all her maids down (Sotah 12b; Ex. R. i. 27); and God filled Bithiah with compassion (Yalk., *l.c.*), and caused the child to find favor in her eyes ("M. W." in Jellinek, *l.c.* i. 41). Thereupon she took the child up, saved him, and loved him much (Ex. R. *l.c.*). This was on the sixth day of the month of Siwan (Sotah 12b); according to another version, on Nisan 21 (*ib.*). When the soothsayers told Pharaoh that the redeemer of Israel had been born and thrown into the water, the cruel edict ordering that the children be thrown into the river was repealed (Ex. R. i. 29; Sotah *l.c.*). Thus the casting away of Moses saved Israel from further persecution. According to another version (Gen. R. xcvii. 5), 600,000 children had already been thrown into the river, but all were saved because of Moses.

His Bringing Up

Bithiah, Pharaoh's daughter, took up the child to nurse him; but he refused the breast ("M. W." *l.c.*). Then she gave him to other Egyptian women to nurse, but he refused to take nourishment from any of them (Josephus, *l.c.* ii. 9, § 5; "S. Y." p. 112b; Sotah 12b; "D. Y." p. 3). The mouth which was destined to speak with God might not take unclean milk (Sotah *l.c.*; "D. Y." *l.c.*); Bithiah therefore gave him to his mother to nurse. Another legend says that he did not take any milk from the breast (Yalk., Wayelek, 940). Bithiah then adopted him as her son ("S. Y." p. 113b). Aside from the name "Moses," which Bithiah gave to him (Ex. ii. 10), he had seven (Lev. R. i. 3), or according to other stories ten, other names given to him by his mother, his father, his brother Aaron, his sister Miriam, his nurse, his grandfather Kehat, and Israel ("D. Y." p. 3; "S. Y." p. 112b; Meg. 13a). These names were: Jared, Abi Gedor, Heber,

Abi Soko, Jekuthiel, Abi Zanoah, and Shemaiah ("Shama 'Yah" = "God has heard"), the last one being given to him by Israel. He was also called "Heman" ([*i.e.*, Num. xii. 7] B. B. 15a).

Removes Pharaoh's Crown

Moses was a very large child at the age of three (Ex. R. i. 32; comp. Josephus; *l.c.*; Philo, *l.c.*); and it was at this time that, sitting at the king's table in the presence of several princes and counselors, he took the crown from Pharaoh's head and placed it on his own ("D. Y." *l.c.*; for another version see "M. W." *l.c.*). The princes were horrified at the boy's act; and the soothsayer said that this was the same boy who, in accordance with their former predictions, would destroy the kingdom of Pharaoh and liberate Israel (Josephus, *l.c.*; "M. W." *l.c.*). Balaam and Jethro were at that time also among the king's counselors (Sotah 11a; Sanh. 106). Balaam advised the king to kill the boy at once; but Jethro (according to "D. Y." *l.c.*, it was Gabriel in the guise of one of the king's counselors) said that the boy should first be examined, to see whether he had sense enough to have done such an act intentionally. All agreed with this advice. A shining piece of gold, or a precious stone, together with a live coal, was placed on a plate before the boy, to see which of the two he would choose. The angel Gabriel then guided his hand to the coal, which he took up and put into his mouth. This burned his tongue, causing him to stutter (comp. Ex. iv. 10); but it saved his life ("M. W." *l.c.*; "D. Y." *l.c.*; "S. Y." *l.c.*; Ex. R. i. 31).

Moses remained in Pharaoh's house fifteen years longer ("D. Y." *l.c.*; "M. W." *l.c.*). According to the Book of Jubilees (*l.c.*), he learned the writing of the Assyrians (the "Ketab Ashurit"; the square script?) from his father, Amram. During his sojourn in the king's palace he often went to his brethren, the slaves of Pharaoh, sharing their sad lot. He helped any one who bore a too heavy burden or was too weak for his work. He reminded Pharaoh that a slave was entitled to some rest, and begged him to grant the Israelites one free day in the week. Pharaoh acceded to this request, and Moses accordingly instituted the seventh day, the Sabbath, as a day of rest for the Israelites (Ex. R. i. 32; "S. Y." p. 115a).

Flees from Egypt

Moses did not commit murder in killing the Egyptian (Ex. ii. 12); for the latter merited death because he had forced an Israelitish woman to commit adultery with him (Ex. R. i. 33). Moses was at that time eighteen years of age ("D. Y." *l.c.*; "M. W." *l.c.*; "S. Y." *l.c.*). According to another version, Moses was then twenty, or possibly forty, years of age (Ex. R. i. 32, 35).

These divergent opinions regarding his age at the time when he killed the Egyptian are based upon different estimates of the length of his stay in the royal palace (Yalk., Shemot, 167; Gen. R. xi.), both of them assuming that he fled from Egypt immediately after the slaying (Ex. ii. 15). Dathan and Abiram were bitter enemies of Moses, insulting him and saying he should not act as if he were a member of the royal house, since he was the son not of Batya, but of Jochebed. Previous to this they had slandered him before Pharaoh. Pharaoh had forgiven Moses everything else, but would not forgive him for killing the Egyptian. He delivered him to the executioner, who chose a very sharp sword with which to kill Moses; but the latter's neck became like a marble pillar, dulling the edge of the sword ("M. W." *l.c.*). Meanwhile the angel Michael descended from heaven, and took the form of the executioner, giving the latter the shape of Moses and so killing him. He then took up Moses and carried him beyond the frontier of Egypt for a distance of three, or, according to another account, of forty, days ("D. Y." *l.c.*; "S. Y." p. 115b). According to another legend, the angel took the shape of Moses, and allowed himself to be caught, thus giving the real Moses an opportunity to escape (Mek., Yitro. 1 [ed. Weiss. 66a]; Ex. R. i. 36).

King in Ethiopia

The fugitive Moses went to the camp of King Nikanos, or Kikanos, of Ethiopia, who was at that time besieging his own capital, which had been traitorously seized by Balaam and his sons and made impregnable by them through magic. Moses joined the army of Nikanos, and the king and all his generals took a fancy to him, because he was courageous as a lion and his face gleamed like the sun ("S. Y." P. 116a; comp. B. B. 75a). When Moses had spent nine years with the army King Nikanos died, and the Hebrew was made general. He took the city, driving out Balaam and his sons Jannes and Jambres, and was proclaimed king by the Ethiopians. He was obliged, in deference to the wishes of the people, to marry Nikanos' widow, Adoniya (comp. Num. xii.), with whom he did not, however, cohabit ("D. Y." *l.c.*; "S. Y." p. 116b). Miriam and Aaron spoke against Moses on account of the Cushite (Ethiopian) woman whom he had married. He was twenty-seven years of age when he became king; and he ruled over Ethiopia for forty years, during which he considerably increased the power of the country. After forty years his wife, Queen Adoniya, accused him before the princes and generals of not having cohabited with her during the many years of their marriage, and of never having worshiped the Ethiopian gods. She called upon the princes not to suffer a stranger among them as king, but to make her son by Nikanos, Munahas or Munakaros, king. The princes complied with her wishes, but dismissed Moses in peace, giving him great treasures. Moses, who was at this time sixty-seven years old, went from Ethiopia to Midian (*ib.*).

According to Josephus' account of this story (see Moses in Hellenistic Literature), after Moses' marriage to the daughter of the Ethiopian king, he did not become King of Ethiopia, but led his troops back to Egypt, where he remained. The Egyptians and even Pharaoh himself were envious of his glorious deeds, fearing also that he might use his power to gain dominion over Egypt. They therefore sought how they might assassinate him; and Moses, learning of the plot, fled to Midian. This narrative of Josephus' agrees with two haggadic accounts, according to which Moses fled from Egypt direct to Midian, not staying in Ethiopia at all. These accounts are as follows: (1) Moses lived for twenty years in Pharaoh's house; he then went to Midian, where he remained for sixty years, when, as a man of eighty, he undertook the mission of liberating Israel (Yalk., Shemot, 167). (2) Moses lived for forty years in Pharaoh's house; thence he went to Midian, where he stayed for forty years until his mission was entrusted to him (Gen. R. xi.; comp. Sifre, Deut. xxxiv. 7).

Relations with Jethro

On his arrival at Midian Moses told his whole story to Jethro, who recognized him as the man destined to destroy the Egyptians. He therefore took Moses prisoner in order to deliver him to Pharaoh ("D. Y." *l.c.*). According to another legend, Jethro took him for an Ethiopian fugitive, and intended to deliver him to the Ethiopians ("S. Y." *l.c.*). He kept him prisoner for seven ("D. Y." *l.c.*) or ten ("S. Y." *l.c.*) years. Both of these legends are based on another legend according to which Moses was seventy-seven years of age when Jethro liberated him. According to the legend ("D. Y." *l.c.*) which says that he went to Nikanos' camp at the age of thirty, and ruled over Ethiopia for forty years, he was only seven years in Jethro's hands ($30+40+7 = 77$). According to the other legend ("S. Y." *l.c.*) he was eighteen years old when he fled from Egypt; he remained for nine years in the camp of Nikanos; and was king over Ethiopia for forty years. Hence he must have been Jethro's captive for ten years, or till his seventy-seventh year.

The Circumcision of Gershom

Moses was imprisoned in a deep dungeon in Jethro's house, and received as food only small portions of bread and water. He would have died of hunger had not Zipporah, to whom Moses had before his captivity made an offer of marriage by the well, devised a plan by which she no longer went out to pasture the sheep, but remained at home to attend to the household, being thereby enabled to supply Moses with food without her father's knowledge. After ten (or seven) years Zipporah reminded her father that he had at one time cast a man into the dungeon, who must have died long ago; but if he were still living he must be a just man whom God had kept alive by a miracle. Jethro went to the dungeon and called Moses, who answered immediately. As Jethro found Moses praying, he really believed that he had been saved by a miracle, and liberated him. Jethro had planted in his garden a marvelous rod, which had been created on the sixth day of the Creation, on Friday afternoon, and had been given to Adam. This curious rod had been handed down through Enoch, Shem, Abraham, Isaac, and Jacob to Joseph, at whose death it came into the possession of Pharaoh's court. Jethro, who saw it there, stole it and planted it in his garden. On the rod were engraved the name of God (Yhwh) and the initials of the ten plagues destined for Egypt. Jethro asked every one who wished to marry one of his daughters to pull up the rod; but no suitor had yet succeeded in doing so. Moses, on being set at liberty, walked in the garden, saw the rod, and read the inscription. He easily pulled it out of the ground and used it for a staff (see Aaron's Rod). Jethro thereby recognized Moses as the deliverer of Israel, and gave him the virtuous Zipporah as wife, together with much money ("S. Y.," "D. Y.," and "M. W." *l.c.*). Jethro stipulated that the firstborn son of the marriage should adopt Jethro's pagan belief, while all the other children might be reared as Jews; and Moses agreed thereto (Mek., Yitro, 1 [ed. Weiss, p. 65b]). According to "M. W." *l.c.*, one-half of the children of this marriage were to belong to Judaism and one-half to paganism. When therefore his son Gershom—who subsequently became the father of Jonathan—was born, Moses, under his agreement with Jethro, could not circumcise him ("S. Y."*l.c.*). Moses, therefore, went with his wife and child (another version says that both of his sons were then already born) to Egypt. On the way he met Satan, or Mastema, as he is called in the Book of Jubilees (xlviii. 2), in the guise of a serpent, which proceeded to swallow Moses, and had ingested the upper part of his body, when he stopped. Zipporah seeing this, concluded that the serpent's action was due to the fact that her son had not been circumcised (Ned. 31b-32a; Ex. R. v.), whereupon she circumcised him and smeared some of the blood on Moses' feet. A voice ("bat kol") was then heard commanding the serpent to disgorge the half-swallowed Moses, which it immediately did. When Moses came into Egypt he met his old enemies Dathan and Abiram, and when they asked him what he was seeking in Egypt, he immediately returned to Midian ("M. W." *l.c.*).

At the Burning Bush

As the shepherd of his father-in-law he drove his sheep far into the desert (Ex. iii. 1), in order to prevent the sheep from grazing in fields not belonging to Jethro (Ex. R. i. 3). Here God appeared to him and addressed him for seven consecutive days (*ib.* iii. 20). Moses, however, refused to listen, because he would not allow himself to be disturbed in the work for which he was paid. Then God caused the flaming bush to appear (Ex. iii. 2-3), in order to divert Moses' attention from his work. The under-shepherds with Moses saw nothing of the marvelous spectacle, which Moses alone beheld (Ex. R. ii. 8). Moses then interrupted his work, and stepped nearer the bush to investigate (*ib.* ii. 11). As Moses was at this time entirely inexperienced in prophecy, God, in calling him, imitated the voice of Amram, so as not to frighten him. Moses, who thought that his father, Amram, was appearing to him, said: "What does my father wish?" God answered: "I am the God of thy father" (Ex. iii. 6), and gave him the mission to save Israel (*ib.*). Moses hesitated to accept the mission (comp. Ex. iii. 11) chiefly because he feared that his elder brother, Aaron, who until then had been the only prophet in Israel, might feel slighted if his younger brother became the savior of the people; whereupon God assured him that Aaron would be glad of it (Ex. R. iii. 21-22). According to another version (*ib.* xv. 15), Moses said to God: "Thou hast promised Jacob that Thou Thyself wouldest liberate Israel [comp. Gen. xlvi. 4], not appointing a mediator." God answered: "I myself will save them; but go thou first and announce to My children that I will do so." Moses consented, and went to his father-in-law, Jethro (Ex. iv. 18), to obtain permission to leave Midian (Ned. 65a; Ex. R. iv. 1-4), for he had promised not to leave Midian without his sanction. Moses departed with his wife and children, and met Aaron (comp. Ex. iv. 27), who told him it was not right to take them into Egypt, since the attempt was being made to lead the Israelites out of that country. He therefore sent his wife and children back to Midian ("S. Y." p. 123a; Mek., Yitro, 1 [ed. Weiss, p. 65b]). When they went to Pharaoh, Moses went ahead, Aaron following, because Moses was more highly regarded in Egypt (Ex. R. ix. 3); otherwise Aaron and Moses were equally prominent and respected (Mek., Bo, 1 [ed. Weiss, p. 1a]). At the entrance to the Egyptian royal palace were two leopards, which would not allow any one to approach unless their guards quieted them; but when Moses came they played with him and fawned upon him as if they were his dogs ("D. Y." *l.c.*; "S. Y." *l.c.*). According to another version, there were guards at every entrance. Gabriel, however, introduced Moses and Aaron into the interior of the palace without being seen (Yalk., Shemot, 175). As Moses' appearance before Pharaoh resulted only in increasing the tasks of the children of Israel (comp. Ex. v.), Moses returned to Midian; and, according to one version, he took his wife and children back at the same time (Ex. R. v. 23).

Before Pharaoh

After staying six months in Midian he returned to Egypt (*ib.*), where he was subjected to many insults and injuries at the hands of Dathan and Abiram (*ib.* v. 24). This, together with the fear that he had aggravated the condition of the children of Israel, confused his mind so that he uttered disrespectful words to God (Ex. v. 22). Justice ("Middat ha-Din") wished to punish him for this; but as God knew that Moses' sorrow for Israel had induced these words he allowed Mercy ("Middat ha-Rahamim") to prevail (*ib.* vi. 1). As Moses feared that Middat ha-Din might prevent the redemption of Israel, since it was unworthy of being redeemed, God swore to him to redeem the people for Moses' sake (*ib.* vi. 3-5, xv. 4). Moses in treating with Pharaoh always showed to him the respect due to a king (*ib.* vii. 2). Moses was really the one selected to perform all the miracles; but as he himself was doubtful of his success (*ib.* vi. 12) some of them were assigned to Aaron (*ib.* 1). According to another version, Aaron and not Moses undertook to send the plagues and to perform all the miracles connected with the water and the dust. Because the water had saved Moses, and the dust had been useful to him in concealing the body of the Egyptian (*ib.* ii. 12), it was not fitting that they should be the instruments of evil in Moses' hand (*ib.* ix. 9, x. 5, xx. 1). When Moses announced the last plague, he would not state the exact time of its appearance, midnight, saying merely "ka-hazot" = "about midnight" (*ib.* xi. 4), because he thought the people might make a mistake in the time and would then call him a liar (Ber. 3b, 4a). On the night of the Exodus, when Moses had killed his paschal lamb, all the winds of the world were blowing through paradise, carrying away its perfumes and imparting them to Moses' lamb so that the odor of it could be detected at a distance of forty days (Ex. R. xix. 6).

At the Exodus

During this night all the firstborn, including the female firstborn, were killed, with the exception of Pharaoh's daughter Batya, who had adopted Moses. Although she was a firstborn child, she was saved through Moses' prayer ("S. Y." p. 125b). During the Exodus while all the people thought only of taking the gold and silver of the Egyptians, Moses endeavored to carry away boards for use in the construction of the future Temple (comp. Gen. R. xciv. 4 and Jew. Encyc. vii. 24, *s.v.* Jacob) and to remove Joseph's coffin (Ex. R. xviii. 8). Serah, Asher's daughter, told Moses that the coffin had been lowered into the Nile; whereupon Moses went to the bank of the river and cried: "Come up, Joseph" (according to another version, he wrote the name of God on a slip of paper, which he threw into the Nile), when the coffin immediately rose to the surface (Sotah 13a; Ex. R. xx. 17; "D. Y." *l.c.*; "S. Y." p. 126). Another legend says that Joseph's coffin was among the royal tombs, the Egyptians guarding it with dogs whose barking could be heard throughout Egypt; but Moses silenced the dogs and took the coffin out (Sotah *l.c.*; Ex. R. *l.c.)*.

On arriving at the Red Sea Moses said to God when commanded by Him to cleave the water: "Thou hast made it a law of nature that the sea shall never be dry," whereupon God replied that at the Creation He had made an agreement with the sea as to the separation of its waters at this time (Ex. R. xxi. 16; comp. "M. W." p. 38). When the Israelites saw Pharaoh and his army drown in the Red Sea (Ex. xiv. 30-31) they wished to return to Egypt and set up a kingdom there; but Moses prevented them, urging them on by force. He also removed the idols which the Israelites had brought with them from Egypt (Ex. R. xxiv. 2).

Receives the Torah

The giving of the tables of the Law and of the Torah in general to Moses is a favorite subject for legends. In contrast to the pithy sentence of R. Jose (Suk. 5a) to the effect that Moses never ascended into heaven, there are many haggadot which describe in detail how Moses made his ascension and received the Torah there. Moses went up in a cloud which entirely enveloped him (Yoma 4a). As he could not penetrate the cloud, God took hold of him and placed him within it (*ib.* 4b). When he reached heaven the angels asked God: "What does this man, born of woman, desire among us?" God replied that Moses had come to receive the Torah, whereupon the angels claimed that God ought to give the Torah to them and not to men. Then God told Moses to answer them. Moses was afraid that the angels might burn him with the breath of their mouths; but God told him to take hold of the throne of glory. Moses then proved to the angels that the Torah was not suited to them, since they had no passions to be subdued by it. The angels thereupon became very friendly with Moses, each one of them giving him something. The angel of death confided to him the fact that incense would prevent the plague (Shab. 88b-89a; Ex. R. xxviii.). Moses subsequently caused Aaron to employ this preventive (Num. xvii. 11-13). Moses, following the custom of the angels, ate nothing during his forty days' sojourn in heaven (B. M. 87b), feeding only on the splendor of the Shekinah. He distinguished day from night by the fact that God instructed him by day in the Scripture, and by night in the Mishnah (Ex. R. xlvii. 9). God taught him also everything which every student would discover in the course of time (*ib.* i.). When Moses first learned the Torah he soon forgot it; it was then bestowed upon him as a gift and he did not again forget it (Ned. 35a).

Worship of the Golden Calf

The Torah was intended originally only for Moses and his descendants; but he was liberal enough to give it to the people of Israel, and God approved the gift (Ned. 38a). According to another version, God gave the Torah to the Israelites for Moses' sake (Ex. R. xlvii. 14). Moses' burnt tongue was healed when he received the Law (Deut. R. i. 1). As Moses was writing down the Torah, he, on reaching the passage "Let us make man" (Gen. i. 26), said to God, "Why dost thou give the Minim the opportunity of construing these words to mean a plurality of gods?" whereupon God replied: "Let those err that will" (Gen. R. viii. 7). When Moses saw God write the words "erek appayim" (= "long-suffering"; Ex. xxxiv. 6), and asked whether God was long-suffering toward the pious only, God answered, "Toward sinners also." When Moses said that sinners ought to perish, God answered, "You yourself will soon ask me to be long-suffering toward sinners" (Sanh. 111a). This happened soon after Israel had made the golden calf (*ib.*). Before Moses ascended to heaven he said that he would descend on the forenoon of the forty-first day. On that day Satan confused the world so that it appeared to be afternoon to the Israelites. Satan told them that Moses had died, and was thus prevented from punctually fulfilling his promise. He showed them a form resembling Moses suspended in the air, whereupon the people made the golden calf (Shab. 89a; Ex. R. lxi.). When, in consequence of this, Moses was obliged to descend from heaven (Ex. xxxii. 7), he saw the angels of destruction, who were ready to destroy him. He was afraid of them; for he had lost his power over the angels when the people made the golden calf. God, however, protected him (Ex. R. xli. 12). When Moses came down with the tables and saw the calf (Ex. xxxii. 15-20), he said to himself: "If I now give to the people the tables, on which the interdiction against idolatry is written (Ex. xx. 2-5), they will deserve death for having made and worshiped the golden calf." In compassion for the Israelites he broke the tables, in order that they might not be held responsible for having transgressed the command against idolatry (Ab. R. N. ii.). Moses now began to pray for the people, showing thereby his heroic, unselfish love for them. Gathering from the words "Let me" (Ex. xxxii.

10) that Israel's fate depended on him and his prayer, he began to defend them (Ber. 32a; Meg. 24a). He said that Israel, having been sojourning in Egypt, where idolatry flourished, had become accustomed to this kind of worship, and could not easily be brought to desist from it (Yalk., Ki Tissa, 397). Moreover, God Himself had afforded the people the means of making the golden calf, since he had given them much gold and silver (Ber. *l.c.*). Furthermore, God had not forbidden Israel to practise idolatry, for the singular and not the plural was used in Ex. xx. 2-5, referring, therefore, only to Moses (Ex. R. xlvii. 14).

Moses and Israel

Moses refused God's offer to make him the ancestor of a great people (Ex. xxxii. 10), since he was afraid that it would be said that the leader of Israel had sought his own glory and advantage and not that of the people. He, in fact, delivered himself to death for the people (Ber. *l.c.*). For love of the Israelites he went so far as to count himself among the sinners (comp. Isa. liii. 12), saying to God: "This calf might be an assistant God and help in ruling the world." When God reproved him with having himself gone astray and with believing in the golden calf, he said: "Lord, why doth thy wrath wax hot against thy people" (Ex. xxxii. 11; Num. R. ii. 14; Deut. R. i. 2). Moses atoned for the sin of making the calf; he even atoned for all the sins of humanity down to his time, freeing men from their burden of sin (Yalk., Ki Tissa, 388, from the Tanna debe Eliyahu; this, as well as the interpretation of Isa. liii. as referring to Moses [Sotah 14a], must be either ascribed to Christian influence or regarded as a polemic against the Christian interpretations referring to Jesus). Moses loved the people (Men. 65a, b), showing his affection on every occasion. During the battle with Amalek he sat on a stone, and not on a cushion which he could easily have procured, because, Israel being at that time in trouble, he intended to show thereby that he suffered with them (Ta'an. 11a). When he begged God, before his death, to recall the oath that he (Moses) should never enter Palestine, God replied, "If I recall this oath I will also recall the oath never to destroy Israel," whereupon Moses said: "Rather let Moses and a thousand like him perish than that one of the people of Israel should perish" (Midr. Petirat Mosheh, in Jellinek, "B. H." i. 121). Moses requested that the Shekinah might rest in Israel only in order that Israel might thereby be distinguished among all peoples (Ber. 7a); that if they sinned and were penitent, their intentional sins might be regarded merely as trespasses (Yoma 36b); and that when Israel should suffer under the yoke of the nations, God would protect the pious and the saints of

Israel (B. B. 8a). All the injuries and slanders heaped upon Moses by the people did not lessen his love for them.

The words "They looked after Moses" (Ex. xxxiii. 8) are differently interpreted. According to one opinion the people praised Moses, saying: "Hail to the mother who has borne him; all the days of his life God speaks with him; and he is dedicated to the service of God." According to another opinion they reproached and reviled him: they accused him of committing adultery with another man's wife; and every man became jealous and forbade his wife to speak to Moses. They said: "See how fat and strong he has grown; he eats and drinks what belongs to the Jews, and everything that he has is taken from the people. Shall a man who has managed the building of the Tabernacle not become rich?" (Sanh. 110a; Kid. 33b; Ex. R. li. 4; Shek. v. 13). Yet Moses was the most conscientious of superintendents (Ber. 44a), and although he had been given sole charge of the work, he always caused his accounts to be examined by others (Ex. R. li. 1). He was always among the workmen, showing them how to do the work.

In the Tabernacle

When everything was prepared Moses set up the Tabernacle alone (Ex. R. lii. 3). He fastened the ceiling of the tent over it, as he was the only one able to do so, being ten ells tall (Shab. 92a). During the seven days of the dedication he took the Tabernacle apart every day and set it up again without any help. When all was completed he gave a detailed account of the various expenses (Ex. R. li. 4). During the seven days of the dedication, or, according to another account, during the forty years of the wandering in the desert, Moses officiated as high priest. He was also king during this entire period. When he demanded these two offices for his descendants God told him that the office of king was destined for David and his house, while the office of high priest was reserved for Aaron and his descendants (Ex. R. ii. 13; Lev. R. xi. 6; Zeb. 102a).

All the different cycles of legends agree in saying that Moses was very wealthy, probably on the basis of Num. xvi. 15 (comp. Ned. 35a, where this interpretation is regarded as uncertain); they differ, however, as to the source of his wealth. According to one, he derived it from the presents and treasures given to him by the Ethiopians when they took the crown away from him ("D. Y." *l.c.*). According to another, Jethro gave him a large sum of money as dowry when he married Zipporah ("M. W." *l.c.*). Still another story relates that Moses received a large part of the booty captured from Pharaoh and, later, from Sihon and Og (Lev. R. xxviii. 4). In contrast to these versions, according to which Moses gained his wealth by natural

means, there are two other versions according to which Moses became
wealthy by a miracle. One of these narratives says that Moses became rich
through the breaking of the tables, which were made of sapphires (Ned.
35a); and the other that God showed him in his tent a pit filled with these
precious stones (Yalk., Ki Tissa, 39b).

Personal Qualities

Moses was also distinguished for his strength and beauty. He was, as stated
above, ten ells tall and very powerful. In the battle against Og, Moses
was the only one able to kill that king (Ber. 54b; see Og in Rabbinical
Literature). His face was surrounded by a halo (comp. Ex. xxxiv. 29-35);
this was given to him in reward for having hidden his face on first meeting
God in the burning bush (*ib.* iii. 2-6; Ber. 7a), or he derived it from the cave
in the cleft of the rock (comp. Ex. xxxiii. 22) or from the tables, which he
grasped while God was holding one side and the angels the other. Another
legend says that a drop of the marvelous ink with which he wrote down
the Torah remained on the pen; and when he touched his head with the
pen he received his halo (Ex. R. xlvii. 11).

Moses was called the "father of wisdom" on account of his great sagacity
(Meg. 13a; Lev. R. i. 15). He possessed forty-nine of the fifty divisions of
wisdom (R. H. 21b; Ned. 35a). The question why the pious sometimes
have bad luck while the sinners are fortunate was solved for him (Ber.
7a). He wished to know also how good deeds are rewarded in the future
world, but this was not revealed to him (Yalk., Ki Tissa, 395). Piety was not
burdensome to him (Ber. 33b). His prayers were immediately answered
(Gen. R. lx. 4). He was so prominent a figure that his authority was equal
to that of an entire sanhedrin of seventy-one members (Sanh. 16b), or
even of the whole of Israel (Mek., Beshallah, Shir, 1 [ed. Weiss, p. 41a]).

His Prophetic Powers

Aside from the Pentateuch, Moses wrote also the Book of Job and some
Psalms. He also introduced many regulations and institutions (Shab. 30a;
comp. Ber. 54; Ta'an. 27; Meg. 4; Yeb. 79; Mak. 24). On account of the
excellence of his prophecy he is called "the father," "the head," "the master,"
and "the chosen of the Prophets" (Lev. R. i. 3; Esth. R. i.; Ex. R. xxi. 4;
Gen. R. lxxvi. 1). While all the other prophets ceased to prophesy after a
time, Moses continued to talk with God and to prophesy throughout his
life (Ex. R. ii. 12); and while all the other prophets beheld their visions
as through nine spectacles ("espaklarya") or through dim ones, Moses
beheld his as through one clear, finely ground glass (Yeb. 49b; Lev. R.

i. 14). Balaam surpassed him in prophecy in two respects: (1) Balaam always knew when God was about to speak with him, while Moses did not know beforehand when God would speak with him; and (2) Balaam could speak with God whenever he wished, which Moses could not do. According to another tradition (Num. R. xiv. 34), however, Moses also could speak with God as often as he wished. The fact that God would speak with him unawares induced Moses to give up domestic life, and to live separated from his wife (Shab. 87a).

Can Not Enter the Promised Land

Moses' modesty is illustrated by many fine examples in the Haggadah (comp. Num. xii. 3). When God pointed to R. Akiba and his scholarship, Moses said: "If Thou hast such a man, why dost Thou reveal the Torah through me?" (Men. 29b; see also Akiba). When Moses descended from heaven Satan came to ask him where the Torah was which God had given to him. Moses said: "Who am I? Am I worthy to receive the Torah from God?" When God asked him why he denied that the Torah had been given to him, he replied: "How can I claim anything which belongs to Thee and is Thy darling?" Then God said to him: "As thou art so modest and humble, the Torah shall be called after thee, the 'Torah of Moses'" (Shab. 89a; comp. Mal. iii. 22). Moses' modesty never allowed him to put himself forward (*e.g.*, in liberating Israel, in dividing the sea, and subsequently also in connection with the Tabernacle) until God said to him: "How long wilt thou count thyself so lowly? The time is ready for thee; thou art the man for it" (Lev. R. i. 15). When Moses had made a mistake, or had forgotten something, he was not ashamed to admit it (Zeb. 101a). In his prayers he always referred to the merits of others, although everything was granted to him on account of his own merit (Ber. 10b). Whenever the cup is handed to him during the banquet of the pious in the other world, that he may say grace over the meal, he declares: "I am not worthy to say grace, as I have not deserved to enter the land of Israel" (Pes. 119b). The fact that Moses, the foremost leader of Israel, who ceaselessly prayed for it and partook of its sorrows (Num. R. xviii. 5), and on whose account the manna was showered down from heaven and the protecting clouds and the marvelous well returned after the death of Aaron and Miriam (Ta'an. 9a), should not be allowed to share in Israel's joys and enter the promised land ("M. W." *l.c.*), was a problem that puzzled the Haggadah, for which it tried to find various explanations. Moses was anxious to enter the promised land solely because many of the commandments given by God could be observed only there, and he was desirous of fulfilling all the commandments. God, however, said that He looked upon Moses as having fulfilled all the commandments, and would therefore duly reward him therefor (Sotah 14a). Moses prayed in vain to be permitted to go into the promised land if only for a little while; for God had decreed that he should not enter the country either alive or dead. According to one opinion, this decree was in punishment for the words addressed by him to God: "Wherefore hast thou so evil entreated this people?" (Ex. v. 22; Ex. R. v. 27). According to another version, this punishment was inflicted upon him for having once silently renounced his nationality. When Moses had helped the daughters of Jethro at the well, they took him home, letting him wait outside while they went into the house and told their father that an Egyptian had protected them (Ex. ii. 19). Moses, who overheard this conversation, did not correct them, concealing the fact that he was a Hebrew ("M. W." *l.c.*). There is still another explanation, to the effect that it would not have redounded to the glory of Moses if he who had led 600,000 persons out of Egypt had been the only one to enter Palestine, while the entire people were destined to die in the desert (comp. Num. xiv. 28-37). Again, Moses had to die with the generation which he took out of Egypt, in order that he might be able to lead them again in the future world (Num. R. xix. 6).

Moses Strikes the Rock

Denying all these reasons, another explanation, based on Scripture, is that Moses and Aaron were not permitted to enter the promised land because they did not have the proper confidence in God in calling water from the rock (Num. xx. 12). Moses asked that this error should be noted down in the Torah (Num. xx. 12) in order that no other errors or faults should be ascribed to him (Num. R. *l.c.*). This story of his lack of true confidence in God when calling forth the water is elaborated with many details in the legends.

Moses was careful not to provoke the people during the forty years of wandering in the desert, because God had sworn that none of the generation which had left Egypt should behold the promised land (Deut. i. 35). When he went to call forth the water he did not know exactly from which rock it would come. The people became impatient and said that there was no difference between the rocks, and that he ought to be able to call forth water from any one of them. Vexed, he replied, "Ye rebels!" (Num. xx. 10) or, according to the Midrash, "fools!" God therefore said to him: "As thou art clever, thou shalt not enter the land together with fools." According to another legend, Moses became angry because some of the people said that, since he had been a herdsman with Jethro, he knew, like all herdsmen, where to find water in the desert, and that now he was merely trying to deceive the people and to make them believe that he had miraculously called water from the rock (Midr. Petirat Aharon, in Jellinek, *l.c.* i. 93 *et seq.*; Num. R. xix. 5; Yalk., Hukkat, 763).

At Aaron's Death

When Moses heard that Aaron also had to die he grieved and wept so much as to occasion his own death (Midr. Petirat Aharon, *l.c.*). This story, as well as the reference to his early death (Yoma 87a), was probably based on Deut. xxxiv. 7, according to which he retained all his faculties and his full strength down to his end; but they contradict the many other versions of his death (see below). When Moses took Aaron up the mountain where the latter was to die, and announced his death to him, he comforted him, saying: "You, my brother, will die and leave your office to your children; but when I die a stranger will inherit my office. When you die you will leave me to look after your burial; when I die I shall leave no brother, no sister, and no son to bury me" (Midr. Petirat Aharon, *l.c.*; Num. R. xix. 11; Yalk., Num. 763, 787)—for Moses' sons died before him (comp. the note in "Zayit Ra'anan" to Yalk., Num. 787). When Moses witnessed the quiet and peaceful death of Aaron he desired a similar death for himself (*ib.*). After Aaron's death Moses was accused by the people of having killed him through jealousy; but God cleared him from this suspicion by a miracle (Yalk., Num. 764).

When Moses was about to take vengeance on Midian before his death (comp. Num. xxxi.) he did not himself take part in the war, because he had at one time sojourned in Midian and had received benefits in that country (Num. R. xxii. 4). When Zimri brought the Midianitish woman Cozbi before Moses (Num. xxv. 6), asking that he might marry her, and Moses refused his request, Zimri reproached him with having himself married the Midianitish woman Zipporah (Sanh. 82a). Later, also, Moses was reproached for this marriage, the Rabbis saying that on account of it he became the ancestor of Jonathan, the priest of Micah's idol (Judges xviii. 30; B. B. 109b). God revealed to Moses before his death all the coming generations, their leaders and sages, as well as the saints and sinners. When Moses beheld Saul and his sons die by the sword he grieved that the first king of Israel should come to such a sad end (Lev. R. xxvi. 7). When God showed him hell he began to be afraid of it; but God promised him that he should not go thither (Num. R. xxiii. 4). He beheld paradise also. A detailed description of Moses' wanderings through paradise and hell is found in the apocalypse "Gedullat Mosheh" (Salonica, 1727; see Jew. Encyc. i. 679).

Death of Moses

The different legends agree in saying that Moses died on Adar 7, the day on which he was born, at the age of 120 years (Meg. 13b; Mek., Beshallah, Wayassa', 5 [ed. Weiss, p. 60a]; comp. Josephus, *l.c.* iv. 8, § 49), the angel of death not being present (B. B. 17a). But the earlier and the later legends differ considerably in the description and the details of this event. The earlier ones present the hero's death as a worthy close to his life. It takes place in a miraculous way; and the hero meets it quietly and resignedly. He ascends Mount Abarim accompanied by the elders of the people, and Joshua and Eleazar; and while he is talking with them a cloud suddenly surrounds him and he disappears. He was prompted by modesty to say in the Torah that he died a natural death, in order that people should not say that God had taken him alive into heaven on account of his piety (Josephus, *l.c.*). The event is described somewhat differently, but equally simply, in Sifre, Deut. 305 (ed. Friedmann, p. 129b). For the statement that Moses did not die at all, compare Sotah 13b. "When the angel of death, being sent by God to Moses, appeared before him and said, 'Give me your soul,' Moses scolded him, saying, 'You have not even the right to appear where I am sitting; how dare you say to me that I shall give you my soul?' The angel of death took this answer back to God. And when God said to the angel the second time, 'Bring Me the soul of Moses,' he went to the place where Moses had been, but the latter had left. Then he went to the sea to look for Moses there. The sea said that it had not seen Moses since the time when he had led the children of Israel through it. Then he went to the mountains and valleys, which told him that God had concealed Moses, keeping him for the life in the future world, and no creature knew where he was."

This simple story of the old midrash follows the Bible closely, making the mountains and valleys the speakers because, according to Deut. xxxiv. 1-5, Moses died on the mountain and was buried in the valley. In the later legends the death of Moses is recounted more fantastically, with many marvelous details. But instead of the hero being glorified, as was certainly intended by these details, he is unconsciously lowered by some traits ascribed to him. He appears weak and fearsome, not displaying that grandeur of soul which he might reasonably have been expected to exhibit at his death.

Wishes to Avoid Death

When God said to Moses that he must die Moses replied: "Must I die now, after all the trouble I have had with the people? I have beheld their sufferings; why should I not also behold their joys? Thou hast written in the Torah: 'At his day thou shalt give him his hire' [Deut. xxiv. 15]; why dost thou not give me the reward of my toil?" (Yalk., Deut. 940; Midr. Petirat Mosheh, in Jellinek, *l.c.* i. 115-129). God assured him that he should receive his reward in the future world. Moses then asked why he must die at all, whereupon God enumerated some of the sins for which he had deserved death, one of them being the murder of the Egyptian (Ex. ii. 12; Midr. Petirat Mosheh, *l.c.*). According to another version, Moses had to die so that he might not be taken for a god (*ib.*). Moses then began to become excited (Yalk., Wa'ethanan, 814), saying he would live like the beasts of the field and the birds, which get their daily food only for the sake of remaining alive (Yalk., Deut. 940). He desired to renounce the entry into the promised land and remain with the tribes of Reuben and Gad in the country east of the Jordan, if only he might remain alive. God said that this could not be done, since the people would leave Joshua and return to him (Midr. Petirat Mosheh, *l.c.*). Moses then begged that one of his children or one of the children of his brother Aaron might succeed him (*ib.* and Num. R. xxi. 15). God answered that his children had not devoted themselves to the Law, whereas Joshua had served Moses faithfully and had learned from him; he therefore deserved to succeed his teacher (*ib.*). Then Moses said: "Perhaps I must die only because the time has come for Joshua to enter upon his office as the leader of Israel. If Joshua shall now become the leader, I will treat him as my teacher and will serve him, if only I may stay alive." Moses then began to serve Joshua and give him the honor due to a master from his pupil. He continued to do this for thirty-seven days, from the first of Shebat to the seventh of Adar. On the latter day he conducted Joshua to the tent of the assembly. But when he saw Joshua go in while he himself had to remain outside, he became jealous, and said that it was a hundred times better to die than to suffer once such pangs of jealousy. Then the treasures of wisdom were taken away from Moses and given to Joshua (comp. Sotah 13b). A voice ("bat kol") was heard to say, "Learn from Joshua!" Joshua delivered a speech of which Moses understood nothing. Then, when the people asked that Moses should complete the Torah, he replied, "I do not know how to answer you," and tottered and fell. He then said: "Lord of the world, until now I desired to live; but now I am willing to die." As the angel of death was afraid to take his soul, God Himself, accompanied by Gabriel, Michael, and Zagziel, the former teacher of Moses, descended to get it. Moses blessed the people, begged their forgiveness for any injuries he might have done them, and took leave of them with the assurance that he would see them again at the resurrection of the dead. Gabriel arranged the couch, Michael spread a silken cover over it, and Zagziel put a silken pillow under Moses' head. At God's command Moses crossed his hands over his breast and closed his eyes, and God took his soul away with a kiss. Then heaven and earth and the starry world began to weep for Moses (Midr. Petirat Mosheh, *l.c.*; Yalk., Deut. 940; Deut. R. xi. 6). Although Moses died in the territory of the tribe of Reuben, he was buried in that of Gad at a spot four miles distant from the place of his death. He was carried this distance by the Shekinah, while the angels said to him that he had practised God's justice (Deut. xxxiii. 22). At the same time the bat kol cried out in the camp of the people: "Moses, the great teacher of Israel, is dead!" (Sotah 13b).

God Himself buried Moses (Sotah 14a; Sanh. 39a) in a grave which had been prepared for him in the dusk of Friday, the sixth day of the Creation (Pes. 54a). This tomb is opposite Beth-peor (Deut. xxxiv. 6), in atonement for the sin which Israel committed with the idol Peor (Sotah 14a). Yet it can not be discovered; for to a person standing on the mountain it seems to be in the valley; and if one goes down into the valley, it appears to be on the mountain (*ib.*).

Bibliography

B. Beer, Leben Moses, nach Auffassung der Jüdischen Sage, in Jahrb. für Gesch. der Jud. iii. 1 et seq.;

M. Grünbaum, Neue Beiträge zur Semitischen Sagenkunde, pp. 15-85, Leyden, 1893.

CRITICAL VIEW

Moses in the Jahvist

In 1753 Jean Astruc, a French physician, published at Brussels a little book in which he advanced the theory that Moses had employed certain documents in composing the Book of Genesis. This work was thought by its author to establish the Mosaic authorship of Genesis upon a more secure basis, but it contained the key which, in the hands of a long line of critics, has led to the modern view that the Pentateuch originated from four great documents, all of which were written some centuries after Moses (see Pentateuch, Critical View). The oldest of these documents, known as J or the Jahvist, contains in its present state no account of the early life of

Moses, but presents him first as a fugitive in the land of Midian. Nearly all the after-events of the life of Moses, enumerated above, are, however, given by J, who has a definite and interesting point of view. Critics differ as to whether Aaron had any place in the original narrative of J or not, Dillmann and Bacon assigning to him an important role, while Wellhausen, Stade, Carpenter, and Harford Battersby hold that such passages as Ex. iv. 13-14 are later interpolations. Be this as it may, J represents Moses as holding the unique position of importance. For example, in J's description of the plagues he pictures Moses as announcing the plague; then he tells how Yhwh sent it, usually through some natural agency (comp. Ex. viii. 20-24, the flies; x. 13, 19, the locusts). Similarly, J tells that Yhwh "caused the sea to go back by a strong east wind all the night, and made the sea dry land" (Ex. xiv. 21). Thus he explains the passage of the Red Sea.

It is J who represents Moses as alone enjoying the privilege of intercourse with Yhwh face to face. He gives the account of the burning bush (Ex. iii. 2); he relates that Moses, Aaron, Nadab, and Abihu, with seventy of the elders of Israel, went up into the mountain, and that Aaron and the seventy beheld Yhwh from afar off and ate and drank in His presence, but that Moses alone went near unto Yhwh (Ex. xxiv. 1-2, 9-11). In Ex. xxxiv. 5 Yhwh descended in a cloud and stood to talk with Moses. In J the basis of Yhwh's covenant are the ten "words" contained in Ex. xxxiv. J, too, in Num. xiv. 11-17, 19-24 presents one of the most noble pictures of Moses. Yhwh was angry, and declared that He would destroy Israel and make of Moses a great nation, but the unselfish leader pleaded against his own interests for the forgiveness of the nation which had so often thwarted him, and the prayer prevailed.

Moses in the Elohist

The second prophetic document in point of age, known as E or the Elohist, contains the account of Moses' birth and exposure on the Nile, together with the incidents which led to his flight to Midian. Aaron and Miriam also played a part in the original E narrative. E gives especial attention to the part of Jethro in initiating Moses into the worship of Yhwh and in the organization of legal procedure (Ex. xviii. 12 *et seq.*). According to E, before the Exodus the Hebrews dwelt in the midst of the Egyptians (not in Goshen, as in J); and E asserts that on the advice of Moses the Hebrews borrowed freely of the Egyptians just before leaving. E pictures Moses as raising the fateful rod when he would have any plague come, at which sign the plague came. At the Red Sea also Moses lifted this rod and the waters parted. In the E narrative Moses had a "tent of meeting" pitched at a distance from the camp, to which he resorted, accompanied only by Joshua, his minister, and there he talked with Yhwh face to face (Ex. xxxiii. 8-11). E makes the basis of the covenant which Moses mediated to be the code in Ex. xx. 24-xxiii. 19. This covenant, however, was not communicated at the tent of meeting, but on the top of the sacred mountain, which E calls "Horeb" and J calls "Sinai." E's narrative contains the chief events of the life of Moses already given. His portrait is dignified and noble, though lacking in the touches of highest heroism which make the picture of J superb.

In the Priestly Code

The writer of the Priestly Code (P), like the two older prophetic writers, includes in his account the chief events in the life of Moses, but in accord with his usual habit tells these events in a few chronicle-like words in order to make them the setting of his history of the sacred institutions. P declares that Amram was the father of Moses, and Jochebed his mother (Ex. vi. 20), and gives to Aaron a prominence much greater than in the older narratives. Moses is a god to Pharaoh, and Aaron is Moses' prophet (Ex. vii. 1). In accord with this view, in P's account of the Egyptian plagues Moses communicates in each case a command to Aaron, who then stretches out the sacred rod to invoke the affliction. Thus Aaron is associated with Moses at almost every point. P increases everywhere the miraculous element. In his account the simple driving back of the waters of the Red Sea by the east wind becomes an astounding miracle (comp. Ex. xiv. 22). P traces to Moses the sacred institutions; the Levitical law was communicated by Yhwh to Moses; Moses received on the mount the pattern of the Tabernacle, which was constructed under his direction; even the duties of the Levites were arranged by him.

The Deuteronomist (D) adds nothing to the knowledge of the character of Moses. The account of the second giving of the Law in Moab, and various notes which expound and interpret the older narratives, constitute the whole Pentateuchal product of this writer.

Moses and Sargon

The cuneiform library of Assurbanipal has furnished a legend of the birth of Sargon of Agade (a Babylonian king who, according to Nabonidos, ruled about 3800 B.C.) which is strikingly parallel to the story of the secret birth of Moses and of his exposure on the Nile. The legend runs:

"Sargon, the powerful king, King of Agade am I. My mother was of low degree; my father I did not know. The brother of my father dwelt in the mountain. My city was Azupirani, which is situated on the bank of the Euphrates. My humble mother conceived me; in secret she bore me. She placed me in a boat of reeds; with bitumen my door she closed. She entrusted me to the river, which did not overwhelm me. The river bore me along; to Akki the irrigator it carried me. Akki the irrigator in goodness . . . brought me to land. Akki the irrigator as his son brought me up. Akki the irrigator his gardener appointed me. While I was gardener, Ishtar loved me . . . four years I ruled the kingdom."

The parallelism between this narrative and the story of the exposure of Moses is thought by many scholars to be too close to be accidental.

Name

The name [Moses] is explained in Ex. ii. 12 (E) as though it were of Hebrew origin, and from [the Hebrew word meaning] ("to draw out"). If this were its real etymology, the name would mean "deliverer," "savior" (comp. Ps. xviii. 17, Hebr.). As an Egyptian princess could not have spoken Hebrew, this etymology has been generally abandoned. A second one dates from the time of Josephus ("Ant." ii. 9, § 6; "Contra Ap." i., § 31), and is built on the Greek form of the name Μωσῆς. This, Josephus claims, is derived from Egyptian "mo" (water) and "uses" (saved)—a theory to which Jablonski gave a quasi-scientific character by comparing the Coptic "mo" (water) and "ushe" (rescued). An Egyptian name with such a meaning would, however, be formed differently (see "Z. D. M. G." xxv. 141). The etymology now generally received regards it as from the Egyptian "mesh" (child), often used as a part of a theophorous name. This view was suggested by Lepsius, and has been accepted by Ebers, Dillmann, Gesenius, and Buhl, by Briggs, Brown, and Driver in their lexicon, and by others. Guthe ("Gesch. des Volkes Israel," p. 20) also regards it as a fragment of a theophorous name. W. Max Müller has objected that the vowel in "mesh" is short, while that in "Moses" is long, and that the sibilants are not those which the philological law would require. Accordingly Cheyne ("Encyc. Bibl.") proposes a Semitic origin, regarding the name as that of a North-Arabian tribe. One is inclined to return to the Biblical account and accept the etymology of E. If it may be supposed that the part of the narrative which attributes the naming to Pharaoh's daughter is inaccurate, the name may well be good Semitic, meaning "deliverer." Possibly it was not a name given in infancy, but an epithet which came to him as the result of his work.

Founder of the Israelitish Nation

It is clear from the different representations of three of the great Pentateuchal documents that some allowance must be made for traditional

accretion in the narratives of the life of Moses. But modern scholars with
much unanimity of opinion regard Moses as a great historical character,
the emancipator of Israel, the mediator of the covenant with Yhwh, and the
real founder of the Israelitish nation. Though few of the laws can be traced
back to him, it is believed that he gave to Israel, by his covenant with Yhwh,
and by his legal decisions at Kadesh, the beginnings of religious law, and
so became the founder of the legal system which prophets and priests
developed as time passed on. It is true that Winckler ("Gesch. Israels," ii.
86 *et seq.*, Leipsic, 1900) regards Moses as a Yhwh-Tammuz myth, that
Cheyne ("Encyc. Bibl.") regards him as a personified clan, and that two
other scholars, Renan ("Hist. of the People of Israel," i. 135 *et seq.*) and
Stade ("Gesch. des Volkes Israel," pp. 129 *et seq.*), regard his historicity
as possible only. The great majority of modern scholars, however, though
differing in details, hold not only to the reality of Moses as a historical
character, but to the reality of his magnificent work as stated. This is the
position of Wellhausen ("I. J. G." pp. 13 *et seq.*), W. R. Smith ("Old Test. in
the Jewish Church," 2d ed., pp. 333 *et seq.*), Kittel ("Hist. of the Hebrews,"
i. 238 *et seq.*), Cornill ("Hist. of the People of Israel," pp. 41 *et seq.*), Budde
("Religion of Israel to the Exile," pp. 12 *et seq.*), Guthe ("Gesch. des Volkes
Israel," pp. 19 *et seq.*), A. B. Davidson ("Theology of the Old Test." p. 110),
McCurdy ("History, Prophecy, and the Monuments," ii. 92 *et seq.*), Kent
("Hist. of the Hebrew People," i. 36 *et seq.*), Barton ("Sketch of Semitic
Origins," pp. 272, 291 *et seq.*), J. P. Peters ("The Old Test. and the New
Scholarship," pp. 116 *et seq.*, and "The Religion of Moses," in "Jour. Bib.
Lit." 1901, xx. 101 *et seq.*), Paton ("Early Hist. of Syria and Palestine,"
pp. 137 *et seq.*), and H. P. Smith ("Old Test. History," pp. 55-65). Such a
consensus of opinion is significant. See Pentateuch.

IN HELLENISTIC LITERATURE

While the Pentateuch represents Moses as the greatest of all prophets, to
whom the Lord made Himself known face to face (Deut. xxxiv. 10; comp.
Num. xii. 7), and who, when descending Mount Sinai, had a halo about
his head which so filled the people with awe that they could not look at
him (Ex. xxxiv. 29), yet there is no attempt made to lift him above the
ordinary man in his nature. He lived for forty days and forty nights on
the mount without eating and drinking (Deut. ix. 9), but this was owing
to the power God lent him while he received the Law; he died and was
buried like any other mortal (*ib.* xxxiv. 5-6). Owing to the contact of the
Jews with the Greeks in Alexandria, Moses was made the subject of many
legends, and in many respects lifted to supernatural heights.

Ben Sira was probably the first to compare him with the angels—a suggestion from Ex. xxxiv. 29 (Ecclus. xlv. 2; the Hebrew text reads "ke-elohim," while the Greek reads "saints"). Especially favorable to the accretion of legends or fictions around the life of Moses was the fact that he was born in Egypt and brought up by the daughter of the king. This suggested that "he was learned in all the wisdom of the Egyptians" (Acts vii. 22). But the Jewish men of letters who lived in Alexandria were by no means satisfied with the idea that Moses acquired the wisdom of the Egyptians; they claimed for him the merit of having given to Egypt, Phenicia, and Hellas all their culture. He taught the Jews the letters, and they then became the teachers of the Phenicians and, indirectly, of the Greeks, says Eupolemus (Eusebius, "Præparatio Evangelica," ix. 26). Artapanus, in his history of the Jews, went so far as to identify Moses with Tot-Hermes (the Egyptian messenger and scribe of the gods, who invented the letters, the various arts of peace and of war, as well as philosophy), and with the Greek Musæus, "the teacher of Orpheus." He even ascribed to him the division of the land into its thirty-six districts, with their various forms of worship. As the foster-mother of Moses, Artapanus names Merris, the wife of Chenephres, King of Upper Egypt; being childless, she pretended to have given birth to him and brought him up as her own child. (Eusebius, *l.c.* ix. 27).

'Jealousy of Moses' excellent qualities induced Chenephres to send him with unskilled troops on a military expedition to Ethiopia, where he won great victories. After having built the city of Hermopolis, he taught the people the value of the ibis as a protection against the serpents, making the bird the sacred guardian spirit of the city; then he introduced circumcision. After his return to Memphis, Moses taught the people the value of oxen for agriculture, and the consecration of the same by Moses gave rise to the cult of Apis. Finally, after having escaped another plot by killing the assailant sent by the king, Moses fled to Arabia, where he married the daughter of Raguel, the ruler of the district. Chenephres in the meantime died from elephantiasis [comp. Ex. R. i. and Targ. Yer. to Ex. ii. 23]—a disease with which he was the first to be afflicted—because he had ordered that the Jews should wear garments that would distinguish them from the Egyptians and thereby expose them to maltreatment [this is characteristic of the age in which it was written]. The sufferings of Israel then caused God to appear to Moses in a flame bursting forth from the earth [not from the bush!], and to tell him to march against Egypt for the rescue of his people. Accordingly he went to Egypt to deliberate with his brother Aaron about the plan of warfare, but was put into prison. At night, however, the doors of the prison opened of their own accord, while the guards died or fell asleep. Going to the royal palace and finding the doors open there and the guards sunk in sleep, he went straight to the king, and when scoffingly asked by the latter for the name of the God who sent him, he whispered the Ineffable Name into his ear, whereupon the king became speechless and as one dead. Then Moses wrote the name upon a tablet and sealed it up, and a priest who made sport of it died in convulsions. After this Moses performed all the wonders, striking land and people with plagues until the king let the Jews go. In remembrance of the rod with which Moses performed his miracles every Isis temple in Egypt has preserved a rod—Isis symbolizing the earth which Moses struck with his rod"

The record closes with a description of the personality of Moses: "He was eighty-nine years old when he delivered the Jews; tall and ruddy, with long white hair, and dignified."

Fantastic and grotesque as these stories are, they are scarcely inventions of Artapanus only. Long contact of the Jews of Alexandria with Egyptian men of letters in a time of syncretism, when all mythology was being submitted to a rationalizing process, naturally produced such fables (see Freudenthal, "Hellenistische Studien," 1875, pp. 153-174), and they have found a place in the Palestinian as well as in the Hellenistic haggadah, in Josephus, Philo ("De Vita Moysis"), and the Alexandrian dramatist Ezekiel (Eusebius, *l.c.* ix. 28), as well as in the Midrash (Ex. R. i.-ii.; Tan., Shemot), the Targum, and the "Sefer ha-Yashar," or the older "Chronicles of Jerahmeel" (xliv.-l.).

Most elaborate is the haggadah from which Josephus drew his story ("Ant." ii. 9, § 2-ii. 10, § 2): (comp. Sanh. 101b; Ex. R. i.; Targ. Yer. to Ex. i. 14; see Jannes and Jambres).

"Egyptian priests skilled in prophesying foretold the birth of a Hebrew who would bring misfortune on Egypt, and thus caused Pharaoh's edict to have every newborn male child drowned in the river" (see Amram; Miriam).

"Amram in his distress at the fate of every newborn child prays to God and receives a revelation" (comp. Ezekiel in Eusebius, *l.c.* ix. 29; "Chronicles of Jerahmeel," xliv. 8; Yalk. i. 166).

"Thermutis was the name of the princess who saw Moses in the water-cradle and conceived a love for him on account of his striking beauty. The child, however, refused to suckle from any other breast but that of his mother." "Moses excelled all by his tall stature and beauty of countenance as well as by his quickness of apprehension." "Thermutis, being without child, brought him up as her own son, and one day when she presented him to her father as her own child, and heir to the throne—a gift she had received from the river-god—Pharaoh took the child on his lap and placed his diadem upon its head; whereupon it cast it down on the ground and trampled upon it. This was taken as an evil omen by the king, and the priestly soothsayer, finding Moses to be the one who would bring upon the kingdom the misfortune predicted for it, wished to slay him, but Thermutis succeeded in saving his life" (comp. "Chronicles of Jerahmeel," xlv.-xlvi.; Yalk. i. 168).

"An attack on Egypt by the Ethiopians caused all to look to Moses for aid, and the king asked his daughter to permit him to go forth as general of an army to Ethiopia. Moses took the short road along the desert, deemed impassable on account of its many flying serpents ('serafim'), and provided himself with numerous baskets filled with ibises, the destroyers of serpents, by the help of which he removed the dangers of the desert. He thus took the Ethiopians by surprise and defeated them, driving them back to Merve, a fortified city. While he was besieging the city, Therbis, the daughter of the king, saw him upon the walls, fell in love with him, and proposed to him to become his wife. He accepted the offer under the condition that the city should surrender to him; finally he married her."

This is obviously a midrashic tale connected with Num. xii. 1, but disavowed at a later stage (see Sifre, Num. 99, and Targ. *ad loc.*).

Philo also shows familiarity with these legends; he refers to the beauty of the babe Moses (*l.c.* i. 3) and mentions the fact that the princess, being childless, contrived to make Moses appear as her own child (i. 4-5). Moses' education in science, art, and philosophy, however, is ascribed to Egyptian masters (i. 6); he was grieved by the sufferings of his Hebrew brethren, many of whom died an untimely death and did not have even seemly burial (i. 7); his prophetic powers were attested at the Red Sea when the Egyptian dead were cast up by the waves and were actually seen by the Israelites, as Moses had announced (iii. 34, with reference to Ex. xiv. 13, 30).

Moses' Preexistence

The end of the great lawgiver especially was surrounded with legends. "While, after having taken leave of the people, he was going to embrace Eleazar and Joshua on Mount Nebo, a cloud suddenly stood over him, and he disappeared, though he wrote in Scripture that he died, which was done from fear that people might say that because of his extraordinary virtue he had been turned into a divinity" ("Ant." iv. 8, § 48). Philo says: "He was entombed not by mortal hands, but by immortal powers, so that he was not placed in the tomb of his forefathers, having obtained a peculiar memorial [*i.e.*, grave] which no man ever saw" ("De Vita Moysis," iii. 39). Later on, the belief became current that Moses did not die, but was taken up to heaven like Elijah. This seems to have been the chief content of the apocryphon entitled "Assumptio Moysis," preserved only in fragmentary form (comp. Charles, "The Assumption of Moses," 1897, Introduction; Deut. R. xi.; Jellinek, "B. H." i. 115-129, vi. 71-78; M. R. James, "Apocrypha Anecdota," pp. 166-173, Cambridge, 1893). No sooner was the view maintained that Moses was translated to heaven than the idea was suggested that his soul was different from that of other men. Like the Messiah, he is said to have been preexistent; he is thus represented in "Assumptio Moysis" (i. 12-14); so too "He was prepared before the foundation of the world to be the mediator of God's covenant, and as he was Israel's intercessor with God during life [xi. 11, 17], so is he to be the intercessor in all the future." While his death was an ordinary one (i. 15, x. 14), "no place received his body"; "his sepulcher is from the rising of the sun to the setting thereof, and from the south to the confines of the north; all the world is his sepulcher" (xi. 5-8). Philo also calls Moses "the mediator and reconciler of the world" (*ib.* iii. 19). Especially in Essene circles was Moses apotheosized: "Next to God," says Josephus ("B. J." ii. 8, § 9), "they honor the name of their legislator, and if any one blasphemes him he meets with capital punishment" (comp. "Ant." iii. 15, § 3). Against such excessive adoration of a human being a reaction set in among the Rabbis, who declared that no man ever ascended to heaven (Suk. 5a).

Bibliography

Beer, Das Leben Moses nach Auffassung der Jüdischen Sage, Leipsic, 1863.

www.ingramcontent.com/pod-product-compliance
Lightning Source LLC
Chambersburg PA
CBHW051951090426
42741CB00008B/1355